Towards the Discovery of Canada

ISBN   7705-0788-3

Essays in this volume appeared originally in the Canadian Historical Association *Report*; the University of Toronto *Quarterly*; the *Journal of Canadian Studies*; Papers and Proceedings of the Canadian Political Science Association; the *Canadian Journal of Economics and Political Science*; the *Canadian Historical Review*; C. T. Bissell (ed.), *Our Living Tradition*, Toronto, 1957; the Historical and Scientific Society of Manitoba *Transactions*; *Saturday Night*; *Maclean's* Magazine; the Laurentian University *Review*.

Printed in Canada

Contents

Part III: Sir John A. Macdonald

Part IV: Continentalism and Biculturalism

Towards the Discovery of Canada

Introduction

THESE ESSAYS, the first of which appeared in 1933, are distributed fairly evenly over the following four decades. More were written in the late 1960s and early 1970s than during any earlier period; but this greater incidence has a simple explanation in the fact that I had far less time for the writing of any kind of Canadian history at the beginning of my academic career than I enjoyed at its close. Nowadays a young scholar who has won his senior degree with a doctoral thesis in Canadian history is normally given an opportunity to teach his specialty in the first year of his appointment to a university; but most of my first two decades at the University of Toronto were spent in trying to instruct students in British or European history. Research in the history of Canada was an indulgence which had to be reserved for weekends, holidays, and summer vacations. I had to economize my time and it seemed to me that I could make the best use of it by writing books rather than essays, articles, and reviews. Young historians of the present generation have acquired the habit of rushing into print with brief introductions to reprints of old works or collections of other people's essays. These easy exercises usually exhibit neither the creative power of youth nor the gathered wisdom of maturity; and I am glad, on the whole, that the book trade of thirty years ago offered no such inducements to quick publications.

There were, in fact, very few possibilities of any kind of publication in those days. The market in Canadian history seemed permanently depressed. It was an act of faith to begin a history book and a triumph of hope and patience to finish it. When I started writing *The Empire of the St.*

Lawrence, I had not the remotest idea of where and how it might be published; and I was well advanced in its composition before Harold Innis suggested that it might be included as a volume in Dr. J. T. Shotwell's new series *The Relations of Canada and the United States*. My second substantial study, *British North America at Confederation*, was commissioned, without any assurance of publication, by the Royal Commission on Dominion-Provincial Relations; and I could only hope, what turned out to be true, that it would be printed as an appendix to the *Report*. A general history of Canada, I assumed, stood an even smaller chance of getting published than a special study; and, when I first conceived the improbable notion of writing one, it never even occurred to me that a Canadian publisher might be interested in it. I happened casually to mention the idea to a travelling representative of an American publishing house; and I was quite literally astonished when about a fortnight later a letter arrived from one of the firm's editors expressing a definite interest in my proposal and requesting a sample chapter—of which, of course, at that point I had written not a single word! This was the unexpected beginning of *Dominion of the North*.

These first three books were large and demanding enterprises which monopolized my time. The essays which I wrote during this period were usually related or incidental to the main work on which I was currently engaged. Thus "The Commercial Class in Canadian Politics" was a first statement of what became the main theme of *The Empire of the St. Lawrence*; "The Economic Background of the Rebellions of 1837" was a by-product of the same work in progress; and "Economic Nationalism and Confederation" grew out of the study commissioned by the Royal Commission on Dominion-Provincial Relations. The origins of "The Victorians and the Empire", which was first given as a public lecture in a series on the Victorian Age, were somewhat more varied; it was a product, in part, of my special studies for *The Empire of the St. Lawrence* and also, in part, of a much more general interest in the history of the British Empire throughout the nineteenth century. "George Brown, Sir John Macdonald and the 'Workingman' ", which appeared some years later, was an early evidence of my growing interest in Macdonald, an interest which was shortly to commit me to the enormous task of writing his biography.

It was during my early studies for this biography that I first became aware of the strength, persistence, and prevalence of the Liberal Interpretation of Canadian history. From the first I was puzzled by the fact that Sir John Macdonald had fared so badly at the hands of the scholars and journalists who dominated Canadian historical writing during the first half of the twentieth century. He was sometimes ignored, his great achievements were frequently undervalued, and all too often he was presented to the Canadian people as a convivial, bibulous, procrastinating, and none too scrupulous politician, virtually untroubled by ideas, principles, or purposes, whose chief specialties were the shabby arts of political expediency and parliamentary manoeuvre. The basic reason for this evaluation gradually became clearer. The Canadian historians of the early twentieth century, I began to realize, had yielded to the seductions of that simplest and most distorting of all methods of viewing the past, the Whig Interpretation of history. Herbert Butterfield, who first invented the name and analysed the nature of the Whig Interpretation, defined it as the study of the past with constant reference to the present, and from the standpoint of present interests and values. Viewed from this eminence, the course of historical change could obviously be nothing but the onward march of progress; and thus the task of the historian was not merely to explain and account for the present, but also to justify and vindicate it historically. Everything in the past which had the appearance of an origin, anticipation, or promise of some valued feature of contemporary society was emphasized by the Whig historians; and everything that seemed incongruous in the eyes of the twentieth century or incompatible with its standards and values was treated briefly or criticized or explained away.

My essay "Sir John Macdonald and Canadian Historians" was, I think, the first attempt to point out the value and relevance of Butterfield's theory for the study of Canadian historical writing. In England the Whig party had utterly vanished, and its successor, the Liberal party, barely survived. In Canada the Liberal party was neither dead nor moribund; it was active, kicking, and immensely powerful and successful. Butterfield had used the term "Whig" simply to designate the reformers, progressives, and radicals of any political faith who looked back on history from the vantage point of the present. But, in Canada, the Liberal party had, with considerable success, attempted to appropriate to itself most of the credit for Canadian progress. The Liberal editors, professors, and deputy-ministers who set the standards of Canadian historical writing in the early twentieth century had gone far to establish a veritable Liberal monopoly of the good men, the great causes, the fine human advances of Canadian history.

I was quickly made aware of the extent to which history had become party property in Canada. In England, the publication of a biography on Disraeli or Churchill would not be automatically regarded as positive proof of its author's Conservative allegiance; but, in Canada, the appearance of my two-volume biography of Macdonald in 1952-5 was more than enough to convict me of the charge of being a Tory. Although I had chosen Macdonald largely because I thought he was a big subject, suited to the kind of history I liked to write, I was instantly placed in the Conservative category; and there, with occasional removals to the Communist or other deplorable political pigeon-holes, I have been kept ever since. In 1957, when the Conservatives

finally gained power, Liberal acquaintances in the academic profession jocosely predicted that I would soon be
given my political reward; and some civil servants, whom I
had scarcely met, insinuated that I had earned it, and not
merely by writing the biography of Macdonald. It was ru-
moured that I had helped to write John Diefenbaker's
speeches; and a few years later, when the Liberals were re-
stored to power, I found that this fiction was evidently still
current, even among the seats of the mighty. I happened to
meet the new Prime Minister, Lester Pearson—whom I
had known during my first, and his last, year in the Department of History at Toronto—in the elevator in the Parliament Buildings. I was accompanied by a Liberal M.P. who
shared my fears of the invasion of American capital into
Canada and who had invited me to dinner in the Parliamentary restaurant. "You see I am in good company," I remarked to Pearson after we had greeted each other. "Better
than I have seen you in recently," he answered sourly.

The elevator continued its upward flight in silence.

II

In the middle and late 1940s, when my studies for the
Macdonald biography were steadily strengthening the
ideas first formed in the writing of The Empire of the St.
Lawrence, I began to realize just how radically the Liberal
Interpretation of Canadian history differed from my own.
I had reached the conclusion that Canada's main object in
North America was the founding of a great continental
empire based in the east-west axis of the St. Lawrence, and
that the most formidable barrier to the realization of this
grand design was the rivalry and hostility of what had been
the Thirteen Colonies and soon became the United States.
The maintenance of her separate and independent po-

sition in North America was thus Canada's first necessity; and since from the beginning she had always been hopelessly inferior to her great antagonist in numbers, economic strength, and military power, she had relied heavily on external assistance. Alone of all the colonies founded in the New World, she had kept her close association with Europe and maintained the imperial tie which bound her to the Motherland. These, it seemed to me, were her distinctive historical characteristics; but it was not long before I realized that the Liberal historians had found in Canadian history a meaning which was almost a complete inversion of my own.

In their eyes, Canada's fundamental purpose was not survival in North America but emancipation from Europe. The winning of responsible government and what used to be called "Dominion status"—the achievement of complete autonomy inside the British Empire–Commonwealth—seemed to them by far the most important theme in Canadian history. They concentrated on constitutional history and the changing nature of the imperial connection; they neglected military history and relations with the United States. Gradually Canada's long, armed struggle for existence in a continent dominated by the United States receded into the dim, forgotten past; and Canadian-American "good neighbourhood" along "the four thousand miles of undefended frontier" was accepted as the natural condition of peaceful North America. Somehow Liberal historians managed to ignore or forget the fact that Great Britain had more often than not taken the initiative in the growth of responsible government and that, at the time of Confederation, she might have been readily persuaded to grant Canada independence. Instead they had converted the achievement of self-government into a long, acrimonious struggle in which every concession had been extorted by eager Canadians from an unwilling and obstinate Motherland.

In 1921 the Liberal Interpretation of Canadian history had nearly reached its full maturity of expression; and the Liberals, under Mackenzie King, recovered power at Ottawa. King and his new Undersecretary for External Affairs, O. D. Skelton, were both convinced that the Liberal historical interpretation explained and vindicated current Liberal ideology, and they were equally eager to alter Canadian policy in accordance with the best Liberal tradition. For the next twenty years, King and Skelton sought, on the one hand, to detach Canada from Great Britain and to break down the co-operative Commonwealth developed during the First World War, and, on the other, to establish increasingly close relations, economic, political, and military, with the United States. By 1939, when the Second World War began, they had virtually succeeded in removing Canada from a British imperial system in which she enjoyed a recognized position and considerable authority and transferring her to an American imperial system in which she had no standing and no influence whatever. The war was the last great manifestation of the still surviving solidarity of the Empire-Commonwealth; but King was determined to prevent even a partial reinstatement of the old co-operative imperial organization. Along with Winston Churchill, he persistently resisted all efforts to re-create the Imperial War Cabinet of the First World War; but nothing could exceed the alacrity with which he hustled down to Ogdensburg and accepted President Roosevelt's invitation to form a Permanent Joint Board on North American defence.

The events of August 1940—the Ogdensburg Agreement and the notorious "destroyers-for-bases" deal, by which the United States acquired a military stranglehold on Newfoundland, Bermuda, and the British West Indies in exchange for two score decrepit American destroyers—threw the great majority of Canadians, including many of my friends and acquaintances, into ecstasies of gratification.

They left me with a new but rapidly increasing sense of disquiet; obviously the United States had gone a long way towards the establishment of a North American military empire. My concern for the future of Canadian independence mounted steadily during the war; but, so far as I could see, I was virtually alone in my worries. It was not until the late 1940s that I began to realize that I had found a powerful ally in my old friend Harold Innis.

Innis's visits to Russia in 1945 and to England in 1948 marked, I think, the beginning and end of a change, even more radical than my own, in his outlook on world affairs. In June 1950, when the Korean War broke out, we discovered how nearly identical our ideas had become. We were both in Ottawa, Innis busy with his work in the Royal Commission on Transportation, and I deep in the writing of the first volume of my biography on Macdonald. We used to meet in the evening before dinner in his room in the Château Laurier for long talks on the Korean situation. We both regarded the action of the United Nations in Korea as a very imperfect disguise for American military intervention in the Far East; but we were quickly made to understand that in Ottawa it was better to keep these reprehensible opinions to ourselves. The members of the Department of External Affairs were united in the exalted belief that the Korean War was a holy crusade in support of the collective system; and one of them informed me curtly that he wanted to hear no more of my sacrilegious aspersions on a noble cause.

Harold Innis's death in the autumn of 1952 was a tremendous loss to me. It deprived me of the support that can come only from a long friendship, based on mutual confidences, common convictions, and shared views. I felt very much alone in the early 1950s; and I quickly realized, with something of a shock, that this sense of isolation was by no means imaginary. In August 1954, I gave the talk "Canada and the Cold War", which is included in this volume, at the Couchiching Conference on Public Affairs. Only a few hours before I was due to speak, I got my first warning of the small storm of disapproval which my paper was to arouse. John G. Diefenbaker was at that time honorary president of the Couchiching Institute and he was to preside over the evening session at which I was to speak. During the afternoon I met him in the park, and he informed me, in a tone of grave reproof, that my talk, of which he had been given an advance copy, was a very extraordinary statement for a "Conservative historian" to make. Later, when I had finished speaking and before discussion had begun, he took occasion to announce publicly that he completely dissociated himself from my strange opinions. The chief critic of the evening, Professor Marcus Long, dismissed my talk as a frontal attack on the United States; and, in those days, this was more than enough to invite a dangerous notoriety and arouse suspicions of Communist sympathies. My remarks were reported on the front pages of the Toronto newspapers and a correspondent to the *Globe and Mail* denounced me as a "professor of lying propaganda" and demanded my dismissal from the University of Toronto. He may have been bitterly disappointed to learn, that autumn, that I had been appointed chairman of the Department of History.

Later, the Public Affairs producers in the Canadian Broadcasting Corporation assured me that there was a fair amount of support for my views among radio listeners; but my reception that August evening at Couchiching was a disturbing experience. It was obvious that dissent from the orthodox Canadian belief in the disinterested wisdom of the American leadership of "the free world" was highly unwelcome. Since I had still to finish the second and more difficult volume of my biography of Sir John Macdonald and had readily agreed to write a memoir on the life of Harold Innis, I kept away from contemporary issues during the middle 1950s. I only gradually came to realize that these same middle years had witnessed an unmistakable change in the attitude of many Canadians to the United States. There was, of course, not the slightest sign of this altered attitude in the policies of the Liberal government; but a good many Canadians were beginning uneasily to feel that American economic power might undermine Canadian independence, and that American foreign policy could endanger the peace of the whole world. A few people even began to suspect that for a whole generation Canada had been fighting the wrong imperialism. Liberal apologists tried to find excuses for this tragic error; but it seemed to me that the Canadian misconception had its origin in a totally mistaken historical theory, the Liberal Interpretation, which misrepresented Canada's essential character, ignored her basic necessities, and altered the direction of her principal trend. I began to express these ideas in my presidential address to the Canadian Historical Association in 1957 and in such essays as "Towards the Discovery of Canada" and "Macdonald and the Anglo-Canadian Alliance", which was first published in *Our Living Tradition*, vol. 1.

III

The Liberal Interpretation of Canadian history placed perhaps its main emphasis on external relations; but there was a second and almost equally important part of the Authorized Version which was concerned with domestic history. It gave pride of place to reformers, early reform movements, the Canadian rebellions, and the winning of responsible government; it relegated Confederation to a much less prominent and honourable position. Soon after 1867, the Liberal party adopted, and fairly steadily maintained, a policy of strong support for provincial rights; and this, of course, quickly had its effect on the Liberal account of the Confederation movement as well as the Liberal concept of Canadian federalism. Liberal historians and political theorists, encouraged by the long succession of provincial victories in the constitutional cases of the nineteenth and early twentieth century, began to question and then to deny the old belief that the Fathers of Confederation had intended a strongly centralized union and a paramount federal government. Later, as the twentieth century reached and then passed its middle point, the Liberal image of Confederation began to change more rapidly. It was deeply influenced by two developments of immense importance—Mackenzie King's transference of Canada from the British to the American empire and the outbreak of the so-called Quiet Revolution in Quebec.

The growing strength of Canada's connections with the United States weakened its attachment to the monarchy and the Commonwealth, reduced the significance of the symbols of royalty and empire, and quickened interest in American constitutional devices. Continentalism threatened Canadian political institutions; the Quiet Revolution carried an equally grave danger for the Canadian federal system. The main aim of the new French-Canadian nationalists was to preserve French Canada's identity and to elevate and strengthen its place in the Canadian nation; and they insisted that these purposes could be attained only by constitutional changes which would recognize the cultural duality of Canada and the special status of the Province of Quebec. These were very large demands; but the federal Liberal party, frantic for office after six unnatural years of Tory rule, hastily acknowledged their justice and, once in power again, made the satisfaction of French Canada its chief obsession. The terms of reference of the Royal Commission on Bilingualism and Biculturalism declared that Canada should be developed "on the

basis of an equal partnership of the two founding races".
The "opting-out" financial formula gave Quebec its first
chance of detaching itself from the other provinces and establishing a special relationship with the federal government.

What followed was a remarkable demonstration of the
influence of party politics on Canadian thought. It soon
became clear that the French-Canadian nationalists had
won over, not only the Canadian government, but also the
Canadian people. For over ninety years of Canada's first
century, the English-Canadian conception of French Canada's place in Confederation had not significantly altered.
Now, almost in a minute, Quebec took on the impressive
and pitiable appearance of the protagonist in a heart-rend-
ing tragedy. The public recitation of the woes, wrongs,
injuries, and tribulations of French Canada became an interminable litany in which nearly everybody joined with
fervour. The mass media had endless time and space for bilingualism and biculturalism; the monthlies and quarter-
lies investigated the political and constitutional implications of French-Canadian nationalism. Universities provided courses, and professors proposed doctoral theses,
in the history of French Canada. Ramsay Cook began to
explore the complexities of the "French-Canadian Question" with the same earnest application that Dawson,
Skelton, and Chester Martin had once devoted to the
growth of responsible government and "Dominion status".
"Justice to French Canada" became an intellectual pursuit
without ever ceasing to be an emotional crusade. Its growing moral compulsion, comparable in the end with that of
an old-fashioned camp meeting or a "moral rearmament"
confessional, proved irresistible; and a large number of
English Canadians became convinced that the lamentable
state of French Canada was a crime of which they were
guilty and for which they must now make reparation.
From these new and exalted heights of repentence and res-

olution, the Constitution of 1867 looked remote, obsolete, and obstructive. Canada, it was assumed, must now escape completely from the rigid letter of the British North America Act, and revive the "true spirit" of Confederation, the essence of which was the "bicultural compact", the unspoken but vital "moral commitment" which bound English and French to realize the equal partnership of the races. With this as the guiding principle of reform, and with a few judicious borrowings from the United States, the Canadian constitution could quickly be remade.

The incessant discussion of French Canada and the Canadian constitution, which filled the 1960s with sound and fury, was invariably called a "dialogue". I soon discovered, when I began to criticize some of the "dialogue's" main arguments, that this was a highly inaccurate description. The lecture which I gave at Trent University in the autumn of 1965, called "The Use and Abuse of History", was a first attempt at a critical examination of the historical and constitutional implications of the French-Canadian nationalist movement. "The Myth of Biculturalism", first given to the Alumnae Association of University College in the spring of 1966, was a much franker attack on the whole idea of Confederation as a bicultural compact. The audience as a whole gave it a fairly warm welcome; but the top brass of the University of Toronto, sitting in close proximity to me at the head of Hart House Great Hall, showed obvious signs of frigid disapproval. That autumn, when the talk was published in *Saturday Night*, and reprinted in the *Toronto Daily Star*, it became clear that this opinion was widespread and deeply rooted.

I began to realize that the alleged "dialogue" on French Canada and the constitution was not a dialogue at all, but an uninterrupted monologue, indeed a chant in plainsong by a chorus of many voices, and that discordant notes were not wanted and would not be excused or condoned. Criticism of French-Canadian nationalism was just as illegitimate in 1966 as criticism of American foreign policy had been twelve years before. Both were offences against an established Canadian consensus and equally deserved censure. A few kind friends gravely informed me that I was behaving like a "bad Canadian" and endangering my reputation; but it was left to Professor W. L. Morton to announce, in a preface to the English edition of Solange Chaput Rolland's *My Country, Canada or Quebec?*, that I had "distorted . . . a lifetime of devotion to the understanding of Canada". Professor Morton sorrowfully charged me with the crime of "invoking cultural continentalism, the fact that North America speaks English", as if I were some modern Owen Glendower who could call spirits from the vasty deep. I didn't invent continentalism: it had, unfortunately, existed for a very long time. What I had done was to remind Canadians—as I had done repeatedly in the past and was to do repeatedly in the future—of the enormous power exercised by the United States on every aspect of their political, economic, and cultural life. I did not believe that our cultural identity could be preserved if our political and economic independence was left undefended, as it had been for virtually half a century; and I also did not believe—and this separates me decisively from Professor Morton—that language is the one indispensable element in that identity and that biculturalism is therefore "the very essence of Canadian national aspirations".

In "Macdonald, Confederation and the West", which was read at a meeting of the Manitoba Historical Society, I returned to the examination of the historical bases of the cultural compact. I then decided that I had said my say on the new compact theory of Confederation; and, since I was eager to finish the manuscript of *Canada's First Century*, I gave all my time to it during the next two years. Inevitably, the writing of this book forced me to take a long view of Canadian history; and in June 1969, when I spoke at the annual meeting of the Canadian Historical Association, I tried to give a brief survey of the nation's troubled journey through time, as I conceived it. The title of my paper, "The Decline and Fall of the Empire of the St. Lawrence", was chosen deliberately. It seemed to me that the penultimate crisis in Canada's career was now at hand. External pressure and internal division were the forces which together could destroy that great nineteenth-century creation, the national state; and in Canada these twin forces had taken on the form of American continentalism and French-Canadian nationalism. Now, and for literally the first time in our history, these two great complementary powers, like upper and nether millstones, were simultaneously grinding the substance of Canadian nationality to shreds. At a moment when national unity was more necessary than ever before to resist the weight of American continentalism, Canadians had permitted themselves to become involved in a divisive cultural problem; and the time and effort which might have gone into defence against the invader was likely to be sacrificed in a prolonged and vain effort to remake Canada and transform its constitution in the interest of cultural dualism. This attempt, it seemed to me, would run its course through frustration and failure to disillusionment, and its only real result would be a still further dilapidation of the original constitution of 1867. These were the chief themes of the epilogue of *Canada's First Century* and of several talks given in 1970-1. "Canadian Nationalism and Its Opponents" and "History and the Constitution", my submission to the Special Joint Parliamentary Committee on the Constitution of Canada, have been chosen as examples of this phase of my work.

The writing of Canadian history had confirmed and strengthened my belief in the value of the Canadian national state; and when, during the last quarter-century, its continued existence seemed threatened by American continentalism on the one hand and French-Canadian provincialism on the other, I could not help feeling deeply concerned and anxious. Somewhat reluctantly, though perhaps inevitably, I became involved in the debates of the period; but this troubled preoccupation with contemporary affairs came late in life and it had no influence whatever on my original intention of writing history. That urge came, not from modern politics, but from English and French literature. I wanted to write history for its own sake, not from the backward glance of the present, but as if what I was describing had happened the day before yesterday. I welcomed the chance of explaining my aims and methods as an historian when I visited York University in the winter of 1971; and the talk I gave there, now called "History and Literature", is, appropriately enough, the first essay in this book.

A final word of explanation is in order. This book was not planned and written as an integrated whole. It is a collection of talks, lectures, and articles composed for different audiences and various journals over a long period of time; and since the essays are printed here in their original form, almost entirely without alteration, there is inevitably some repetition. Ideas which are basic in my view of some general subject appear, variously expressed, in talks given months or years apart to quite different audiences. I have not tried to eliminate these recurrences. To do so would be to spoil the continuity of a few of the essays and change the character of the book.

Part I
The Craft of
History

History and Literature

THE SUBJECT OF this talk is my view of what history is, and my aims and methods as an historian. This means, I am afraid, a prolonged but unavoidable exercise in the first person singular. I am also going to make the assumption, an even more obvious indication of vanity, that history is, or can be, a branch of literature. It is certainly so regarded in England and France: *The Times*, *Le Monde*, and *Figaro* give history an honourable place in their literary pages. Not so in Canada; Canadians, even more than Americans, have a frontier conception of literature as something completely detached from the reality of historical fact. Nothing can be truly creative unless it is wholly imaginary: and only two categories of writing— poetry and fiction—qualify for this distinction. Everything else in prose is relegated to a large, third residual heap called "remaining material" (it used to be so termed in the *University of Toronto Quarterly*'s annual survey) or is briefly and simply designated as "non-fiction". Fiction and poetry are, of course, "creative"—I am repeating the dis-

First delivered as a lecture at York University in February 1971 and published here for the first time.

tinctions originally established for the Governor General's Awards. A work of "non-fiction" may conceivably be creative, but never when it has been written by a member of a university. All "non-fictions" written by university people are "academic". I am thus driven to the inescapable conclusion that I have been writing uncreative, academic nonfiction all my life.

These generous classifications, which, you will notice, are defined chiefly by negatives, do not get us far towards an understanding of what history is and provide no explanation at all of what I am trying to do when I write it. All too frequently, even in university curricula, history is consigned to a large category labelled "the social sciences", which, on the whole, is very unsuitable and uncongenial company for it. History differs from political science, economic theory, and sociology, and also from philosophy, not only and obviously in its subject matter, but also in its method, which is mainly narrative and descriptive rather than analytical and expository. History's closest affiliation is with literature: it is not a science, and is, or should be, a literary art or craft, and its most appropriate form is narrative. Narrative history, represented by Gibbon, Macaulay, Froude, Trevelyan, Bryant, Runciman, and Taylor, is the main English tradition; and the historians who have had any influence on my work are almost exclusively British historians.

To say that history is an art or craft does not mean that it can dispense with the disciplined and systematic procedures of the scientific method. The search for evidence must be comprehensive and exact; scrupulous care must be used in its evaluation; and the historian should try to equip himself to make good use of the semi-scientific tools of the social sciences—politics, economics, and sociology. Scientific practice is highly desirable; but its use does not convert history into a science, not at least in the sense in which the word is understood by the logical positivists.

They believe that the business of history is the discovery and elucidation of general laws and universal truths, of which particular events are merely illustrations or examples. This theoretical concept seems to me untenable; and on this fundamental question, I take my stand, not with the positivists, but with the so-called idealists, such as R. G. Collingwood, Michael Oakeshott, and my friend William Dray of Trent University. "Covering laws", if they are really valid, are so vague and general that they illuminate nothing of interest. Historical events are unique and basically incomparable; and the only way to their understanding is to get beneath them into the human hopes, ideals, purposes, and intentions by which they were inspired. The historian's first task is the elucidation of character; but characters—human beings—are not totally free and independent. They have a definite and significant position in time and space. The historian's second task is the re-creation of the circumstances—the situations, problems, opportunities, and difficulties—which confront his characters. He must make clear and vivid the setting in which they are compelled to act. Thus, to me, history is the record of an encounter between character and circumstance.

History—the course of events, that is—is an unending and bewildering torrent of multitudinous, unique facts. The historian must choose from this vast, formless mass the elements he thinks essential to its understanding, and compose them in such a way as to reveal their meaning and significance, as he sees it. His task is selection and arrangement. His aim is pattern—the composite of the leading qualities or features of his period. His purpose is the discovery of the significant form or design which will reveal the essential meaning beneath the chaos of facts. It ought to go without saying, of course, that the historian's truth is only partial truth: real truth is laid up in the mind of God. But even partial truth has value in a chaotic and bewildering world. Men need not be ignorant and helpless victims of the historical process. History can help men to understand their nation's distinctive character, and to recognize the main direction of its advance in time.

Historical pattern or form as the essence of history can, it seems to me, best be realized through the development of themes. A theme is an idea which underlies the historical material; the material is organized around the idea; and the idea summarizes and interprets the material. The themes, in short, are the principal components of the pattern or design; it is realized through their arrangement, just as, to compare small things with great, one of Claude Monet's enchanting pictures of the Seine at Argenteuil is realized through the disposition of masses and the choice of colours. Or perhaps more appropriately, since a picture is a captured moment which survives unchanged through time, a theme should be likened to a musical motif, and particularly to Richard Wagner's leitmotif, or "leading motif". In "The Ring of the Nibelung", the leading motif is a short melodic passage representing physical elements, forces of destiny, individual characters, emotional states, and heroic purposes and achievements; and these motifs keep on recurring throughout the four operas with every conceivable change of phrase or tone or mood. My musical friends used to regard my enthusiasm for Wagner with majestic condescension; but I felt sustained by the fact that though Wagner may not be a musician's composer, he is certainly a writer's composer, as the views of Moore, Shaw, Proust, Mann, Maugham, and Eliot attest.

It is, of course, absurd and pretentious to compare an historian's prosaic method with Wagner's beautiful, haunting musical device. And yet perhaps a basic similarity does exist. It is only by the recurrence of a theme through a variety of changing phases that its nature and development will be fully understood. It is only through the development of all the themes as an interrelated whole that the significance of the entire period will become clear. One of the primal themes in my books, the St. Lawrence as the east-west axis of Canadian transcontinental expansion, finds expression in western exploration, the westward march of the fur trade, the settlement of the prairies, the building of the transcontinental railways, and the growth of the wheat economy. A second basic theme, the exact antithesis of the first, is continentalism, the American urge towards continental empire; and this appears and re-appears in such varied manifestations as armed invasion, commercial competition, political pressure, financial take-over, and cultural influence.

Narrative, it seems to me, is the only way in which a theme can be fully developed and all its changes and phases revealed. At times, of course, there must be exposition, analysis, and criticism; but history's main emphasis should surely be placed on the sequence of events and on the thoughts and actions of men and women in the changing situations of their lives. The encounter between character and circumstance is essentially a story; and therefore, for me at least, history's most closely affiliated literary form is the novel. I cannot help feeling that novelists have taught me more than historians have about the craft of narrative. I do not, of course, mean all novels, and not many contemporary ones. Mainly I have been influenced by the great realistic or naturalistic novels of the nineteenth and early twentieth centuries, and primarily by novels which are concerned with a group, a family, a class, or a community at a particular time and place, with a large cast and a comprehensive and detailed background or setting. English literature is extremely rich in this form; one thinks of Dickens, Thackeray, George Eliot, Trollope, Hardy, Bennett, Galsworthy, C. P. Snow. The novels of Dreiser and Dos Passos are obvious American examples; and Thomas Mann's *Buddenbrooks* and Tolstoy's *War and Peace* must also be remembered. But it has always seemed to me that the greatest achievements in this, the "grand style" of the novel, have been French. Balzac, Zola, Proust, and Jules Romains set out to tell the story of a whole generation or entire epoch.

A common feature of all these novels is a sensitive awareness of time. Time is obviously the protagonist of *La Comédie humaine*, *Les Rougon-Macquart*, *A la recherche du temps perdu*, and *Les Hommes de bonne volonté*. Time, and not Constance Povey or Sophia Scales, is the chief character in Arnold Bennett's *The Old Wives' Tale*. This is made poignantly explicit in a scene which occurs towards the end of the book. Gerald Scales, Sophia's husband, who deserted her thirty-six years before, has at length returned, old, broken, destitute, and ill, to England. Sophia, who has never seen him in all these years, is informed of his arrival at the house of a distant connection in Manchester, and goes to see him. He is dead before she gets there. She stands in the dim upstairs room facing his body, and her past crowds through her mind in disordered snatches.

> She was not sorry that Gerald had wasted his life, nor that he was a shame to his years and to her. The manner of his life was of no importance. What affected her was that he had once been young, and that he had grown old, and was now dead. That was all. Youth and vigour had come to that. Youth and vigour always came to that. Everything came to that. . . . By the corner of her eye, reflected in the mirror of a wardrobe by the bed, she glimpsed a tall, forlorn woman, who had once been young and now was old. . . . He and she had once loved and burned and quarrelled in the glittering and scornful pride of youth. But time had worn them out. "Yet a little while," she thought, "and I shall be lying on a bed like that! And what shall I have lived for? What is the meaning of it?"

It is a terrific scene in which Time seems to be physically present, just as he does, perhaps even more portentously, in the last lines of the second part of T. S. Eliot's *The Waste Land*. There the scene is a public house at closing time. The proprietor keeps calling out, "Hurry up please, it's time, hurry up please, it's time." And Time seems suddenly to stand in the doorway, a dreadful figure, bidding the company begone. Time is the essence of history; and any young student who wants to be an historian and hasn't a sensitive feeling for time—for growth and change and decay—had better alter his plans and take up a timeless and lifeless study such as political science or economic theory.

The passage of time can be conveyed only through narrative; and no narrative can be vital unless it deals with the thoughts and actions of intelligible human beings responding to the changing circumstances of their lives. The revelation or disclosure of character is just as important for the historian as the creation of character is for the novelist; and the chief defect of many history books is that their characters are not real people at all. They are lay figures, papier-mâché figures, roughly moulded from the pulp of dispatches, pamphlets, and parliamentary papers. Such lifeless models would not satisfy a good novelist and they ought not to satisfy an historian. It is possible, though difficult, to get at the real person through private letters, diaries, memoirs, and contemporary reminiscences; and a character's reflections and statements, and particularly his casual, colloquial comments, can be used as conversation. I have been reproached on occasion for putting particular thoughts, aims, and plans in the heads of my historical characters at particular moments. How do I know, is the derisive question, that these specific ideas were passing through their minds at this exact point of time? The answer is, of course, that I don't know. But there is ample evidence to prove that these hopes, beliefs, or intentions did preoccupy my people at a time close to my chosen moment.

My moment is chosen because it is dramatically effective; it is usually the moment of action. And the thought explains the action.

Historical characters take action in response to circumstance; and the second major task of narrative is to present the changing situations in which people have to live and act. Here also the historian can emulate the practice of the realistic novelist. The principal defect of a great many descriptions of historical settings or situations is their abstract, unsubstantial nature; all too often they are composed of broad generalizations about the political, economic, and social conditions of the time. Concrete detail, pictorial in quality, can alone invest a scene with an air of vivid actuality; but to achieve this kind of effect, an historian must laboriously acquire a detailed knowledge of the scenery, architecture, costume, manners, and speech of his historical setting and period. Background can be best indicated by occasional light touches; elaborate period descriptions are rarely necessary. Nothing is more unreal than heavily costumed, over-dramatized history, dressed up to look like romance or melodrama. The aim of the historian should be the feeling of actuality, the sense of immediacy. The reader should be induced to accept the illusion that he is reliving the historical experience. All history is contemporary history.

There is another important lesson that the novelist can help to teach the narrative historian. This is that he should never forget that he is telling a story; events should be put down, in the main, as they occur in time. There are, of course, legitimate exceptions to this rule; the novelist himself uses the "flashback", the interruption of the story in order to introduce a previous incident or incidents. Similarly, the historian will sometimes have to go back into the past in order to explain a particular development, or he may feel it necessary to subject some issue to a detailed analysis, or to examine, at some length, the contradictory points of view in a debate or controversy. Unfortunately, historians are often tempted to go much further than this. They are always finding themselves burdened by awkward or intractable materials which are extremely difficult to fit into the main body of the narrative; and the easy way out of this predicament is to reserve the unmanageable residue for a separate topical chapter. This desperate expedient may be inevitable on occasion; but some historians resort to it with regrettable frequency and the sad result is a series of discrete essays, like the chapters of a doctoral thesis, and not a narrative history at all.

History, I believe, should attempt to give a total impression of the course of events as it moves forward in time. Obviously it is impossible to write about everything at once, except in the broadest generalizations. This is perhaps the greatest difficulty that a narrative historian has to face, but there are at least a few devices by which he can try to cope with it. Often it is possible to treat several closely related themes together, or, by the use of what might be called cross references, to remind the reader of one subject at a significant point in the development of another. Often, however, and particularly in a general history, which attempts to cover a wide range of human activities, it is necessary to concentrate on one theme alone; but here again the storyteller's habit of dividing a chapter into scenes or episodes can be helpful. In a true narrative history, the span of time covered by a single chapter will be short enough to permit the historian to deal with the development of several, if not all, of his principal themes and thus to give the reader a total impression of the onward movement of events in that period.

My subject was my view of history and my aims and methods as an historian. I have talked enough, and perhaps more than enough, about them. Only two remarks remain to be made. The first can be put briefly. I have been talking about narrative history, which I regard as "pure" history, but I am ready to concede that there are other, to me somewhat adulterated, varieties of the same subject. I do not mean, though I may seem to have implied it, that young historians should accept this evaluation and follow my example. "There are nine and sixty ways of constructing tribal lays, and every single one of them is right". I believe Rudyard Kipling was right also.

The second point can also be briefly put. I do not for a moment regard this talk as a solid contribution to the theory or philosophy of history, or even as a detailed plan for writing it. When I began to write, I had no plan at all, and not much knowledge of what the philosophers of history had said. I designed and wrote my books instinctively and not in conscious accordance with any literary principles. It is only fairly recently that I began to look back over my work in an effort to define what my aims and methods were. I may have systematized the results of this inquiry too much, but I have given them to you for what they are worth.

Doctrine and the
Interpretation
of History

CANADIAN HISTORICAL ASSOCIATION presidents, like all Gaul, are divided into three parts. Faced with the annual necessity of composing and delivering a presidential address, they almost invariably follow one of three possible courses. On the one hand, a small but hardy number compose philosophic discourses on the nature and meaning of history; and, on the other, a much larger and more cautious group prepare good, solid papers on the subjects of their current research. Obviously the first of these two courses represents the extreme of presidential daring, and the second the maximum of presidential prudence. The third course leads through middle ground. Presidents who modestly follow the third course are accustomed to choose, not the vast and terrifying problem of history as a whole, but the more manageable yet still impressive subject of what is called in North America their "field". And they then compose a critical report or evaluation of the state of historical studies within this chosen area. There is, as will be instantly appreciated, a good deal to be said for this third course. It combines a high degree of safety with a fair amount of latitude. It is the wise way, the good way, the middle way. It is what, from all Canadian experience, will be instantly known and

---

First given on 14 June 1957 at the University of Ottawa at the annual meeting of the Canadian Historical Association and published in the C.H.A. *Report*, 1957, p. 1, under the title "Presidential Address".

recognized as the Liberal way. And it is the way which, both gratefully and admiringly, I propose to take tonight. What follows is a brief review of historical writing about Canada, its chief problems and its main tendencies, during the past quarter-century.

This, surely, is an appropriate moment for such a survey. It is true, of course, that historians are always discovering appropriate moments, always making convenient punctuation marks in the writings of time. Ending epochs, beginning new periods, and delimiting ages of transition are questionable professional habits in which historians are only too apt to over-indulge. And yet there are some very substantial reasons for feeling that, at the present moment, we stand in a particularly favourable position for looking back into the past, and forward into the future, of historical writing about Canada. During the last few years, Canadian historical studies may be said to have come to an end of a fairly well-defined stage in their development. It has been a curious, paradoxical period, the stage which has just drawn to its conclusion. During the nearly thirty years which elapsed from the Imperial Conference of 1926 to the accession of the second Queen Elizabeth, Canadian historians did some of their best creative work, and yet, at times, hardly knew, or seemed to care very much, whether they could call their souls their own. They became, all too easily, the too susceptible victims of others' intimidation and their own credulity. On the one hand, history was subjected to a fair amount of pressure from related academic disciplines, and from journalists and politicians. And, on the other, the historians themselves showed an inveterate disposition to lose their own spiritual independence through the uncritical acceptance of currently fashionable theories of historical change. The intellectual atmosphere of these decades was not particularly favourable for historical studies in general; the currently popular theories of historical change were seriously misleading when applied to Cana-

dian history in particular. And it was not really until the
first decade after the war of 1939-45 that these circumstances began markedly to alter and these prepossessions to
lose their stultifying grip. In the past few years Canadian
history has recovered its sense of autonomy, its conviction
of the worth of its subject matter and the value of its own
independent approach. It has also—and this is still more
important—shaken itself free from the rigid doctrinaire
obsessions which dominated Canadian thought in the inter-war years.

In this description of Canadian history's attainment of a
new-found maturity, there lies, of course, an obvious para-
dox. For history is the oldest, the most solidly established
of all Canadian studies. It is the most articulate of the humanities, the most productive of the social sciences. As the
annual reports of university presidents reveal very clearly,
the economists, political scientists, lawyers, literary critics,
and art critics of Canadian universities share a marked
preference for the historical method. Canadian scholars, in
any and every academic discipline, are far more likely to
be historians than they are to be theorists or philosophers.
Outwardly this might have seemed highly flattering as well
as extremely valuable to the professional historians; but, in
actual fact, they found it to be almost as much a curse as a
blessing. History has dominated the humanities and the social sciences; but its domination was one which the
professional historians found, to their cost, that they did
not exercise themselves. Everybody—or nearly everybody—was his own historian. Everybody was intimately
convinced that he wrote superb history and was prepared
shyly to admit the fact at the slightest provocation. Everybody was perfectly ready at all times to instruct the
professional historian in the infinitely superior methods by
which he could improve his own miserable performance of
his task.

This amiable business of hectoring, instructing, and supervising historians goes back a very long time indeed. It may be said to have had its beginning in the unhappy tribulations of one of the earliest and best-known of Canadian professional historians. A great teacher, a wise scholar, a writer of learned and gracefully written books, this historian enjoyed, and still enjoys, a very considerable reputation; and it may occasion a start of surprise for some to realize that he spent a good part of his early professional career in fighting manfully for the autonomy of his subject. Yet so, incredibly enough, it was. A colleague of his, the head of a fairly closely related department in the university, claimed, and tried energetically to exercise, some mythical superintendence over the Department of History. And when, inevitably, it proved impossible to make this absurd and impertinent claim good, the would-be superintendent went around the university, chattering with rage behind his bushy beard. The historian, who was a Christian and a gentleman, was distressed and perplexed by his colleague's exhibition of angry presumption. He no doubt put it down to some private aberration of that person's character. But succeeding generations of historians have discovered that these delusions of grandeur, these infatuated claims of empire, seem to be a regularly recurring phenomenon among the disciplines with which history is most closely associated.

Either some other subject appears to be going to take over history holus-bolus, or else the professors of some other subject are proclaiming, with self-righteous confidence, that history *ought* to be taken over holus-bolus. In the 1920s, when most Canadian nationalists were passing through what might be described as a species of frenzy over the question of Dominion autonomy, it looked for a while as if lawyers and neo-legalists were going to make Canadian history a branch of constitutional law. In the 1930s, when the influence of Harold Innis was at its height and everybody was writing and talking about staple production, it began to seem possible that history would degenerate into a sub-department of Political Economy. Finally, just at the opening of the 1940s, came what can only be regarded as the challenge of that great new discipline, Canadian sociology. It was a resounding, a stentorian challenge. It could in fact be described with justice only as a Defiance. And it irresistibly recalls that other famous Defiance, the Pogram Defiance, as recorded by Charles Dickens in *Martin Chuzzlewit*. Martin Chuzzlewit and his servant, Mark Tapley, you will remember, encountered Elijah Pogram during their unhappy travels in the United States. Elijah Pogram was a Member of Congress, "one of the master minds of our country, sir", and he was the author of the Pogram Defiance.

"What is the Pogram Defiance?" asked Martin, thinking, perhaps, it was the sign of a public-house.

"An o-ration, sir," returned his friend.

"Oh! to be sure," cried Martin, "What am I thinking of! It defied—?"

"It defied the world, sir," replied the other gravely. "Defied the world in general to com-pete with our country upon any hook . . ."

Now this was almost exactly what sociology proceeded to do. It defied Canadian history in general to com-pete with Canadian sociology upon any hook. Leading sociologists, in tones of mingled condescension and reprimand, deplored what they referred to as the "limitations of conventional historical method". The real trouble with conventional history, they confidently announced, was that it had in fact no method at all. All that professional historians possessed was a primitive sense of chronology; and all that they could do was to hang their material, like so many hats, coats, and scarves, upon little rows of chronological pegs. They had no ideas; they had no analytical theories; they lacked—and this was the crowning charge of the whole awful indictment—they lacked "conceptual tools".

Is it any wonder that the historians grew red with shame and mortification? They were acutely, painfully conscious of the dreadful deficiency which had been imputed to them. They hung their heads miserably. And then by degrees they plucked up sufficient courage to begin to wonder about the "conceptual tools" of other disciplines. What, they asked themselves, were the much vaunted methods of the sociologists? It certainly did not take them very long, or require very much effort, to find out. The "conceptual tools" of sociology turned out to be a rather small collection of simple implements which looked a little as though they had been turned up by a party of archaeologists investigating a Neolithic campsite.

It was not only other academic disciplines such as law, geography, economics, and sociology which had tried to make off with history. Similar attempts were made by politics and journalism; and it must be conceded that politics and journalism proved to be fairly practised hands at the business of abduction. They were, for one thing, quite closely united and very powerful. For the past half-century, Canadian politics—with the exception of a few brief lapses into Tory bondage—have been Liberal politics; and by a similar and not entirely unrelated process of the survival of the fittest, Canadian journalism began to take on a predominantly Liberal hue. In short order, these Liberal journalists realized that a political party, in order to be respectable, must have a tradition, and that really respectable traditions are created by books, not newspapers. They began to write books. They began to write histories and biographies, essays, and learned articles. Sir John Willison started the pious labour. Dr. John Wesley Dafoe continued it with equal ability and even greater fervour. And it has been carried on to this day by that large company of distinguished men which one can best describe respectfully as Dafoe's journalistic progeny. Today, Dafoe's journalistic progeny are still conspicuous in the Parliamentary Press Gallery; they occupy many of the strategically located seats of the mighty in Canadian journalism. It is a consoling, a fortifying thought that, wherever you are in Canada, you can still and always, through the local daily or a national weekly, hear the "voice of Dafoe" ringing sonorously and authoritatively through the land.

It was in this way that the Liberal Interpretation—or Authorized Version—of Canadian history was begun. Its respectability steadily increased—successive Liberal victories and the personality of Mackenzie King were enough to ensure that. And as it grew in favour with serious-minded Canadian nationalists, others besides Dafoe and his journalists began to have a hand in its elaboration. Historians and political scientists lent their professional talents to the task of enlarging and filling in the Liberal Interpretation; and there were not a few like Dr. O. D. Skelton, who wrote the official life of Sir Wilfrid Laurier and subsequently found himself called, by a grateful Canadian people, to the position of Deputy Minister of External Affairs. At first, when these professional scribes of the Authorized Version were called to Ottawa, it was usually to accept a post in the civil service or to become a member of some Royal Commission. But in the meantime the Liberal Interpretation grew steadily in authority and dignity; and it finally began to be realized that the task of enlarging and perfecting the Sacred Text was a full-time occupation which required the undivided services of specially designated, specially dedicated, and particularly pious clerks. A national Liberal shrine, in short, was imperatively necessary. What building could serve more appropriately than Laurier House in Ottawa? National Liberal scribes were required to devote themselves to the service of the Word. Who could be more appropriately chosen than those scholars who had dedicated themselves to the lives of the blessed Liberal saints and martyrs of the past?

It was in this way that the Liberal Interpretation of Canadian history took on something of the awful grandeur of
divine revelation. Last Monday, the impregnable rock of
this Authorized Version, as Mr. Gladstone would have
called it, was suddenly and strangely shaken.* But in the
past it was Truth; and Truth must be accepted literally, in
a becomingly fundamentalist spirit. There was no place in
Canada for regrettable evidences of Modernism, or what
used to be called the Higher Criticism. If a passage in the
Authorized Version was in doubt or in dispute, then occasionally—and rather more frequently of recent years—a
member of the Canadian government, speaking *ex cathe-
dra*, would settle the matter by a final pronouncement. Recently, for example, the Canadian government permitted
the people of Canada to become aware of the fact that Sir
John Macdonald and the Fathers of Confederation had *not*
intended to call Canada the Dominion of Canada or to refer to the central administration as the Dominion government. Here was a most providential addition to our stock
of historical knowledge. "Revealed religion," a learned
divine once reflected, "furnishes facts to other sciences
which those sciences, left to themselves, would never
reach." A more beautiful illustration of this truth could
scarcely be found than the government's discovery about
Canada's title! It is perfectly certain that historical science,
left to itself, would never have attained this priceless fact.
The truth is that historical science, left to itself, would
have quite definitely decided that the Fathers of Confederation *did* intend Canada's title to be the Dominion of Canada. In other words, we were saved from error by the revelations of the Authorized Version; and we have one reason
the more for humbly contrasting our own poor, puny human intelligence with the godlike wisdom of the Canadian
government.

*The reference is to the Federal Election of June 10, 1957, which returned
the Progressive Conservatives under John Diefenbaker.

History—human history, that is, as written by professional historians—has thus led a rather embarrassed
existence for some time. It has been corrected, repriman-
ded, intimidated, overawed, and silenced. The professors of the other social sciences have questioned the value
of history's method; the scribes of the Liberal Interpretation have shattered history's poor findings with devas-
tating revelations from the Authorized Version. Geogra-
phers, lawyers, political scientists, economists, newspaper-
men, civil servants, and Liberal statemen have all tried
energetically to abduct Canadian history to a lifetime of ser-
vitude in their own particular salt-mines. These repeated
and continued tribulations would have been bad enough
in all conscience, even if they had stood alone. But, most
unfortunately, they were only a part of the ordeal which
history was called upon to endure. The pressure from outside was extremely serious; but perhaps its worst effect was
that it helped to foster and strengthen certain basic misap-
prehensions and delusions among the historians themselves. At any rate, they forgot their own proper business,
which was the careful and imaginative study of the facts of
Canadian history. Instead they accepted, for historical
purposes, the two highly fashionable political theories
which dominated the thought of the inter-war and war
years.

Each of these two political theories provided their believers with a satisfactory general view of world affairs at
the time. They were general political philosophies, adapt-
able for most occasions and nearly all purposes. But it is
highly significant that they were both based fundamentally
upon quite definite theories of historical change. Both
these theories of historical change were revolutionary theories, in the sense that they had had their origins in revolutionary programs and had been confirmed by revolutionary
experience. Both also were deterministic, materialistic,
and anti-intellectual theories—a combination of qualities

which effectively ensured them popularity in the inter-war years. And finally—and this may be perhaps the most significant point of comparison—each theory had become the official doctrine, or the widely accepted belief, of one of the two greatest continental states of modern times. They were, in short, very much alike in many ways. Yet there was one essential point of difference. The one theory found the origin of historical change in economic organization; the other discovered it in physical environment. The first was, of course, the Marxian doctrine of the class struggle; the second was that characteristic expression of the American Revolution and American western expansion, the frontier theory.

The popularity of the Marxian economic interpretation of history is one of the most interesting features of the 1930s and early 1940s. It supplies an excellent example of how the claims of the Canadian social scientists and the circumstances of Canadian politics combined to induce the historians to accept a doctrine which was alien to their experience and unremunerative for their purposes. Once again, they were the victims of superior propaganda. Everything about them seemed to emphasize the primacy of economic phenomena. On the one hand were Innis and his disciples, whose reconstruction of Canadian economic history was soon to be given impressive popular expression in the first, historical volume of the *Report of the Royal Commission on Dominion-Provincial Relations*. On the other hand was the depression, and the economic and social distress which it had caused, and the political protest movements which it had helped to inspire. Of course, most of the professional economists—and especially Innis—refused to accept the simplified Marxian version of historical determinism which the circumstances of the moment made so popular; but these timid academic scruples did not deter those party historians, party economists, and party political scientists who made up that superbly confident body, the League for Social Reconstruction, and who were recognized respectfully at the time as the "brains trust" of the Co-operative Commonwealth Federation. The members of the "brains trust" knew what was wrong with the Canadian economy. They knew what was the mainspring of Canadian development. And it was even more necessary for them than for other party theorists to make off with Canadian history in a hurry. They confronted the majestic orthodoxy of the Authorized Liberal Version. Self-respect imperatively required them to obtain a rival interpretation. And what could be more highly satisfactory than the Marxian doctrine of the class struggle?

There were, however, difficulties—grave difficulties, it turned out—in applying the great historical truth of the class struggle to Canadian conditions. On closer inspection—though, indeed, the inspection was never particularly close—it began to appear that Canadian history was a sadly imperfect vehicle for the exemplification of the Marxian verities. Canadian history—to put it bluntly—was so regrettably, so deplorably un-European! In Europe, the members of the C.C.F. brains trust agreed, political parties divided in a respectable, proper Marxian fashion, according to Class; and consequently English and European party battles were always charged with deep significance. English party battles were battles over principles; and principles were those political ideas—and only those political ideas—which had had a respectable parentage in feudal struggles or seventeenth and eighteenth century revolutions in Europe. Judged by these exacting standards, Canadian history seemed to make a very poor showing. Canadians were imperfectly class-conscious, they had had no revolution, and they kept getting politically excited about all the wrong things. Canadian history, in short, was disappointing. The members of the C.C.F. brains trust let it be known that they could not entirely approve of Canadian history. They kept on trying bravely, of course, to inject a little real Marxian meaning into what they regarded as the empty sound and fury of Canadian affairs. They insisted perseveringly that the real work of the Fathers of Confederation had been to establish an economic empire for the *entrepreneurs* of Montreal, that the concentration of wealth and power within this empire was rapidly producing a class structure similar to that of Europe, and that the depression of the 1930s was in fact a crisis of capitalism which would likely end in a destructive class struggle.

Blinding flashes of insight such as these could scarcely fail of their effect. And yet it must be confessed that the little group of serious socialist thinkers of the 1930s and 1940s did not have a very profound impression upon Canadian historiography. The class struggle was attractive as an explanation of historical change; but, on the whole, it was decidedly less attractive than the frontier thesis. For the frontier thesis was an environmental interpretation and environmental interpretations of almost anything have an irresistible appeal for North Americans. North Americans are fascinated by geography—they have so much of it. They regard the vast stretches of their continent with all the infinitely complacent satisfaction of a Buddha contemplating the broad expanse of his belly. The size, the self-sufficiency, the power of North America, and North America's significant isolation from the rest of the world, have all helped to create in the minds of its inhabitants, and particularly among the citizens of the United States, a very emphatic and a very exclusive sense of identity. The continent had, in fact, created its own distinctive world-view, continentalism. Obviously continentalism would have to have a theory of historical change as its basis; and obviously also this theory would have to prove the truth of North America's intellectual and spiritual autonomy and North America's independent cultural creativity. This is precisely what the frontier thesis, as established by American historian Frederick Jackson Turner and his disciples, succeeded in doing. Turner, responding instinctively to this deep-seated North American need, fixed upon the movement of settlement across the continent as the most important fact in its history. The frontier, "the hither edge of free land", was "the greatest formative influence" in the development of America. Out of the frontier had come American individualism, freedom, egalitarianism, adaptability, vigour, and idealism. The frontier had created the institutions, convictions, and habits which were most characteristic of America. Thus the source of creative inspiration and action was found not at the centre, but at the periphery, of western culture; and the older view that the progress of its civilization had been an outward movement from an original source was exactly reversed.

For obvious reasons, the frontier thesis received a vociferously cordial reception in the United States. The theory then crossed the border, a somewhat delayed import, into Canada, where the circumstances of the 1930s and early 1940s combined to ensure the rapid growth of its popularity. Once again, as in the case of the Marxian doctrine of the class struggle, it was the union of an intellectual movement with a peculiarly appropriate set of political circumstances which made the success of the frontier thesis. On the one hand were Turner and his American disciples, who, in the respectful eyes of colonially minded Canadians, were invested with the same majestic doctrinal authority which clothed European socialists and British Labour party theorists. On the other hand were the members of the Canadian government who, particularly in the period after 1935, were making those preliminary cordial approaches to the United States which formed the prelude to the astounding concessions of the summer of 1940. In that August of 1940, the Canadian government took two supremely important North American actions. It benevolently accepted, in the first place, a ninety-nine-year American military leasehold in the island which the Fathers of Confederation had always hoped would be a province of Canada, and which, at the moment, was Canada's chief strategic outpost. In the second place, the Canadian government, acting apparently on the assumption that mere geographic propinquity meant absolute and eternal identity of interest, agreed to establish, with the United States, a Permanent Joint Board on Defence for North America. Canada, like a dutiful child that has learned to like what its parents think good for it, had actually accepted American continentalism. It had even been sold the idea of North American community fellowship, which may be said to be the Rotarian version of Manifest Destiny. North America was that psychologists' ideal—a great, big, happy family, in which all the members were perfectly adjusted. It was a gigantic international Elks convention where all the delegates went around hand-shaking and back-slapping and exuding cordiality from every pore.

In these inspiring circumstances, Canadian historians found it easy to convince themselves of the ineffable wisdom of the frontier thesis. In North America, we were, thank God, just folks; and here was a simple, straightforward, homespun, honest-to-gosh theory, which glorified the backwoods and the frontier and extolled the independent creative power of rugged simplicity. Here surely was God's truth for God's continent. And yet—it was very sad—when one actually got down to the business of applying this continental revelation to the facts of Canadian history, painful difficulties were immediately encountered. Once again, as in the case of the Marxian doctrine of the class struggle, Canadian history seemed to be a curiously imperfect vehicle for the exemplification of historical truth. In Canada the frontier had not advanced in that free, unspoilt, untutored fashion in which it ought to have done, according to Turner. Its onward creative progress had been evidently modified by all sorts of extraneous and unnatural things such as railways, efficient police, and governmental supervision, both provincial and federal. The western disturbances of 1869-70 and 1885 turned out to be decidedly unsatisfactory illustrations of frontier resistance; and the Upper Canadian rebellion of 1837 was simply deplorable, for the rebels had come, not from the frontier, but from the older settled parts of the province, while the real frontiersmen, who evidently lacked the benefit of Dr. Turner's direction in their true historical role, were unaccountably discovered marching into Toronto to defend the cause of law and order. These, certainly, were disheartening difficulties. Yet the believers in the frontier thesis, like the supporters of the Marxian doctrine of the class struggle, nobly persevered. They kept insisting that Canadian democracy was "forest-born", that all sound, progressive, democratic forces in the Canadian community were the beneficent products of the backwoods and the prairie, and that all dynamic, free-born, forward-looking elements in Canadian politics had had their origin on the frontier.

Yet this did not by any means exhaust the uses to which the frontier thesis and the doctrine of the class struggle were put by Canadian historians and political scientists. The popularity of the two theories was only partly shown in the interpretation of domestic Canadian history; it was equally well revealed in writings on Canadian external relations. Once again, the intellectual supply offered by the two theories happened exactly to coincide with the intellectual demands of Canadian politics in their first great attack upon the problems of foreign policy. The 1920s and 1930s were the decades, above all others, in which Canadian national policy, and its supporters and interpreters, required a simple-minded, anti-imperialist doctrine which could be used as a club against Western Europe in general and West European and British imperialism in particular. Mackenzie King was revolutionizing the Commonwealth through the implementation of Dominion autonomy; Dr. O. D. Skelton and the newly established Department of External Affairs were systematically reducing our commitments and limiting our connections with Europe and the League of Nations; and Canada, for what was really the first time in its history, was luxuriating to the full in that sense of physical and spiritual isolation from the rest of the world, that moral superiority to the unfortunate remainder of mankind, which is one of the chief characteristics of North American continentalism.

In these circumstances, the frontier thesis and the doctrine of the class struggle came pat to the purpose of Canadian historians and historical publicists. Both Marxism and North American continentalism were obviously, in their different ideological ways, profoundly hostile to Western Europe; and both, moreover, were professedly anti-imperialist systems. In retrospect, and from the vantage point—if, indeed, it can be called a vantage point—of our present position, we can bitterly appreciate the horrible irony of these fraudulent anti-imperialist claims. We can realize now—what, if we had been passable historians, we ought to have realized long before—that both Marxism and North American continentalism are essentially revolutionary systems; that revolutionary systems rest on the assumption of the discovery of political truth valid for all countries and all ages; and that revolutionary states, either in the short or the long run, are propagandist, missionary, and imperialistic. Finally, it ought to have been obvious, particularly to Canadians, that the planting of these traditional revolutionary impulses in two nations of such enormous continental extent threatened even graver dangers for the future. Canadians ought to have been aware of the implications of the mystical North American obsession with geography, with space, with the irresistible onward march of the frontier across vast expanses. They could possibly have foreseen the ultimate consequences of the union of the idea of manifest destiny of God's chosen people with the idea of territorial expansion on a continental scale. They might even have anticipated that, once the period of glutted continental isolation was finished, the mastodon-like battle between the continents would begin.

Yet, in fact, the Canadian intellectuals of the 1920s and 1930s remained complacently oblivious to all or most of this. In their imitative colonial fashion, they took over the Marxist and American conception of European and British imperialism; and without scarcely even bothering to make a perfunctory adjustment or two, they clapped it on to the story of the achievement of Canadian autonomy inside the British Empire–Commonwealth. It was, of course, an extraordinarily bad fit. The trouble which the Canadians had had in wearing these mass-produced, machine-made garments from the Marxian and American ideological factories was enormously increased when they tried to change from home attire to going-abroad costumes. The simple truth was that the revolutionary tradition was completely incompatible with Canada's historic position in the external world. Canada had never broken with Europe; Canada had never identified herself solely with the Western Hemisphere. British North America had, in fact, consciously stood aloof from the familiar, commonplace western revolutionary movement, which had been originated by the United States and faithfully copied by every duodecimo South American republic. British North America had sought to achieve a distinct and separate political existence in the Western Hemisphere; she had tried to preserve her identity against the levelling, standardizing impact of American continentalism; and, to a very large extent, the measure of her success could be attributed to the maintenance of her vital connection with Europe. It was British military and diplomatic support which ensured the survival of Canada in a continent which otherwise would have become the prey of Manifest Destiny. For Canada, the imperial connection was not a parent-and-child relationship which ended in an appalling row, but an adult partnership which was prolonged more at the instance of the junior than of the senior partner.

How wrong we were! How imitative, how gullible, how truly colonially minded! Only now has it become possible for us to realize the enormous extent of our deception. The war and the twelve years which have elapsed since its conclusion have ended our dreams and given us instead a continuous existence of terrible reality; and, in all this grim period, there has been no disillusionment greater than the worldwide disillusionment in the twin revolutionary doctrines of Marxism and North American continentalism. The supposedly anti-imperialist ideas, by which Canadians complacently believed they could offset the weight of British domination, have become themselves the basis of new imperial systems, as powerful as any since the beginnings of Western civilization and potentially far more dangerous; and the abortive revolution in Hungary and the mass riots in Taiwan have revealed how hated or disliked these new imperialisms have become even in the states which they are said to maintain and among peoples whom they are supposed to benefit. Everywhere the disenchantment has been shattering; but it is safe to say that no people were less prepared than the Canadians to stand the shock of the revelations of the last ten years. It was not simply, as George Ferguson said in an illuminating paper given a year ago at the annual meeting of the Political Science Association, that we were fighting modern battles with the broken-down ideas of the day before yesterday. Of course we were doing that. We were trying to stand up to the Russians and the trigger-happy strategists down in the Pentagon Building with notions which would have been relatively up-to-date at the time of the colonial-secretary-ship of Joseph Chamberlain. Yet it was not the rusty antiquity of this mental armour that was its chief defect. Its chief defect was that it was irrelevant to our circumstances, alien to our tradition, and useless for our fundamental purposes.

For all this the Canadian historians, like the other intellectuals and pseudo-intellectuals of the inter-war generation, must bear their share of the blame. They played their part in letting the Canadian people down. They did their little bit in producing that state of silenced, frightened bewilderment in which it seems impossible to do anything but accept what Mr. Pearson calls, with happy originality, the American leadership of the free world. The Canadian historians, if they had stuck firmly to their real job, might have given their countrymen some valuable positive direction in the difficult business of being Canadian in a time of global conflict. But, instead, they let themselves be lectured and intimidated by people who claimed to know what history was all about. They looked on tamely—they even applauded—while other people, social scientists, publicists, journalists, outriders for this or that political party, made off with Canadian history; and, worst of all, they let themselves be persuaded, by the sales-talks of two smart international advertising agencies, into purchasing a couple of suits of imported intellectual reach-me-downs which were as ill-fitting as they were fashionable. They did all this, and for years we have been suffering the consequences. Our tribulations are not over. All we can say is that the delusions which partly created them are gone, and that the authors of the delusions are no longer unquestioned oracles. A definite epoch in the history of Canadian history has come to an end. A new generation of professional historians has arisen, is arising; and although the character of their work has not yet definitely declared itself, it can be predicted with some confidence that they will have less deference for imported theories of historical change and more respect for the manifold facts of Canadian experience.

Towards the Discovery
of Canada

"NON-FICTION" is an inelegant and unflattering description, invented no doubt by librarians, which is firmly established in Canadian usage. The literary journals of Great Britain and Western Europe still attempt to be more discriminating. In their old-fashioned and pedantic way, they go on recognizing the separate categories of history, biography, politics, economics, and world affairs; but in Canada these refined European distinctions are cheerfully disregarded. A survey of Canadian literature, by Canadians, normally begins with an article on Canadian poetry, which is followed immediately by an article on the Canadian novel; and then everything that is left over, philosophy, history, economics, as well as literary and art criticism, is swept summarily into a huge residual heap, labelled "remaining material". Poetry and fiction are, of course, "creative". But the claims of "remaining material" to this proud distinction are regarded, in Canada, as decidedly more dubious. A few small items in the vast, amorphous mass of "non-fiction" may be accepted as "creative", but only on the inflexibly enforced condition that they have not been written by members of universities. Works by members of universities are in all cases dismissed as "academic"; and in Canada, as in other parts of the English-speaking world, "academic" is very definitely a pejorative word.

It may be worth while to lift Canadian history and Ca-

First published in the *University of Toronto Quarterly*, vol. xxv. no. 3. April 1956.

nadian work in the social sciences out of the undifferentiated mass of "remaining material" for a brief inspection. In Canada, as in the United Kingdom and the
United States, sales of novels have been steadily declining;
and throughout the English-speaking world, poetry has become almost unsalable. The calamity which has overtaken
creative literature in the post-war years may have a number of causes; but a satisfactory explanation cannot be
found in the alleged decline of reading or in the supposed
transfer of interest from the book to other forms of communication. The misfortunes of creative literature are its
own; and the uncreative rejects of "non-fiction" are enjoying what, in the twentieth century, is an unprecedented
vogue. Canadian historians and writers in the social sciences have had their own small share of the benefits of this
mysterious shift in popular favour. They have always had a
good deal to say for themselves; but they now find that
their books are more readily published and even frequently read. Can it be that the contributors to "remaining material" have something to say to their fellow Canadians that the contemporary poets and novelists are incapable of saying? Have they succeeded more fully in interpreting Canadian experience? Have they, within the limits
of their subject-matter, done more to enable Canadians to
understand themselves and their world?

It may very possibly be so. Certainly the writings of Canadian historians and social scientists supply a candid and
painfully revealing record of the development of the colonial mind, And, to a large extent, the fidelity of the record is to be explained by the very narrowness of their approach. Every author, in every country, is subject to the
egocentric delusions born of his time and place. But the
writer in a colony approaching nationhood is under a special compulsion to be parochial. He knows very well that if
he attempts subjects of international significance, the outside world will very probably not pay the slightest atten

tion to him. Great authors are normally born in great countries; great literary reputations are the product of great communications systems; and fine writing is a function of power politics. It was only a few years ago that the editors of a majestic English university press explained with complacent candour to a Canadian scholar that his book would almost certainly be damned if he committed the ghastly error of confessing, on its title page, that he was a member of a Canadian university.* A writer in a young country has to be very good indeed before he will even be granted that brief perfunctory hearing—that species of literary "children's hour" which comes only at the very end of an exhausting day devoted to serious writing and high scholarship. A writer from a young country will find it extraordinarily difficult to break into those great-power literary monopolies which are guarded so vigilantly and tenaciously by the thoughtful little groups of friends and acquaintances who do each other's reviewing in the literary capitals of the Western world.

And in the meantime, while his application for admission into these imperialistic literary preserves is being subjected to such a frigid scrutiny, the writer of a young country will find that his own nation is clamouring for interpretation. Only very infrequently will scholars from other parts of the Western world give any real help towards satisfying this instinctive demand. Once the young country has ceased to be a recognized dependency open for imperial exploitation, they will quickly lose interest in it; and their curiosity will not revive until the young country has grown to be a very considerable power in its own right. In the meantime, scholars and journalists from the outside world will visit it only occasionally, on journeys undertaken with the inducement of substantial expense accounts; and what will interest and impress them most will not, in the main, be the signs of the new nation's increas-

*The scholar was Charles Norris Cochrane, and his book, *Christianity and Classical Culture*, London, 1940.

ing cultivation, but the evidences which will confirm them in their assumption of its continuing barbarism and primitiveness. The prestige of great literary empires requires the existence of a rude intellectual hinterland, a recognized literary "external proletariat", just as the military might of the great modern power blocks depends upon the submissive adhesion of young undeveloped countries which can be induced to believe that it is a privilege to have their policies controlled and their natural resources ransacked by others. A half-century ago, the prairie west was the only part of Canada in which Europe and America had much interest; but now, of course, the north has become the fashionable area for literary and economic exploitation. If a Canadian novelist wishes to sell his wares in England, he would be well advised to dress his characters in Eskimo parkas; and a Canadian economist, seeking an attentive audience among the entrepreneurs and cold-war strategists of the United States, could do no better than to devote himself to Canada's great northland, the arsenal of Western democracy.

These highly selective approaches may occasionally flatter a Canadian; but mainly they leave him bewildered and annoyed. He remains profoundly, angrily dissatisfied with the treatment that he receives from his more powerful neighbours; and it is this dissatisfaction, this hungry urge towards greater self-knowledge, that Canadian writers find themselves both persuaded and compelled to appease. It is mercifully true, of course, that this task has never absorbed all their energies: their preoccupation with continental Canada has never converted them into cultural isolationists. Charles Cochrane's *Christianity and Classical Culture* and A. S. P. Woodhouse's *Puritanism and Liberty* are both contributions on the highest level to studies which are the common concern of the whole of Western Europe and America; and Alexander Brady's *Democracy in the Dominions* deals not merely with Canada but with all the senior nations of the British Commonwealth. These are distinguished pieces of work; but they are also distinguishable from the great mass of Canadian writing in history and the social sciences by their subject-matter. The main concern of Canadian writers is Canada: they are volunteers or conscripts in the service of national self-realization and self-determination.

Subject-matter, however, is not the only thing they have in common. To a very large extent they also share a common method. Their first, instinctive approach to any question is historical. They are concerned with developments in a given time and place which they regard as distinctive, if not unique. They have so far given relatively little time to theory, to the search for regularities, uniformities, and recurrences, to the formulation of laws and the elaboration of systems. In Canada, economists are very frequently economic historians; and B. S. Keirstead's contributions to economic theory are clearly exceptional. A political scientist like R. M. Dawson might quite reasonably be described as a Canadian constitutional historian: and the sociologist S. D. Clark has departed so completely from the comparative methods prescribed by the Logical Positivists that at times he might be pardonably mistaken for a social historian. History has dominated, if it has not overwhelmed, the social sciences; and economists, sociologists, and political scientists have taken their places alongside historians in a vast co-operative effort to explain to their fellow Canadians how they have come to be what, and where, they are.

II

Canada, like other nations which have emerged from colonialism, has, as the main theme of its development, a great, simple, archetypal plot. And the title, *Colony to Nation*, of A. R. M. Lower's recent general history of Canada, states this plot with classic simplicity. Canada, in short, is the outcome of an encounter between the two forces of nationality and imperialism; and Canadian history is the record of the struggle—prolonged, difficult, but noble—by which Canadians have ascended from the lowly status of dependent colonialism to the serene heights of autonomous nationhood. The fable is basically a simple one; but the early nationalist Canadian historians—G. M. Wrong, Chester Martin, and R. G. Trotter—perceived that its enactment in Canada was full of complexities. They saw that the achievement of Canadian nationality was a dual, not a single, process. They did not make the mistake of identifying national autonomy simply and exclusively with emancipation from British control; and they realized that the maintenance of a separate political existence in a continent dominated by the United States was a more important and more difficult achievement. In other words, there had been two goals of nationhood, not one; and the methods by which they had been attained differed profoundly. Autonomy inside the British Empire–Commonwealth had been acquired by a peaceful, gradual process of compromise and adjustment. A separate political existence in North America had been won at the cost of two armed struggles, the American Revolutionary War and the War of 1812.

It was not long, however, before Canadian writers began to be dissatisfied with this specifically Canadian version of the fable of nationality against imperialism. It was, they considered, too complicated. It lacked immediate popular appeal. It differed regrettably from the immensely fashionable drama on the same subject which had been playing to crowded houses in the United States ever since 1776. The American version, considered as a tribal myth, was infinitely superior. In it there were no complications, subtleties, and compromises. There was simply a straightforward, knock-down conflict between liberty and tyranny, progress and reaction, good and evil. A single hero, democratic virtue embodied in the revolting Thirteen Colonies, confronted a single villain, Great Britain, steeped to the lips in the iniquities of autocratic imperialism. Here, surely, was the prototype, the pattern, the model of all subsequent re-enactments of the stupendous encounter between imperialism and nationality. Here was orthodoxy; and any departures from its sacred simplicity were to be regarded with suspicion and disfavour. Had not the Canadians erred in fondly imagining that they could have their own distinctively Canadian version of the truth about colonies? Were not they guilty of a serious democratic deviation?

Some such impression began to extend its influence over Canadian writers in the brave days when that squat knight-errant, Mackenzie King, was breaking the last fetters which bound Canada to British policy. Great Britain, it was now realized, was and always had been the real opponent of Canadian nationalism. The only really serious struggle which Canada had had to wage had been the struggle to win autonomy inside the British Empire; and the achievement and maintenance of a separate political existence on the North American continent had been, by contrast, an easy and almost perfunctory affair. Statements about the "century of peace" and the "four thousand miles of undefended frontier" underwent the process of transmutation from after-dinner pleasantries into great historical truths. A new and exclusive sense of identity with North America, of community inside North America, began to affect Canadian writing. A new generation of journalists and publicists arose to extol the self-sufficiency and normality of Canada's Americanism. Canadians were perhaps slightly retarded, but potentially as good, Americans as their cousins south of the international boundary; and Canada was a normal, respectable American community, virtually indistinguishable from the United States. The two countries were, in fact, children of the same parents, who had passed through similar stages of development and endured similar tribulations. They had, of course, had frightful difficulties with the "old folks", but they had always got on exceedingly well themselves.

Even the series of volumes "The Relations of Canada and the United States", sponsored by the Carnegie Endowment for International Peace and edited by Dr. James T. Shotwell, was affected, to some extent at least, by the prevalence and popularity of these views. These twenty-five volumes, most of which appeared in the years immediately before the Second World War, embodied some of the best Canadian scholarship of the last quarter-century. Canadian social scientists and historians—H. F. Angus, G. P. deT. Glazebrook, F. Landon, H. A. Innis, and A. R. M. Lower in particular—made a notable contribution to the series; but it was a contribution which was concentrated upon certain areas of Canadian-American relations and which almost completely neglected others. There were, for example, several volumes on the diplomatic relations between the two countries; and it was an odd but perhaps not entirely insignificant fact that all these volumes, without exception, were written either by native Americans or by Canadians born who had become permanent residents of the United States. The Canadians themselves were complacently uninterested in the long and acrimonious struggle by which Canada, with essential British assistance, had maintained its separateness in the North American continent. They took their political survival for granted, as something which just occurred, not as something which had had to be won; and they tended to look upon the occupation and exploitation of the continent, not in terms of competition and conflict, but as a peaceful and co-operative process in which the international boundary had played a very insignificant part. *The Mingling of the Canadian and American Peoples* was the title of the volume which M. L. Hansen and J. B. Brebner contributed to the

Canadian-American Relations Series; and in it the settlement of Canada was regarded simply as a subordinate but integral part of the occupation of North America as a continental whole. To the student of population, Professor Brebner remarked in another essay, "the settled regions of Canada . . . appear on the whole to be outward projections of the settled regions of the United States . . . rather than as interlocked units of a separate people which has systematically expanded its occupation from Atlantic to Pacific."

The Canadians were not a separate people; the North Americans were one great big happy family. It would be unneighbourly to give any very serious consideration to the international boundary, and it would be highly unnatural, not to say indecent, to presume to regard the United States for one moment as an aggressive, imperialistic power in North America. The only aggressive imperialistic power with which Canada had ever had anything to do was of course Great Britain; and the only important theme in Canadian history was the heroic struggle between legitimate colonial demand on the one hand and obscurantist imperial resistance on the other. In the 1920s and 1930s, with the publication of the Balfour Report and the passage of the Statute of Westminster, the principle of Dominion or national status was obviously approaching its apotheosis. Autonomy in domestic affairs had been long ago obtained; freedom in external relations had now been secured; and Canada's foreign policy, liberated from the entangling meshes of British imperialistic power politics, soared upward, in a somewhat uncertain but surely edifying fashion, heavenwards. The whole thing was clearly a miracle; and a little group of devoted hagiographers now appeared to record the saintly lives and the pious episodes by which the miracle had been brought to pass. There were lawyers and civil servants, such as O. D. Skelton, the author of *The Life and Letters of Sir Wilfrid Laurier*; there were journalists such as John W. Dafoe, who wrote

Canada: An American Nation and *Laurier, a Study in Canadian Politics*; there were political scientists such as R. M. Dawson and R. A. MacKay. Professor Dawson's book *The Development of Dominion Status* was really a collection of documents; but beneath the academic restraint of its lengthy introduction there swells irrepressibly that note of moral indignation and moral unction with which a righteous man records the reclamation of a naturally innocent soul from undesirable associates and wicked courses.

III

The Canadian version of the great fable of nationality versus imperialism had thus been purged of its errors and heresies. Its scribes had become resolutely anti-British and complacently pro-American. The political scientists and the political historians were the first to be affected, for Dominion status was outwardly a political achievement; but the influence of the new attitude and the new outlook did not stop here. It spread rapidly and pervasively over a wide range of Canadian writing in history and the social sciences. Canada, after all, had not simply proclaimed that she was a sovereign North American state; she had also announced, as an essential part of the publicity campaign, that she was a typical North American community. The independence which had been declared had an economic, social, and intellectual significance, as well as a political and constitutional meaning. "Britain Overseas", if it had ever been true of the Dominion in the past, was true no longer. The Canadian demand for nationhood was solidly rooted in the native North American environment. It found its complete justification in the North American way of life.

Here, of course, was a much more fundamental break with the past. During the nineteenth century the Canadians had had the best of reasons for assuming that they were part of a general West European–American civilization; and, if they had ever stopped to theorize about the matter, they would doubtless have reached the unremarkable conclusion that British North America was the outcome of an encounter between the West European inheritance and the North American environment. In the 1920s and 1930s, however, these old-fashioned opinions began to be regarded as painful evidences of the continuance of the colonial mind. The Canadian historians and social scientists, like the Canadian journalists and politicians, sought instinctively to depress the importance of Europe as the source of Western civilization and to exalt the creative power of North America. North America was single, self-sufficient, and all-powerful. North America had become a faith; and what was needed was a cultural Book of Genesis which could serve as a first chapter in the new religion's Holy Writ.

Where was such a Book of Genesis to be found? The Canadians did not have to continue their search very long, for they found, as was to be expected, that an American prophet had supplied them with the required article. His name was Frederick Jackson Turner, and he and his overzealous disciples among them had elaborated what came to be called the frontier thesis. From the point of view of a North America eager to be assured of its intellectual independence and cultural creativity, no more completely satisfying doctrine could possibly have been invented. It did not simply amend or qualify the old view of the outward movement of civilization; it exactly reversed it. The source of inspiration and action was found not at the centre, but at the periphery, of Western culture. The frontier, "the hither edge of free land", was "the greatest formative influence" in American history. Out of the frontier had come American individualism, freedom, egalitarianism, adaptability, vigour, and idealism. The frontier had created the institutions, convictions, and habits which were most characteristic of America. The west, in short, had made Americans out of Europeans. The west was the real America. It was the true source of the American way of life.

The frontier thesis—which may be regarded as an American version of the eighteenth-century doctrine of the Noble Savage—was to have a profound influence on Canadian writing in history and the social sciences. And one of its first and most obvious functions was to help to awaken interest in the Canadian northwest as a region for study. No encouragement could have come more pat. During the first two decades of the twentieth century, the west had gone through the vast disturbance of occupation and commercial exploitation; and it now lay waiting, a community which had endured the first terrible phase of its existence, and was ready for examination and interpretation. Canadian writers accepted its challenge very readily. Just as the new-found sense of community in North America had helped to inspire that enormous scholarly undertaking "The Relations of Canada and the United States", so the exciting experience of the discovery of the west found expression in another great collective enterprise, "Canadian Frontiers of Settlement", edited by W. A. Mackintosh and W. L. G. Joerg. The first volume in the series, *Prairie Settlement: The Geographical Setting*, was the work of the Canadian editor, W. A. Mackintosh. The sociologists, led by C. A. Dawson, made a notable contribution; and there were volumes by such veteran Canadian economists and historians as H. A. Innis, Chester Martin, A. R. M. Lower, and A. S. Morton. It was the most important, but by no means the only, expression of that absorbed concentration which Canadian scholars had developed in the northwest. D. A. MacGibbon examined the workings of the Canadian grain trade; G. E. Britnell began his studies of the wheat economy; and a group of still younger writers found fascinating themes in the growth of such typically western political movements as the United Farmers, the Progressive Party, and Social Credit. In short order, the west became the most fashionable subject in Canadian scholarship. The universities and the great foundations were ready to pour money into such studies; Canadian historians and social scientists were eagerly prepared to lavish time upon them. So far as scholarship was concerned, the west had become a "have" rather than a "have not" region.

But this was not all. The west was not only a geographic area superlatively worthy of study; it was also, as Turner and his disciples had proved, the inspiration of an historical philosophy and the source of a set of value judgments. The west was important because it was the last manifestation of the frontier; and in Canadian, as well as in American, history the frontier had been a great, if not the greatest, formative influence. The frontier was the energizing source of the sound, progressive, democratic forces in the Canadian community. It explained almost everything in the country's development—everything, in particular, which looked new, dynamic, and vaguely forward-looking. North American democracy, on both sides of the international boundary, was largely "forest-born"; every Canadian radical party was discovered to be an expression of the frontier in Canadian politics. The frontier explained W. L. Mackenzie and the rebellions of 1837; it explained the rise of the Clear Grits in the 1850s; and when, with the beginning of the twentieth century, political radicalism winged its way out to the prairies, the frontier once again produced as an explanation of this last and presumably final Canadian manifestation of the reforming spirit. W. L. Morton's *The Progressive Party in Canada* emphasized the western origins of the movement and found in Progressivism "the latest upsurge of agrarian and frontier democracy". Canadian social scientists, in short, had become environmentalists; and they had identified national progress with the advance of the agrarian frontier.

The frontier thesis, of course, had been based upon the idea of conflict. That was why it had been such a useful doctrine in the narration of the great struggle between nationality and imperialism. In frontier mythology, the edge of settlement was invariably pitted against the centre of civilization; the virtuous west, the source of progressive, egalitarian, and democratic forces, was confronted by the sinister east, the home of privilege, reaction, and exploitation. This conception of a terrific moral conflict had first been pressed into service to dignify the story of British North America's struggle with the imperial government; but it was quickly seen that the fulfilment of this prime function did not exhaust its usefulness. Canada as a whole was obviously more righteous than Great Britain: but western Canada—the area which the frontier had reached at any given moment of time—was also and unquestionably better than the Canadian east. The Hudson's Bay Company might be a great, monopolistic fur-trading organization; but in A. S. Morton's *History of the Canadian West to 1870-71*, there was no question of its moral superiority over the commercial corporations and governments of Montreal and Ottawa. The Red River Rebellion and the Northwest Rebellion might be somewhat dubious revolts and Louis Riel an equivocal hero; but even in the pages of such a scholarly study as G. F. G. Stanley's *The Birth of Western Canada*, the resistance of the *Métis* against a harsh, dilatory, and niggardly government began to take on a pathetic grandeur.

This application of the frontier thesis to Canadian domestic affairs was accomplished smoothly and with little apparent confusion. Of course there were changes. There had to be. But the changes, though drastic, were astonishingly few. Ottawa was quickly substituted for London as a metropolitan centre. The federal cabinet was summarily placed in the unsympathetic position which had just been vacated by the British government; and Macdonald, Laurier, and Borden, who had been received with acclaim as the intrepid defenders of insurgent Canadian nationalism and self-government, were now abruptly required to adopt the unpleasant rôle of the imperialistic ogres whom they had been defying to resounding applause only a little while before. These sudden changes might have bewildered a more sophisticated audience. A sophisticated audience might have been affronted by elements of unreality in the performance. But the steady supporters of Canadian historical melodrama were not disturbed at all. For they knew the good old plot and the good old plot remained the same. Here once again was the affecting North American morality play of the vigorous and progressive west triumphing over the effete and reactionary east. The frontier thesis had become a formula, a stereotype, worn down and greasy: but it had left a lasting mark on Canadian thought. It had made popular a simple-minded environmentalist method, a parochial, self-regarding nationalist feeling, and a suspicious, isolationist attitude to the rest of the world.

IV

To a very large extent, it was H. A. Innis who freed Canadian writing in history and the social sciences from these narrow restrictions. Innis was an economist, an economic historian; and in the existing circumstances his special approach gave him a definite advantage. He was not likely to be much affected by the romantic nationalistic assumptions which so easily coloured the views of the historians and political scientists; he would not be irresistibly impelled to produce a Hollywood western out of Canadian settlement or a *Cavalcade* out of the upward and onward march towards Dominion status. The fashionable academic game of making new tribal lays out of old tribal myths did not greatly interest him; and the grandiose con-

ception of a new and greater civilization arising from the
mystic union of Nationality and the North American Environment did not, curiously enough, become the inspiration of his thoughts. Instead he devoted himself to the outwardly prosaic business of examining the successive staple
trades and industries by which British North Americans
had supported the burden of existence in the new world.
He went from furs to fisheries and from fisheries to wood-
pulp, paper, and printing, and the "communication industries" which they sustain. Each of his three greatest books
brought its own kind of enlargement to the field of Canadian studies. *The Fur Trade in Canada* traced the rise and
fall of the first truly transcontinental organization in Canadian history. *The Cod Fisheries*, with its significant sub-
title, *The History of an International Economy*, brought
the whole of the North Atlantic within the limits of Canadian interest; and *Empire and Communications*, which began with Egyptian papyrus and ended with twentieth-century wood-pulp, placed the Canadian newsprint industry
in a setting which was vast in space and deep in time.

Innis succeeded more than any other writer of the
twentieth century in giving both breadth and depth to Canadian studies in history and the social sciences. Here he
performed an enormous general service; but at the same
time he also made a special contribution which, in the existing Canadian preoccupation with the twin concepts of nationality and environment, had a more precise and immediate value. A large part of Innis's work was a criticism, express or implied, of the fashionable notion that Canadian
nationality had had only one goal—the achievement of autonomy inside the British Empire—and only one opponent—the imperial government of Great Britain. He rein-
troduced the idea of competition, of rivalry in North
America. He broke down the conception of the continent
as a geographic unit, an undivided whole. In his view, the
main influential lines of its geography did not run north

and south; economically, Canada was not simply an unrelated series of northern projections of the main economic
regions of the United States. On the contrary, the
Dominion had its economic basis in a great competitive
east-west trading system, based upon the St. Lawrence
River and the Great Lakes, which had been extended westward from Montreal and which had as its aim the winning
of a politico-economic empire in the heart of the continent.

The commercial empire of the St. Lawrence was at once
a transcontinental and a transoceanic system. One end of
its long trading line lay in the North American west, the
other in the commercial capitals of Europe. The frontier
was important, but so also was the metropolitan centre;
and both New France and British North America had
been dependent upon the markets, commercial organizations, and military and naval power of their respective
mother countries. The St. Lawrence became a pathway by
which men, and capital, and goods were brought outward
from the centre to the limits of Western civilization. Europe and Great Britain were the sources of ideas, enterprises, and creative power; and for Canada, engaged in an
unequal struggle with a North American power vastly
greater than herself, the assistance which Great Britain
could bring was an absolute essential. Help alone could
bring success: help was necessary to ensure mere survival;
and Canada remained British, not by accident or through
sentiment, but by reason of its own strongest impulse and
deepest necessity. For Canada the imperial connection was
not a family relationship which had ended in a row with
the approach of colonial maturity; it was a partnership
which had been maintained in large measure for practical
reasons and chiefly at the instance of the junior member of
the association. The drama of nationality versus imperialism, in the original "American" version, had never been
re-enacted in Canada at all.

Innis founded a new school of Canadian scholars and provided a new framework for Canadian studies in history and the social sciences. It began to be appreciated that the attainment of Dominion status was not the sole end of man, and that everything bright and beautiful in North America was not necessarily "forest-born". Writers lifted their eyes from their absorbed, almost Buddha-like contemplation of the interior of the continent and became aware of the fact that they were members of a great civilization which for long generations had had its focus in Western Europe. In the case of Innis himself, this widening of the intellectual horizon had strikingly revealed itself in the vast extension of the range of his studies; and at least a few of his followers were similarly inspired to pursue new themes in strange climes and past ages. But this enlargement of the scope of Canadian studies was not the most immediate or, perhaps, the most important evidence of Innis's influence. Canada remained the main subject of Canadian scholars; but they attacked it now in a fashion which began significantly to alter. They were less inclined to rely upon exclusively "American" methods of interpretation. They were less parochial in outlook, less nationalistic in spirit, less environmentalist in approach.

The series of volumes edited by S. D. Clark under the general title "Social Credit in Alberta: Its Background and Development" is, of course, another large-scale co-operative venture devoted to the Canadian west. It attempts to do for a single western political movement what "Frontiers of Settlement" did for the west as a whole; and as a result, a small bit of the frontier is being examined on an unprecedented and impressive scale. Yet the treatment differs from that of the earlier series: the Albertan experiment is placed in a wider setting of political experience and political and economic theory; the frontier hypothesis is either modified or, in the case of C. B. Macpherson's *Democracy in Alberta*, tacitly dismissed. And, in the meantime, while the sacred west was being regarded with this detachment and so-phistication, another group of scholars was rediscovering the North Atlantic and the world that lay beyond. Innis's *The Cod Fisheries* extended the frontiers of British North America not westward, but eastward, over a vast area of in-ternational competition and conflict; and the military and naval historians C. P. Stacey and G. S. Graham saw Canada as part of an imperial defence system based on transoceanic and intercontinental strategy. Even the Canadian-Amer-ican Relations Series, that characteristic expression of North America's sense of isolation and self-sufficiency, had a curious and unexpected ending in the publication of J. B. Brebner's *North Atlantic Triangle: The Interplay of Canada, the United States, and Great Britain*. Brebner, as he explained in his preface, had begun with the intention of setting forth the interplay between Canada and the United States; but in the end he had come to the conclu-sion that "these activities could not be explained in merely North American terms." This realization of the inad-equacy of a purely North American interpretation of the relations of two North American powers was a significant indication of a new and different trend of thought. A fun-damental change of attitude had, in fact, taken place. Ca-nadian scholars had made a rediscovery of Europe; and in the process they had gone a long way towards discovering Canada itself.

The Use and Abuse
of History

IN HIS SPEECH at the laying of the cornerstone of Champlain College, Premier Jean Lesage made a remark which provides an appropriate introduction for this discussion. "To those who keep repeating 'What exactly does Quebec want?' " Mr. Lesage said, "I ask, 'What exactly do you want Quebec *not* to want?' " Well, I have no intention of picking up Mr. Lesage's challenge in the form in which he so dramatically flung it down. I suspect that a Canadian from any one of the other nine provinces would have as little relish for specifying what he *does not* want Quebec to want as Mr. Lesage evidently has for specifying what Quebec *does* want. But the embarrassment of being specific, which everybody feels, is not my main reason for declining to submit an itemized list of refusals to Mr. Lesage. My main reason is that his challenge appears to rest on an assumption which I do not find acceptable. His words seem to imply that Canadians are divided into two great classes: those in Quebec who have wants and those outside Quebec who want to deny those wants.

This is surely, at the least, a very large oversimplification of the present confused and agitated state of public opinion in Canada. Obviously the "wants" of which Mr. Lesage speaks are concerned with the position of Quebec Province, and of French Canada as a whole, in Canadian Confederation; but these are not the only "wants" that are being felt in Canada today, and, equally impor-

First delivered at Trent University, 4 November 1965, and published in the *Journal of Canadian Studies I*, 1 May 1966, p. 9, under the title "Confederation: The Use and Abuse of History".

tant, they are not the only wants that imply changes in the Canadian constitution. All over the country Canadians are advocating changes, or discussing the advisability of changes, or—and this is perhaps most important of all— making demands, reaching decisions, drawing up plans which, though they realize it only partly if at all, may mean still more drastic, though indirect, changes in the future. It is not enough to examine the wants of Quebec or of French Canada in isolation; it is necessary to review the whole range of recent developments which either directly or indirectly alter the form or upset the balance of the Canadian constitution. If a "quiet revolution" has been going on in Quebec, another revolution, quieter still but just as significant, has been going on in Canada as a whole.

Revolution means the complete overthrow of an established form of government, or, more generally, of an established political and social régime; and it is obvious at once that changes on such a grand scale are not in many Canadians' minds at the present time. A considerable part of our constitution, like most of the British, is unwritten; and with these venerable conventions, by which free men are ruled in a constitutional monarchy, nobody wants to tamper seriously. When we talk about constitutional change what we almost invariably mean is change in the purely federal part of our constitution, which is, of course, set out in the British North America Act of 1867. This act has been amended in the past; but the amendments have not been frequent and few of them are really substantial in character. In its written form, our federal constitution is thus fairly close to what it was a hundred years ago; and that brings us back to the intentions of the Fathers of Confederation, which is the subject of this paper. What I should like to do is re-examine the intentions of the Fathers in the light of the new demands and changed circumstances of the present day. What were those intentions and why are they now regarded by some as inadequate? What arguments are advanced to justify constitutional change and how valid are they?

All revolutionaries—including "quiet" revolutionaries—have got to make up their minds about history. The past inexorably confronts all those who advocate sudden and major changes. The question of how history is to be regarded, of how it is to be interpreted so as to justify drastic reforms, is inevitably a crucially important problem for revolutionaries. They have, of course, found extremely varied solutions to it over the centuries; but, at bottom, these varied solutions are simply different expressions of two main approaches or attitudes to history. The past can either be represented as an era of misery and oppression from which society must try to escape, or it can be pictured as a lost golden age to which a defrauded people must seek to return. Either history can be the "bad old times" whose harsh enactments should be abolished; or it can be the "good old times" whose wonderful spirit has been forgotten or killed by the letter of the law.

These two revolutionary attitudes to the past, here contrasted sharply for the sake of clarity, have, of course, been modified and toned down in a variety of ways. It is obviously not necessary, for example, to look back upon the past as completely evil—as nothing but the record of the crimes, follies, and misfortunes of mankind. It can be, and sometimes is, dismissed just as effectively by holding it up not as the "bad old past" but simply as the past without any adjectives at all—the past which is irrelevant and useless to the present merely because it is history. This assumption comes naturally and readily to modern town and city dwellers who live in oblongs of space in high-rise apartments with not much room, no privacy, and lots of chrome, arborite, and gadgets. They have been taught by journalists and television personalities that anything older than ten years is positively medieval; they have been convinced by advertisers that rapid obsolescence is the greatest principle of the good life yet discovered by man.

To dismiss the past as outworn and unsatisfactory for the needs of the present is a favourite revolutionary approach to history. But, as has already been noted, there is another, more sophisticated approach which may be equally effective. This is not to reject the past as completely valueless for the modern generation, but to discover in it a new meaning or significance, which has been lost or forgotten, and which fortunately happens to provide a complete justification for the revolutionary demands of the moment. In this case, history becomes the "good old times", or the "better old times", with rights and liberties which have since been violated, promises and agreements that have not been kept, and a fine generous spirit that has not been lived up to. Obviously the type of revolutionary who takes this approach does not want to wash his hands of the past; his aim is to reinterpret it so as to bring out its lost or forgotten meaning; and if the black letter of the historical document seems to cast doubt on this new interpretation, he is apt to appeal to something beyond it, to some unwritten agreement or unspoken major premise which underlies the bare historical record and gives it its real meaning. This "real meaning" is often just another way of stating the revolutionary demands; and history is thus made to give its authority and sanction to a major program of change.

II

There are, of course, other approaches to history. Historians are human beings with individual biases and prejudices; and they can differ widely in their interpretations. But for the moment we are concerned with revolutionary approaches, for revolutionary approaches are more popular when great changes are under consideration; and Canadians are ill-equipped to judge their validity, for they have no great body of historical knowledge to fall back upon. Colonies, which have no clear sense of an identity separate from that of the empire to which they belong, are very apt to be indifferent to, and ignorant of, their own history. Canada ceased entirely to be a dependent entity in the British Empire–Commonwealth at a time well within the memory of many people now living; and there are many occasions now when she seems to be becoming, if she has not already become, an even more thoroughly assimilated and tractable portion of the Empire of the United States. There are signs, perhaps increasing in number during the past two decades, that Canadians are growing more interested and concerned about their history, as a result possibly of some obscure fear of the extinction of their collective personality. But it still remains true that Canadians, as they face the future, cannot rely upon any substantial body of knowledge about the past. They are confused and uncertain about the direction they should be taking, partly because they do not know whence they have come, or by what route, or with what aims and ideals as guides for the journey. Ignorance readily accepts myth and is vulnerable before propaganda.

Yet there is no real reason for this ignorance. There is, for example, a large body of records on the making of Canadian Confederation; and in the past there has never been any substantial difference of opinion as to what the intentions of the Fathers of Confederation really were. With the utmost clarity and precision, in speech after speech and resolution after resolution, the Fathers set out their purpose of establishing a great transcontinental nation in the form of a constitutional monarchy under the British Crown. Constitutional monarchy on the British model meant, of course, parliamentary sovereignty—the concentration of legislative power in a single sovereign legislature; and, if they could have had their way, most Cana-

dians, including in all probability a majority of the Fathers of Confederation themselves, would have preferred
to see all the British North American provinces joined in a
legislative union under one common parliament. Legislative union was their first choice; but legislative union was,
they realized, impossible, partly because French Canada
wished to guard its distinctive culture with some measure
of local autonomy, and partly because the Maritime
provinces, which had not developed municipal institutions, would have been left literally without any local government at all if their provincial legislatures had been
abolished.

For these reasons, the union could not be legislative, it
would have to be federal; but though most Canadians in
the years 1863-7 recognized the inevitability of federalism, they could not help regarding it with the greatest
doubt and suspicion. Up to that time, there had never
been a federal union in the British Empire; in the whole
history of the English-speaking world the only federal union was that of the United States of America; and in 1864
when the British American union was being planned, the
United States appeared to be fatally divided by a terrible
civil war. In the eyes of British Americans, the explanation
of that civil war was to be found in the very large powers
granted by the American constitution to the individual
states and in the extravagant demands they had based upon
them. As one British American journalist put it, federalism
was the Guy Fawkes lurking under the structure of the
American union who had eventually succeeded in blowing
it to pieces. Was there not a terrible possibility, he and
other British Americans asked, that history might repeat itself north of the international boundary, and that the cen-
trifugal forces of federalism would in their turn destroy the
union of British America?

The realization that federalism was necessary was therefore almost exactly balanced by the conviction that federalism was dangerous. The greatest task facing the northern

provinces was the task of preserving their separate collective identity in a continent dominated by the United
States; and if they formed a union that broke up through
internal weakness, it would likely mean that the fragments
would be devoured at its convenience by the great republic. The only union which could ensure the survival of
British America was a strong union; and if federalism had
to be accepted as unavoidable, the forces of disruption la-
tent within it must be systematically weakened and rigidly
controlled. This was the sober and deliberate judgment of
the Fathers assembled in the Charlottetown and Quebec
Conferences; and out of it came what, it seems to me,
should be regarded as the "Great Compromise" of Canadian Confederation. The union, it was admitted, would
have to be federal in character; but at the same time it
must also be the most strongly centralized union that was
possible under federal forms. It was on this condition, and
on this condition alone, that a federal framework was accepted by the architects of Confederation.

The spirit of this basic compromise pervades the whole
of the seventy-two Quebec Resolutions on union. The Fathers openly declared and avowed that they proposed to
correct the mistakes and remedy the weaknesses of the
American constitution by reversing the decentralist federal
principles upon which it was based. The American states
had granted small and insufficient powers to the federal
government, retaining all the rest, the so-called residuary
powers, themselves; the British American provinces, on
the contrary, were to be given only the limited authority
necessary for local needs, and all the remaining or residuary powers were to be held by the central government.
In two crucial debates in the Quebec Conference—the debates on the residuary clause and on the federal controls
over provincial legislation—these basic principles of the
proposed federal scheme were challenged by a small minority of delegates, and in each case the challenge was decisively beaten. The provinces and the Dominion were not

to be co-ordinate in authority, as a purist definition of federalism would have required them to be; on the contrary, as John A. Macdonald openly explained, the provincial governments were to be subordinate to the central government. Their functions and responsibilities, it was generally expected, would be relatively small and unimportant, and most people hoped and believed that they should be organized in a very simple and inexpensive fashion. So important a delegate as George Brown would have preferred to give the "local" legislatures a frankly municipal organization and to have reduced them to the level of glorified county councils.

To the great disappointment of some Canadians, who cannot believe they are free men until they have tried to imitate the United States, the British North America Act makes no attempt to provide a complete constitution for Canada, as the American Constitution of 1787 does for the United States. The main purpose of the British North America Act was to establish the new federal institutions and to divide legislative power between the provinces and the Dominion; and unlike the American constitution, it does not start out with a preamble setting forth the aims of government, nor does it include a bill of rights. In general, the liberties of the subject are assumed as part of the unwritten constitution inherited from Great Britain; and it is only in a few particular cases that the act concerns itself with rights or liberties, and then in a characteristically practical and empirical fashion. It provides safeguards for the distinctive Civil Code of the Province of Quebec, for the already established sectarian schools of religious minorities, and for the use of the English and French languages in the Parliament and courts of Canada, and in the legislature and courts of the Province of Quebec.

It goes no further. Canada was not declared to be a bilingual or a bicultural nation—the modern use of the latter term was unknown in 1867. Such a declaration of general principle was never even suggested. It must always be remembered that the aim of Confederation was not simply to settle the sectional rivalries of Canada East and Canada West—the future Quebec and Ontario. That problem might have been solved just as well, as George Brown wanted to solve it, by changing the legislative union of Canada into a federal union. The main aim of Confederation was to found a strong transcontinental nation; and the first great step in this enterprise, and the most difficult and decisive achievement of the Fathers, was the union of Canada with the Maritime or Atlantic provinces. This union was also to be called Canada; but the name did not imply by any means that the rights and liberties peculiar to the Province of Canada were now to be exported to the Maritime provinces. The new Dominion of Canada was not to be a duality, as the old Province of Canada had been; on the contrary, it was designed and organized as a triumvirate of three divisions, Ontario, Quebec, and the Atlantic provinces, which would become fourfold with the addition of the Northwest Territories and British Columbia. The rule of the Civil Code and the use of the French language were confirmed in those parts of Canada in which they had already been established by law or convention. But that was all. They were not extended to the Maritime provinces or to Ontario. Alexander Galt's original resolution on language, presented on behalf of the Coalition government to the Quebec Conference, is nothing more than a draft of Section 133 of the British North America Act. There is no evidence that French-speaking ministers or ordinary members of the legislature ever proposed that the French language be given legal status in Ontario or the Maritime provinces. There is a good deal of evidence which strongly suggests that Tilley, Tupper, and Brown would not have listened for a moment to such a proposal.

III

Now it is obvious from even the most casual glance at the state of the Canadian nation that enormous changes have occurred in our federal system since 1867. In a number of important ways, the intentions of the Fathers have not been realized; some of their most confident expectations have failed of fulfilment; and the relations between the provinces and the Dominion and between English-speaking and French-speaking Canadians have altered, shifted, veered in new directions, and taken new courses in a fashion which the Fathers of Confederation clearly never anticipated. The various aspects of this constitutional revolution, at times "quiet", at times stridently vociferous, are of course extremely numerous; but for the sake of brevity they can be grouped into two main trends or tendencies. On the one hand, the balance of power between federal and provincial governments, which the Fathers believed should incline decisively towards the Dominion, has now fallen sharply towards the provinces; and on the other the Province of Quebec, which the Fathers recognized as different in only a few particulars, has asserted the pervasiveness of its distinct character and has claimed a special status in Confederation as a result.

The provinces which George Brown regarded as glorified county councils have become great and powerful states, with large resources and a wide variety of functions; and the Federal-Provincial Conference, in which they are directly represented in their own right, seems at times to have grown into a paramount legislature which may threaten to supersede the authority of the Dominion Parliament. The Province of Quebec has pointedly withdrawn from many of the enterprises in which the other provinces and the Dominion are co-operating, insists that it must have direct superintendence over most of the activ-

ities of the Canadians living within its boundaries, affects
at times to assume a kind of protective guardianship over
French Canadians in other parts of Canada, and on occasions even appears to claim that it is an international person capable of making binding agreements with foreign
powers.

This, in very general terms, is the revolution that threatens to change the whole nature of Canadian federalism.
And, like every other revolution, it is now confronted by
history. It is confronted in the first place by the British
North America Act of 1867, the formal embodiment of the
intentions of the Fathers of Confederation. But the British
North America Act is not the only obstacle in the path of
its onward career. Its way is also impeded or embarrassed
by our more general knowledge of the aims and purposes
of the men of 1867 and of Sir John Macdonald in particular, by our instinctive feeling that radical changes might
perilously weaken the fabric of our federal union, and
finally by the haunting fear that the survival of Canada as a
separate and autonomous political society in North America is still by no means assured. The past is not dead. It
stands at bay, confronting the revolution with its legal barriers, historical memories, and inherited convictions; and,
if the revolutionaries are to succeed, they must overcome
these obstacles, silence these fears, eradicate these inhibitions.

This is what, with increasing vigour, they have been
trying to do for the past few years. This is, in part, the explanation of the revived interest in the amendment of the
British North America Act and the drafting of what is
popularly called the Favreau-Fulton amending formula. It
may also turn out to be the explanation of the ultimate
failure of the Favreau-Fulton formula to win acceptance
and establishment as part of the constitution. In the end,
the formula may be dropped as intolerably inflexible; and
an attempt may be made, not to thread a difficult path

through the obstacles of the British North America Act, but to go round the act or to jump over it. The earlier belief that an informed "dialogue" on the constitution would do good has now been followed by suggestions that an informal or formal conference would be advisable, and even by the hint that in the end a constitutional assembly or convention, specially called for the purpose, may be found necessary.

But this is only the beginning. It is not enough to devise ways and means of carrying out radical changes; it is also necessary to justify them. And it is here that the inevitable encounter with history takes place. The "quiet" revolutionaries must get rid of history or they must make it serve their purpose. They must either demonstrate that the recorded intentions of the Fathers of Confederation have been invalidated by the passage of time and are therefore obsolete; or they must prove that the recorded intentions do not constitute the whole of the great plan of Confederation, that beyond them was another and a more important general purpose, an inarticulate major premise, which underlay the whole scheme of the British North America Act, but never found adequate expression in it. As a result, it must be argued, the spirit which might have humanized our federal union has never been lived up to, and the implicit agreement which formed its basis had never been properly carried out.

Both these arguments have in fact been used. It has been urged, in the first place, that economic and social developments have made the intentions of the Fathers of Confederation irrelevant and their plans obsolete; and in the second place it has been contended that Confederation was not, as most people have always believed in the past, a union of several provinces, but a union of two cultures or two nations, French and English. The evidence for the first of these propositions is stronger on the face of it than that for the second; it is always easy to make an impressive list of differences between the present and the past of a hundred years ago; and proving how much better—and how much better off—they are than their ancestors has always been a favourite indoor sport of each generation. Thus the "quiet" revolutionaries argue that the Fathers of Confederation obviously did not foresee the tremendous expansion of education, or the coming of the welfare state, with its pensions, family allowances, medical care, and various forms of insurance. The Fathers also mistakenly assigned natural resources to the provinces under the impression that most of the best land had already been alienated and that public domain would never bring in a large revenue. These confident expectations, the "quiet" revolutionaries argue, have been largely falsified by the discovery of enormous mineral deposits in central and western Canada, by the exploitation of forest resources, and by the development of hydro-electric power. Finally, it is claimed, the Fathers were also sadly mistaken in their expectation that the great public improvements of the future would be federal enterprises such as transcontinental railways. On the contrary, it is provincial and municipal public works— schools, universities, hospitals, and roads—that now constitute the bigger part of the public enterprises of Canada. In short, the whole trend of modern development has placed more power and more responsibility in the hands of the provinces; and this inevitably means such a large degree of decentralization as to make the centralist scheme of the Fathers seem obsolete.

In the meantime, while the Fathers were meeting with this frontal attack, their position was also menaced by a more subtle flanking movement. Confederation, the revisionists of Canadian history explained, was not, or not mainly, a union of provinces; rather it was an agreement between two cultures or two nations, French and English. There was, some of the revisionists admitted, very little evidence for this thesis in the Charlottetown or Quebec Conferences, or in the proceedings that led up to the enactment of the British North America Act. In 1867, therefore, they say, the agreement could perhaps best be described as an extra-legal agreement, an unspoken moral commitment, which was meant to inform the whole union with its spirit. It was only when Manitoba and the North-west Territories were incorporated in the union that the Fathers of Confederation and their immediate successors took positive steps to ensure that this bicultural compact should prevail in the new western domain and that it should thus become the common possession of both English-speaking and French-speaking Canadians. In this spirit, it is claimed, the first Conservative government gave legal status to the French language in Manitoba and the first Liberal government after Confederation did the same for the Northwest Territories. Finally, it is argued that this agreement between the two cultures, with which Confederation started out, has not been honoured as it should have been, and that substantial amends must now be made.

The uses to which the two-nation theory can be put are manifold. It can give support to the promotion of French in the public service or the increase of French-taught schools in areas where the character of the population requires it. But its advocates are not usually content with such modest programs. The two-nation theory can be made to justify a bicultural Senate and a bicultural Supreme Court, with equal representation for French- and English-speaking Canadians. It is also the basis of the proposal that Quebec be made an associate state.

IV

Such are the two radical views of the Fathers of Confederation and their work; such are the arguments on which they are based. It is obvious at once that these interpretations have been used to support very large claims and sweeping conclusions; and this very fact invites us to exam ine their supporting evidence closely. As soon as we begin to do so, it is immediately clear that there are very serious weaknesses in the case for radical change.

We are deceived by the theory of inevitable decentralization. It has such an air of sweet reasonableness about it. How could the Fathers of Confederation be expected to make provision for the welfare state and the modern Canadian economy? The answer is *not* "Of course they couldn't", as the "quiet" revolutionaries assume. The answer is that the Fathers *did* make ample provision by founding a strong central government which could have coped very effectively with modern social and economic problems. And the fact that it is not now capable of playing the role which the Fathers intended it to play is not the result simply of natural social evolution and economic change, but also, and more importantly, of arbitrary human intervention—of the decisions of the courts and the arrangements of politicians. The British North America Act, as I have said, has not often been formally amended; but its whole character has been drastically changed, and, indeed, almost exactly reversed, by the decisions of the courts, and particularly of the Judicial Committee of the Privy Council, which in effect have transferred residuary authority from the central government, where it was intended to lie, to the provinces, which were never meant to have it. There was nothing natural or inevitable about this at all; it might, it ought, to have happened the other way. With infinitely more justification than in the United States, the trend of judicial interpretation could have favoured the central government. But it did exactly the opposite. And the tragic irony of our present plight is that the Canadian constitution, which was designed to prevent the defects of decentralization from which the United States was supposed to suffer, has in fact acquired far more of these defects than the American constitution itself.

The judges began the process of decentralization by

transferring powers and responsibilities to the provinces; the politicians have continued and hastened it by transferring vast sums of money. During the depression of the 1930s and the war of the 1940s, the Dominion government still maintained its dominating economic and financial control; but since then provincial pressures and federal concessions have altered this state of affairs, and with accelerating rapidity. The recent financial agreements between the provinces and the Dominion have steadily increased the provincial share of the Canadian tax dollar. The "opting out" or "contracting out" formula may give the provinces more complete administrative and financial control over development and welfare programs which they have previously shared with the federal government. Finally, the new Canada Pension Plan will put in the hands of the provincial governments enormous capital sums which can be used quite independently to carry out provincial economic and social projects. This huge increase in the provincial share of the public or government sector of the economy could threaten serious trouble for the future. It might weaken the Dominion's power to support its monetary and fiscal control, and hence its capacity to maintain the nation's economic well-being. It might help to break down those common minimum standards of public services and welfare which most people believe a nation ought to try to achieve.

The arguments for the theory of inevitable decentralization are certainly defective; yet its consequences may be serious. The same general comment might very well be made about the two-nation theory of Canadian Confederation. The obstinate historical facts will simply not bear the weight of this massive generalization. The Manitoba Act of 1870, which gave provincial status, the French language, and sectarian schools to the first prairie province of Canada, was not at all the original intention of the Fathers of Confederation. Their original intention was expressed in an act passed one year earlier, now generally forgotten, the

Act for the Provisional Government of Ruperts Land, which gave the northwest the government of a territory, not of a province, and made no mention of languages or schools. What forced the Fathers of Confederation to abandon their original plans for the northwest was, quite simply, the Riel Rising of 1869-70. It was Louis Riel, backed by five thousand *Métis*, the partial support of the Red River community, together with British pressure and Anglo-Canadian fears of American intervention in the northwest, which compelled the Fathers of Confederation to fix the institutions of Manitoba prematurely, before the true character of the province had declared itself.

Even if one concedes, which I do not, that the settlement of 1870 was wise, it by no means follows that the Manitoba Act established a bicultural pattern for the northwest which was carefully confirmed and followed thereafter. The North-West Territories Act of 1875, which first set up a territorial government for the prairies beyond Manitoba, made no mention whatever of language rights; and the amendment which in 1877 gave the French language legal status in the territories was proposed, not by the Liberal government of the day, but by a private member in the Senate. Anybody who cherishes the fond delusion that these early bicultural provisions in the west were the result of a settled policy followed by both Conservative and Liberal governments would be well advised to read the speech with which David Mills, then Minister of the Interior, greeted this Senate amendment when it was brought down to the Commons in April 1877. He reminded the members that the prevailing language of the region was Cree. He regretted the amendment; and he reluctantly accepted it because otherwise it would be impossible to get the revised bill through before the end of the session.

The Fathers of Confederation were neither political philosophers nor political dreamers, but hard-headed, practical, empirical statesmen. They had come through some very bitter disputes over the controversial subjects of religion, education, and language; and it was not in their nature to provoke trouble by laying down abstract declarations of general principle. On these contentious cultural matters, they contented themselves with a few provisions which were precise, definite, and limited. Yet these limitations have not prevented a liberal enlargement of the original privileges, by usage and convention, far beyond the letter of the law. The British North America Act merely requires that French as well as English shall be used in the records and journals of the Houses of Parliament; but what a vast extension has already taken place here, and entirely without the sanction of the theory of the two nations! The use of French as well as English on stamps and banknotes, in federal stationery, forms, and notices, in all the publicity, information, and publications of a modern state, and in such national enterprises as the Canada Council, the Film Board, Air Canada, and the Canadian Broadcasting Corporation, has come about gradually but steadily, and a great advance has been made within the past twenty-five years. The Royal Commission on Bilingualism and Biculturalism may usefully help this process on its way; but it would be dangerously unwise for its members to regard themselves as the Stepfathers of Confederation and to assume that their terms of reference empower them to propose fundamental changes in the Canadian constitution. They should remember—we should all remember— that the attempt to impose a bicultural pattern by law on the Canadian west was resisted with the utmost determination as soon as the west had formed its character and come of age. The resulting controversy was as prolonged and bitter as anything in Canadian history and it ended with the west's total rejection of biculturalism.

Thus the theory of natural decentralization and the theory of Confederation as a bicultural agreement, both of which have such a plausible appearance, become doubtful and suspect in the hard light of history. This realization ought to strengthen our resolve to understand and respect our past. History must be defended against attempts to abuse it in the cause of change; we should constantly be on our guard against theories which either dismiss the past or give it a drastically new interpretation. Such theories are likely to abound in an age of doubt and uncertainty about the future; and most of them, whether consciously or unconsciously, have been developed to serve the radical programs of the moment. From this the path to historical propaganda is short and easy; and as George Orwell has shown in his terrible satire, *Nineteen Eighty-Four*, the systematic obliteration and re-creation of the past may become the most potent weapon in the armoury of a collectivist dictatorship. A nation that repudiates or distorts its past runs a grave danger of forfeiting its future.

Part II
Commerce and Empire

The Commercial Class in Canadian Politics, 1792-1840

THERE WERE TWO occupations of Canada at the conquest, the military and the commercial. And this dual occupation sums up much of the history of the past and suggests the development of the future. The long struggle on the North American continent had been not only a war between two great European powers, France and England, but also a conflict between two purely American societies—the society of the St. Lawrence and that of the Atlantic seaboard; and the significance of the conquest lies less, perhaps, in the fact that it extended British imperial control over the old Province of Canada than in the fact that it made possible the conjunction of these two dissimilar colonial societies within the confines of a single state. British control might mean either arrogance and ineptitude or impartiality and wisdom. But the great issues in Canada, as in all America, were not to be decided by imperialistic virtues and vices; they were to be decided by

First published in *Papers and Proceedings of the Canadian Political Science Association*, vol. v, 1933, p. 43.

American capacities and by the promptings of the American spirit.

And this American spirit was, fundamentally, materialistic. It was the response of a middle-class population in a commercially minded age to the apparently unbounded possibilities of an unworked continent. On the Atlantic seaboard, this spirit was, perhaps, best typified by Massachusetts, where the New Englanders were creating a commercial prosperity with that ingenious efficiency which, in the seventeenth century, had been devoted to the establishment of a Puritan paradise. It was this energy and commercial aggressiveness which the "miserable sutlers and traders" brought to Quebec and Montreal. They came to the newly conquered province with the single, simple, and essentially American objective of making money by trade. And they were to be an incalculably disturbing force, not, in the main, because they were English-speaking Protestants, but because they were the pure, distilled spirit of British American commercialism dropped into the tepid colonial society of the St. Lawrence.

The most important products of the New World were its new men. The French, like the Spaniards, Dutch, British, and Germans, crossed the Atlantic Ocean as Europeans; but they and their descendants remained in the new continent as Americans. It is impossible, in comparing the society of the St. Lawrence with that of New England, to insist exclusively upon such old-world factors as race, language, or religion. The French Canadians were also distinguished from their southern neighbours by the peculiar responses of their spirit and by the characteristic adjustments of their social heritage, to the promises and demands of a vast and empty continent. The population—a scant sixty-five thousand—huddled together comfortingly along the lower reaches of the river. The inward pull of church, family, and seigniory was enormous. The little colony peopled itself slowly without expanding and the earthy, solid frontier of New England and Virginia was replaced here by the vast, unsubstantial empire of the fur trade. In that trade the courage and resource of the French Canadians had been lavishly expended. Their use of the St. Lawrence River system, their transportation units, their commercial technique, and their cultural borrowings from the Indians, were all distinctive features of their colonial civilization.[1] So was their economic dependence on the fur trade; for efforts at more extended and diversified commercial enterprises had been unsuccessful. And back in the seigniories between Quebec and Montreal, the *habitant*, ruled by an old-world system of tenure, sale, and inheritance, toiled tranquilly away at his subsistence farming. It was a curious little society, stolid, comfortable, and unaspiring; and to the commercial seaboard and the land frontier of British America it appeared—in all its aspects—alien and almost incomprehensible.

The initial results, however, of the introduction of American commercialism into the culture of the St. Lawrence valley were naturally, but somewhat deceptively, limited. The conquest, it is true, brought not merely an administrative but also a commercial decapitation. And this gradual but inevitable concentration of commercial leadership in the hands of the British traders accentuated the basically peasant and professional character of French-Canadian society. This presaged darkly for the future; but at the moment it meant little, for the merchants, from motives of self-interest as strong as those of the government, were determined to maintain the bases of the St. Lawrence system. Just as Carleton attempted to erect an aggressive political structure upon the foundation of French-Canadian institutions, so the merchants built up a competitive commercial structure upon the basis of French-Canadian

[1]H. A. Innis, *The Fur Trade in Canada* (New Haven: Yale University Press, 1930), pp. 170-1, p. 393; H. A. Innis, *Problems of Staple Production in Canada* (Toronto: Ryerson Press, 1933), p. 3.

organization and technique.[2] So long as the fur trade dominated the horizon, so long as the large-scale immigration
forecast in the Proclamation of 1763 failed to material-
ize, the merchants could afford to be largely indifferent to
other aspects of the St. Lawrence culture. They spoke
French, intermarried with the French Canadians with a
readiness which has surprised later generations, and acquired seigniories, tacitly accepting a land system alien to
their own.

In consequence, the political action of these merchants,
though outwardly persistent and occasionally offensive,
lacks, during this period, a really revolutionary core. Their
campaign was directed against the military and conciliar
British administration in Quebec as much as it was against
the colonial society of the St. Lawrence; but in neither case
was it a massed and determined attack. Their profound
but narrow commercial interests, their concentration in
the old French staple, fur, kept the merchants dependent
upon the native French-Canadian economic system, just as
it kept them loyal to the British connection. Shut out from
the Council, despised by the lordly potentates of the mess-
room and the battlefield whom Great Britain sent out to
govern Quebec, the merchants, to be sure, organized their
own political machine. Petitions, agents such as Fowler
Walker, Maseres, and Lymburner, and the political co-operation of the English merchants were the main instruments in their employ. But they employed them only
where their interests as traders and consequently as the purest type of civilians were really involved. Their attempt to
influence western policy, their campaign against French
commercial law, their quarrels with military governors,
and their adroit opposition to conciliar taxation, all exemp-
lify the spirit behind their persistent campaign for an Assembly. Not unnaturally, they wished to make Quebec safe

[2]Innis, *The Fur Trade in Canada*, pp. 180, 265.

for civilians and commercialism. It was their belief that they would find in the Assembly the independence and progress which the middle-class and commercially minded New Englanders had found in the Charters. Obviously they hoped to use the Assembly as a taxation engine, just as they attempted later to employ it as a credit instrument.[3] And it was characteristic of the French that this was one of the features of the scheme which aroused their bitter opposition.[4] The merchants did not campaign as Protestants; they had abandoned, among the earliest, all serious thought of religious tests. It was a straight conflict between an aggressive mercantile body and a dormant peasantry. And it was, very significantly, the first really serious rift in a concord which had been solidly based upon the commercial interests of the merchants, their acceptance of the economic system of the St. Lawrence, and the consequent contentment of the French.

II

The period from 1783 to 1821 witnessed the first great economic revolution in Canada. It opened, on the morrow of the Peace of Paris, with the appearance of the Loyalists on the shores of Lake Ontario, and it closed appropriately in 1821, with the collapse of the vast fur-trading organization centralized at Montreal. French Canada, which had survived the American Revolution, succumbed to the Peace; and the Loyalists, who entered where the Republicans had been repulsed, brought equally a revolution to the old life of Quebec. They were followed by the first American settlers in the Eastern Townships; and before

[3]A. Shortt and A. C. Doughty, *Documents relating to the Constitutional History of Canada, 1759-1791* (Ottawa: King's Printer, 1918), pp. 745, 961, 972.
[4]Ibid., pp. 758ff., 972-3.

1821 forces were at work in Scotland and Northern Ireland to produce the great Canadian immigrations of the twenties and thirties. While the first frontiersmen in Upper Canada began to produce and to consume, the North West organization, centralized to pursue a retreating trade across a half-continent, was directed inevitably into the last furious struggle with Hudson Bay. But already, years before the long contest between the canoe and the York boat had been concluded, capital and labour were being shifted to the new staples, timber and wheat. Population grew; farmers settled where fur traders had roved; the whole commercial technique and transportation system of the French was altered and then abandoned.[5] Gradually the limitations and deficiencies of the St. Lawrence system of communications became startlingly distinct to a new population in which optimism, restless energy, and materialistic ambition were the dominant traits.

The slow course of this revolution masked for a time its inevitable consequences; but it was from the beginning big with menace for the French Canadians. And it ended by completing the divorce between the merchants and the colonial society of the St. Lawrence. By 1821 the fur trade had passed away; but while the merchants who had directed it grasped eagerly at fresh opportunities, the society which had been based upon it endured unchanged on the lower reaches of the river. Aloof and dogged, the French Canadians clung to the nerve centre of a communication system which restless aliens were determined to exploit in new and unfamiliar ways; and the merchants began to feel annoyance at the very time when the Canadians experienced their first cool thrill of apprehension. The attack was no longer against single features of their culture, such as their commercial law or their devotion to the paternalistic form of government; it was an attack from all sides,

[5]Innis, *Problems of Staple Production in Canada*, pp. 6-8.

against the position as a whole, and it was led by merchants whose commercial interest, which had once directed
them to maintain the economic system of the St. Lawrence,
now forced them to undermine it. Immigration threatened
to submerge the culture of the French Canadians. Free-
hold tenure in the Eastern Townships menaced the seigniorial system in the very province which they believed
their own.[6] Merchants and land speculators began sharply
to question their system of notorial records, their bankruptcy laws, their fines on sales of land. The slowly elaborated program of banks, land companies, roads, canals, harbours, and ship channels was conceived to gain objectives
which they did not cherish and was to be implemented by
methods of which they did not approve. Private enterprise
on a grand scale through banks and public works on a
grand scale through taxation and credit were alien to them
and distrusted instinctively. By 1821 the issue was joined
between a peasant community producing for consumption
and led by lawyers and priests, and a frontier community
producing for export and led by a business class whose primary interest was trade.

During this period, the commercial class was adapt-
ing its program and its methods of political action to the
slowly changing exigencies of the situation. The agitation for an Assembly, reinforced now by the petitions of
the Loyalists, was satisfied at last by the Constitutional Act.
But the projected division of the province robbed the concession of much of its savour; and Lymburner, the merchants' agent, fought to the last to preserve the economic
unity of the country. His defeat and the division of the old
province of Quebec into Upper and Lower Canada condi-
tioned largely the economic and political activity of the
merchants for the next half-century. Political division be-

---

[6]The French Canadians realized this very quickly, as the early numbers of *Le
Canadien* show.

came inevitably the chief check upon their commercial program, just as union became the chief article of their political creed.

Rapidly, their political position under the Constitutional Act became paradoxical in the extreme. Cut off from their friends in the Upper province who in all essentials accepted the same gospel of expansion and prosperity, surrounded by a peasant and professional society at once dormant and suspicious, the merchants acquired an outward aspect of extreme political conservatism as naturally as they developed a revolutionary economic creed. In 1792, when the first legislature opened, they were weak in the Councils and fairly strong in the Assembly. But in 1821, when the Canadian commercial revolution had run its course, all this had altered. The governors of the teens and early twenties turned to the traders as the French Canadians turned away from them; and the commercial class, along with the bureaucrats, judges, and French-Canadian landowners, became intrenched in the Legislative and Executive Councils as it was extruded from the Assembly. This union with governors and councillors, not often intimate, was frequently interrupted. The interests of the merchants were immensely practical and unemotional; they could scarcely sympathize with Ryland's unreasoning bigotry nor could they understand, later on, Lord Gosford's feeble wooing of French-Canadian popularity. In the Councils, moreover, they could not always win their point. They were unable, in 1805, to persuade the Legislative Council to vote down the new customs duties and they failed to induce it to support the Union Bill of 1822.[7] But while the Council was a defective institution for their purposes, it was the only institution which they could hope to dominate. And the whole trend of events from 1783 to

[7]*Journals of the Legislative Council of the Province of Lower-Canada*, 1823, pp. 24-8.

1821 was forcing them to depend less upon their private capacities and more upon the public instruments of legislation and finance.

But if their union with government was never perfect, their divorce from French Canada became inevitably complete. Yet it was not until the crowding economic changes had begun this alienation, and had stamped the commercial minority with a faint tinge of red, that symptoms of serious trouble first appeared. It is surely significant that the first embittered clash in Lower Canada occurred, not during the governorship of Craig, the terrorist, but during the administration of the mild and ineffective Milnes; and that it concerned, not the lofty questions of religion and language, but the prosaic problem of financing the construction of gaols.[8] It was a straight dispute between a peasant community which hated all taxation and land taxation in particular and a commercial class which wished to escape part of a burden which rested, in the first instance, almost entirely upon its shoulders. The abusive articles in the Quebec *Mercury* and the founding of *Le Canadien* followed the quarrel; and thereafter the war of newspapers and pamphlets never really ceased. While *Le Canadien* attacked the fur traders and criticized the American frontiersmen in the Eastern Townships, British publicists began to laud American enterprise and prosperity and to reflect sadly that unprogressive Canada "exhibited its infant face, surcharged with all the indications of old age and decay".[9] The merchants, as they established steamboat services and founded banks, realized acutely that they had only half escaped from a society which remained un-

[8]The French-Canadian Assembly voted to arrest Edwards of the *Montreal Gazette*, and Cary, of the Quebec *Mercury*, for alleged libels in connection with the dispute. See *Journals of the House of Assembly of Lower-Canada*, 1806, *passim*.

[9]*Le Canadien*, November 22, 1806 (vol. I, no. 1); December 12, 1807 (vol. II, no. 3), pp. 9-10. *An Apology for Great Britain* (Quebec: J. Neilson, 1809), p. 22.

changed to provoke and to impede them. As this period closes, they began to organize for the repeal of the Constitutional Act and the establishment of Union.

III

In rapid succession, at the beginning of the new period, the North West Company passed from existence, the first little canal at Lachine was started, the financial struggle in Lower Canada broke out, and the ill-fated Union Bill was debated and withdrawn. These apparently haphazard events constitute at once a warning and a prophecy; they reveal the basic problems of the period only to suggest their final solution; and they symbolize the intimate and vital connection between new staples, transportation, public finance, and union which dominates the situation and which creates the maladjustments, efforts, and tensions of the next few years. The period of gradual change is over; the pace is enormously accelerated. A new world confronts the men of 1821 imperiously. Its opportunities and problems crowd in upon them faster than the immigrants who land by thousands in the ports of Quebec and Montreal. And beneath all the shifting perplexities of immigration, settlement, roads, staples, currency, and credit lay the immense problem of the St. Lawrence, which complicated all the joint and several difficulties of the provinces and upon the solution of which their future, as a going American concern, depended.

But if the new age produced problems, it created confidence to meet them. The country was full of hope, naïve optimism, and driving ambition; exhortations and grandiose programs crammed the press; an army of surveyors, engineers, and promoters invaded the provinces, and land companies, canal companies, railway organizations, and banks sprang into existence. Inevitably men were driven back to the provincial and imperial parliaments; and, as the political pressure increased, as the petitions and programs continued to rain upon the heads of unhappy governors and recalcitrant assemblies, the antagonism, deep and irremediable, between the spirit of colonial France and that of colonial America was now at length completely revealed. The American culture, expressed by merchants and frontiersmen, was in the ascendant; and, as the tide closed in around them, the French Canadians realized its menacing significance and were driven into violence and hysteria.

The position of the merchants in this period was central. A few hundred feet from their banks, their warehouses, and their homes, the massive river pursued its way to the sea. They dreamed dreams and grasped at concrete realities. They saw the whole of northern North America as an east-west network of lakes and rivers—a system whose natural centripetal force, if increased by artifice, would attract irresistibly the commerce of a half-continent and direct it to the trunk line past their doors. It was Canada's great commercial age; and though it would be absurd to deny the differences between the merchants and the frontiersmen in the townships of Upper Canada, yet, as compared with the French, they thought alike on broad essentials, and the merchants saw with clarity and imagination what was dimly and confusedly understood elsewhere. Time pressed. The Americans were energetically building canals and the Upper Canadians were restive and impatient; and the merchants organized with an exasperation and a conviction which portended trouble for the future. They improved their position in the Councils. They supported favourable governors like Dalhousie with the same realistic readiness that they condemned impartial administrators like Gosford.[10] They began to fight elec-

---

[10]For British criticism of Gosford, see Adam Thom, *Anti-Gallic Letters* (Montreal: The Herald Office, 1836).

tions bitterly. They furnished their lobby over in London, the North American Colonial Association, with pabulum for its campaign at the Colonial Office.[11] And, as the colony drifted towards revolution in the crucial decade of the eighteen-thirties, they were forming political associations with as much zest as they were floating companies.[12]

Their program, though outwardly more aggressive, remained almost purely commercial in essence. It was their conviction that the seigniorial system acted as a positive barrier to improvement and prosperity; and they campaigned for registry offices, for changes in the bankruptcy law, and against the incidents of feudal tenure. They applauded and helped to finance the British American Land Company, with the triple purpose of making money, increasing settlement, and galvanizing the dormant activities of the province. They suggested the Commission for the Improvement of the Harbour of Montreal, organized the Champlain and St. Lawrence Railway to tap the trade of the Eastern Townships, pointed out the deficiencies of the ship channel across Lake St. Peter, and pressed incessantly for canals on the St. Lawrence. Always they were conscious of time, of American competition, of the immense possibilities of their country. And as their difficulties mounted, the conviction became unshakable that union, or the annexation of Montreal to Upper Canada, could alone deliver them from bondage.

To most of this the old society of the St. Lawrence was either indifferent or hostile. The control of commerce had long ago passed from the French Canadians; the lawyers who led them were mainly interested in legal and political questions; and their indifference to change lapsed quickly into definite hostility, as, in this latter period, the merchants and their supporters became more aggressive and

[11]Nathaniel Gould, Chairman of the North American Colonial Association, was accustomed to include long extracts from Canadian correspondence in his letters to the Colonial Office during the eighteen-thirties.
[12]The Constitutional Associations, formed in the autumn of 1834.

importunate. On the subject of the seigniorial system, the popular party was either evasive or downright in opposition.[13] The British American Land Company was fiercely opposed. Immigrants were frequently characterized as paupers whose chief contribution to the country was disease, and the legislature clapped a capitation tax on immigrants which was bitterly resented by the merchants.[14] When in 1834 Stuart demanded a large loan to get the St. Lawrence canals going, Papineau talked sadly of burdening a young country with debt.[15] The French-Canadian Assembly discontinued grants to the Harbour Commission for the simple reason that it disliked one of the British Commissioners. It failed to renew the bank charters and the merchants, in desperation, appealed to London. "Whether there be banks or not," said Papineau in the election campaign of 1834, "one acre of land will not be cultivated more or less"; and he proceeded to suggest the run on the banks which occurred in the autumn of that year.[16] At the same time, in extreme exasperation, the merchants organized their political associations. They appealed, as well as the French Canadians, for a complete change in the existing system; and contributed equally to the total paralysis of government which followed.

They were true to their character. From the first a purposeful and disturbing group, they became, as the movement of change rushed to a crescendo, a revolutionary body; and their uneasy alliance with government and their respectable position in the Councils fail to mask the dynamics of their program. The rebellion in Lower Canada was not a revolt of maddened liberals against a dormant

[13]The French-Canadian party was opposed, not only to provincial legislation on the subject, but also to the Canada Trade Act (1822), which permitted change in tenure by article xxxi; *Journals of the House of Assembly of Lower-Canada*, vol. 33 (1823-4), pp. 246-7.

[14]The *Montreal Gazette*, February 15, 1834 (vol. xlii).

[15]Ibid., March 6, 1834 (vol. xlii).

[16]Ibid., December 11, 1834 (vol. xlii).

and oppressive government; it was, as Lord Durham saw, a little civil war, and the betting was even as to which side would first appeal to arms. As early as March 1835, Aylmer feared that the British party would soon be roused to take the law into its own hands.[17] In December of the same year, a section of the party, under Adam Thom, attempted to create the nucleus of an extra-legal force.[18] And Lord Durham later suggested that the British had themselves helped to precipitate the rebellion in order to bring on a crisis before the French Canadians were prepared.

IV

The rebellions in Upper and Lower Canada were both, to a considerable extent, the result of the efforts made by two politically divided colonies to adjust themselves to a geographical background which demanded their union. But, while the basic economic problem was the same for both colonies, the two societies which wrestled with it were profoundly different and the resultant political struggles were fundamentally distinct. The conflict in Upper Canada conformed to a type which the history of the Thirteen Colonies had made wearisomely familiar; but the origins of the dispute in Lower Canada are more mysterious and obscure. One theory, that the conflict was a quarrel between frontier liberalism and a conservative oligarchy, Lord Durham speedily rejected; another, that the dispute was a racial struggle between French and English, he confidently believed. But surely both theories are inadmissible; the first because, as we have seen, it is a patent misinterpretation of the facts, and the second because it is an un-

[17]Canadian Archives, *Series Q*, vol. 221, part 2; Aylmer to Hay, March 14, 1835.
[18]Ibid., vol. 223, part 2; Gosford to Glenelg, December 28, 1835.

due simplification of them. When Lord Durham found in race a *primum mobile* external to the facts, he became a victim to the monotheistic determinism common to most philosophers of history. Race, as a universal, automatically operating constant, is a myth. There were two races and two religions in Quebec in 1763; but there was no rebellion until 1837. And North America, in this case as in others, has proved tolerant of religions and races, when those races have accepted its social uniformity and bowed to the materialistic gospel of its inhabitants.

It was precisely this that the French Canadians refused to do. Their program was essentially a broad social program—the preservation of a distinct colonial society unimpaired in all its basic essentials; and they insisted, not merely upon their racial purity, their religion, and their language, but also upon the legal system, the land system, the agrarian social structure, and the simple economic activities which had always distinguished their community. The Quebec Act, to which they began to appeal, is an instrument for the preservation of an old order, just as the Declaration of the Rights of Man and the Citizen is an instrument for the creation of a new. Decades after the French Revolution and the Napoleonic régime had transformed the land and legal systems of continental France, the French Canadians were still descanting upon the nobility and simplicity of the Custom of Paris and earnestly debating the advantages and disadvantages of the feudal system. They saw greed in American commercialism and turbulence in the American frontier; and they desired to protect their little society from the onslaught of both. Their methods varied, but their purpose remained the same. Distrustful at first of democracy, they learnt to use it, and later demanded its extension. But they opposed an elective Assembly in the seventeen-eighties and demanded an elective Council in the eighteen-thirties for basically the same reason—the preservation of the old colonial society of the St. Lawrence.

We have seen, on the other hand, that the merchants represented, not merely another religion and language, but also a different colonial view of life, a different response to the problems and opportunities of an undeveloped continent. They brought commercialism to Canada, one of the purest and most aggressive forms of American materialism; and from 1760 to 1840 their political activity was very largely directed by their conception of the economic and social future of the country and of the role which they should play in it. For a time their commercial interest led them to maintain the French-Canadian system, just as it later directed them to alter it. When the fur trade had disappeared, when the commercial revolution and immigration had changed the face of the country, when the horizon of opportunity widened and the vast magnitude and complexity of their tasks stood fully revealed, they turned impatiently from the French-Canadian system only to find that French Canada remained, inert and unresponsive, to baffle their progress. Then, and not until then, did they resolve on desperate action. And if, like the French Canadians, they were led by an artificial political system into devious paths and uneasy alliances, this does not conceal their real character. The dynamics of Canadian commercialism were decked out in the smug garb of political reaction, just as the statics of Canadian feudalism masqueraded in the bright hues of democracy. But when they campaigned for an elective Assembly in the seventeen-eighties and against an elective Council in the eighteen-thirties, their purpose was fundamentally the same, the development of the country as they conceived it and the profit of commercialism therein.

V

Lord Durham's Report, which capped the climax of this struggle, serves also, and very appropriately, as a finale to the thesis of this paper. The Report contains two great recommendations—responsible government and union. The second recommendation, as well as the first, offers a key to the significance of the Report and the character of its author. For those who stress responsible government, Lord Durham is a great liberal imperialist, with a regrettable tendency to ruthlessness and bias; for those who neglect union and its implications, the Report is a magnificent treatise on colonial government, marred by certain omissions, inaccuracies, and prejudices. But these limitations of the Report and these deficiencies of its author, if they are to be mildly deprecated from one point of view, can perhaps be explained from another. That point of view is union and the necessities which lay beneath it. Union is the cure for the economic and social maladjustments of Canada, just as responsible government is the corrective for its political distempers. And the man who saw the necessity of union was not only the first missionary of liberal imperialism, but the first great English convert to the American gospel. He was not concerned to give impartially equal treatment to artificial political units like Upper and Lower Canada; for he was thinking in terms of North America. He could not be fair to French Canada, for he was dreaming typically American dreams of expansion and prosperity.

The man's whole character—his optimism, restless energy, and brusque aggressiveness—seems to sum up the spirit of a confident, questing, commercial generation. He could respond to America's way of life, he could see America's future; and this instinctive sympathy determines considerably the attitude, ideas, and temper of the Report.

Obviously, he was interested in the institutions of the United States just as he was fascinated by their progress and material prosperity. And there lies deep in the Report the apparently instinctive conviction that Canada's progress must be measured largely in terms of its successful emulation of American achievement. This explains the constant references to American conditions, the emphasis upon land policy and immigration, the preoccupation with communications and public works which are such characteristic features of the Report. Characteristically, also, Lord Durham criticized Canadian institutions and deplored Canadian political quarrels as obstructions to a broad policy of improvement. It is surely no disrespect to say of him that, if he worked to make Canada a self-governing British Dominion, he also hoped to make it a going American concern.

This strong, instinctive hope dictated largely Lord Durham's treatment of Lower Canada. From a standpoint of politics, Lower Canada was merely one of several provinces; but from the standpoint of society and economics, which bulked large in Lord Durham's consideration, it was of unique importance. He gave to the province a peculiar prominence and a peculiar treatment which are explicable only by his materialistic aims. He saw that the struggle in Lower Canada was a social and not a political conflict; and he viewed these two contending societies, their institutions, aptitudes, and spiritual impulses, mainly in relation to the opportunities and tasks of a great unworked continent.[19] He stressed the commercial genius, the organizing ability, the instinct for expansion and prosperity which he believed characterized the British. He emphasized the feudal institutions, the peasant interest, and the inertia of the French. He believed that North America could scarcely accept such a fundamental contra-

[19]*Lord Durham's Report* (C. P. Lucas, ed., Oxford: Clarendon Press, 1912), vol. ii, pp. 48-50.

diction of its spirit. He believed that it was justified in refusing to tolerate such opposition at the gateway to a river system which was the common property of all who lived upon its banks.[20] And these beliefs measure the completeness of his acceptance of the aggressive commercial philosophy of America.

Responsible government may have been conceived originally by Lord Durham or by the Canadian reformers; but union, and the whole philosophy of expansion and commercial prosperity which lay behind it, was the product of Montreal. Responsible government comes first in the Report, but is is permissible to doubt that it came first in Lord Durham's mind; for the British Canadians would never have accepted responsible government without union, nor would Lord Durham have proposed it. Union was the primary and indispensable step; union was first established; and if it was followed by responsible government, it was followed also by local government, large loans, the canal-building program, and the extinction of seigniorial tenure. Lost in the obscure background of the Canadian picture, half hidden by the elbow of some governor or by the peremptory visage of some second-rate politician like Mackenzie or Papineau, these merchants—the Ermatingers, McTavishes, Richardsons, Auldjos, and Moffatts—had a policy, fought for it, and triumphed in the end.

[20]Ibid., vol. II, p. 290.

The Economic Background
of the Rebellions of 1837

I N 1837, THE Canadian economy was subjected both to
the stresses inherent in its own unstable organization
and to the strains of a temporary financial and commercial panic. The last crucial stages of economic change
and social conflict within the Canadas coincided unhappily with a general financial collapse in the English-
speaking world; and the coincidence of these two crises
produced a violent exaggeration of all the weaknesses to
which the Canadas had been subject. From the very beginning the trades of the St. Lawrence had suffered from persistent fluctuations and shared a common instability; but
to these chronic infirmities were now added all the special
difficulties of the shift from the trades in fur and timber to
the production of wheat and flour. The discord between
trade and agriculture, the disagreement between the organization of the commercial system and the demands of
the rural communities, had reached the last stages of their
development. While the old trading system of the St. Lawrence was expressed politically in the commercial state, the
agricultural interest had become vociferously articulate in
the reform parties of both provinces. And these economic
contradictions and social conflicts were evidently nearing
their climax at the very moment when the financial panic
broke in England and the United States.

The special maladjustments and conflicts which distracted the Canadas in the 1830s were, in the main, the

First published in the *Canadian Journal of Economics and Political
Science*, vol. 3, August 1937, p. 322.

product of that great series of changes which began with the advent of the Loyalists in 1783 and closed approximately at the middle of the nineteenth century. In the past the Canadas had formed a commercial state. The St. Lawrence, in the minds of those who controlled and directed its activities, was a great imperial trade route rather than a centre of populous North American communities. The northern trading system, which was the obsession of successive generations of Canadians, was vast in its extent. It bound Canada to the metropolis of the Empire; and in North America it had inspired a continental strategy which extended far beyond the international boundary between Canada and the United States. The first tiny settlements on the St. Lawrence and the lower lakes were dwarfed by a commercial system which was largely independent of their existence and which, in fact as well as in design, transcended their limited activities. The fur trade, which had been hostile to the last against settlement, had ended only in 1821. The trade in square timber which succeeded it was, in a large measure, carried on independently of the new settlers. And it was not until the early 1830s, which witnessed an enormous increase in the exports of wheat, that the value of the wood shipped to Great Britain was exceeded by the total value of all other commodities exported from Quebec to British ports.[1]

Yet within this commercial system, which had been organized to serve interests largely different and far more ambitious than their own, the little agricultural settlements developed, at first slowly and then with rapidly increasing speed. The French Canadians on the St. Lawrence and the Richelieu and the Loyalists on the edges of the lower lakes had been steadily recruited by the advent of American frontiersmen and assisted British immigrants; and in the late 1820s there began the first great spontaneous migration of British peoples to Canada. It arose

[1]*Montreal Gazette*, March 5, 1836.

out of the chronic, only occasionally relieved depression which in Great Britain followed the conclusion of the Napoleonic wars; and its volume, the calamities which were associated with it, and the amazing consequences to which it led, astonished, dismayed, and delighted the people of the Canadas. The population of the two puny provinces shot upward. In 1827 the number of inhabitants in Upper Canada had been estimated at 177,174; in 1837 the total population of the province was reckoned at 397,489.[2] The immigrants, who were packed away in the holds of the empty timber ships returning to Canada, helped to solve some of the problems of the heavy one-way traffic in the timber trade.[3] But this temporary balance was purchased at the price of a more important disequilibrium. The shift from the older trades to agriculture was accelerated; the demand for new markets and a better transportation system grew more imperative; and the intensification of the agricultural interest created new requirements, new commitments, and new problems which unsettled the bases of the old commercial state.

These weaknesses and maladjustments in the Canadian economy were reflected in the social disputes and political rivalries which in 1837 approached their climax. Though it drew inspiration from various different sources and assumed a variety of forms, the conflict in the Canadas was in large measure a social conflict which grew naturally out of the disturbed economy of the St. Lawrence. The governing class—the "Château Clique" in Quebec, the "Family Compact" in Upper Canada—was less a company of blood-relations than it was a fraternal union of merchants, professional men, and bureaucrats; and the Reformers of both provinces, though they are usually described in terms of their ethnic characteristics, their religious affiliations, or

[2]*Census of Canada*, 1870-1, vol. IV, pp. 83-171.

[3]H. A. Innis, "Unused Capacity as a Factor in Canadian Economic History" (*Canadian Journal of Economics and Political Science*, vol. II, February 1936, pp. 1-15).

their political principles, drew their main support from the countryside and took on all the characteristics of a rural protest movement. The controversy between agriculture and commerce, farmlands and trade routes, North American parochialism and the old colonial system, had already found expression, a quarter-century before, in the quarrels between the merchants of Quebec and Montreal and the peasants and lawyers of Lower Canada; and now, as the migration peopled the western part of Upper Canada, the conflict was extended territorially and deepened in import. In Lower Canada, which was still devoted to subsistence agriculture and to a debased feudal land-holding system, the peasants' opposition to commercialism was embittered by a touch of archaic misunderstanding and hatred. But in both provinces there was the same struggle against the institutions and programs of the commercial class and the same dislike of commercial wealth and privilege.

As it developed, the conflict aroused political loyalties and expressed itself in rival political philosophies; but action continued, nevertheless, to hover around definitely economic issues. In the new age, with the emergence of the agricultural west, the merchants were determined to solve the few problems which seemed alone to delay the realization of their enormous opportunities; and it was their design to build a new international commercial empire upon the bases of the staples, wheat and timber, to reconstruct a second unity of the St. Lawrence upon the ruins of the fur-trading unity of the past. They intended, by free trade, to encourage the import of American products into Canada, and they hoped, through the old mercantile system, to obtain protected imperial markets for the exports from Quebec; and the St. Lawrence trading system which connected these far markets and these distant depots of supply was to be improved by canals, harbours, and ship channels, developed by banks, commercial companies, and government enterprises, and peopled by a horde of immigrants from the British Isles. The governing class was the party of commercialism, the party which hungered to develop the country by private capital and public expenditure; and in support of a commercial system which was at once transatlantic and transcontinental, the merchants were prepared to break by force through feudal law, antiquated custom, and rural inertia.

The Radicals in both provinces viewed all this with indifference, suspicion, or positive hostility. It was true that among the frontiersmen of Upper Canada these feelings of apathy and distrust were not so instinctive or so obstinate as they were among the peasants, priests, and lawyers of the lower province; but in time, as the political engagement became general, the attitude of the Upper Canadian Radicals came to differ comparatively little from that of the *Patriotes* of Montreal. It was the belief of the leaders of both parties that the institutions, projects, and expenditures desired by the commercial class would either divert attention from rural needs, or would impose intolerable burdens and inflict definite injuries upon the countryside. While in Lower Canada the Assembly absolutely refused to begin its part of the St. Lawrence Canals, the Radicals in Toronto criticized Upper Canada's share of the undertaking and repeatedly attacked the Welland Canal.[4] "My opinion is," declared Perry, in opposing a new provincial loan in aid of the Welland Canal, "you would injure the agricultural interest of Upper Canada . . . and I never will give up the interest of Upper Canada for the Welland canal. Is all to be subservient to this great Moloch, and everything bow to it?"[5]

It was the same with all the other institutions and projects characteristic of the commercial state. The Canada Company was attacked by the Radicals in Toronto with only less ferocity than the British American Land Com-

[4] *Montreal Gazette*, March 6, 1834; *The Patriot*, February 14, 1834; *Colonial Advocate*, February 17, 1831.

[5] *The Patriot*, February 4, 1834.

pany was denounced at Quebec; and Papineau's hostility to the Montreal Bank was paralleled by Mackenzie's relentless pursuit of the Bank of Upper Canada. "Let them run to the Banks," declared Papineau, anticipating Mackenzie's language of a few years later, "and, in the terms of the law, demand gold and silver for their notes. . . . The most efficacious and the most immediate means which the Canadians have to protect themselves against the fury of their enemies, is to attack them in their dearest parts— their pockets—in their strongest entrenchments, the Banks."[6] The Radicals engineered a run on the Lower Canadian banks in 1834 and on the Bank of Upper Canada in 1837. While Papineau and his followers criticized the timber trade and questioned the timber preference, the Radicals in Upper Canada campaigned against the free-trade policy by which American products were admitted into Canada for export by the St. Lawrence.[7] Fundamentally, Mackenzie was hostile to the whole Canadian commercial system; and he was even anxious that the United States should be requested to permit Upper Canada to import and export *via* the New York route.[8] These economic disputes were not unimportant, subsidiary, and ephemeral. They were continually agitated; they helped to bring on the deadlock in the Canadas and to prepare both parties for politics of force; and when in 1834 the Montreal Tories formed their Constitutional Association, they solemnly declared that they would no longer "submit to the domination of a party averse to Emigration, to commerce, to internal improvements, and to all those interests which may be regarded as British. . . ."[9]

[6]*Montreal Gazette*, December 11, 1834.

[7]*Colonial Advocate*, October 2, 1834; *Belleville Intelligencer*, quoted in *The Patriot*, November 28, 1834.

[8]*The Patriot*, January 19, 1836.

[9]Public Archives of Canada, *Secretary of State's Papers*, Lower Canada, Molson *et al.*, to Craig, November 22, 1834.

The economic changes which disturbed the old commercial system, the economic issues which embittered the conflict between the farmers and the governing class, were not, however, the only material factors in the political situation of 1837. The weaknesses and inconsistencies in the Canadian economy, the growing animosities among the Canadian people, were paralleled by the increasing financial instability of the commercial state. Its obligations and resources, which ought to have been consolidated, were, in fact, divided between the two provinces; and these two quarrelling provinces could not combine in joint policies or share a common burden. The disputes over the division of the customs revenue collected at Quebec were settled periodically, though with difficulty; but though it was possible to divide income, it was impossible to equalize expenditure. The problem of the canals was as indivisible as the river they were designed to improve; but while Lower Canada obstinately refused to begin its part of the construction, the upper province optimistically took up its own heavier share of the task. The province, which was financially stronger, made no attempt to use its borrowing power, while the financially weaker province proceeded to acquire a large debt. Before 1837, Upper Canada had exhausted the market for provincial bonds within the Canadas and had placed debentures to the value of £600,000 with Baring Brothers and Thomas Wilson & Co. in England.[10] Upper Canada was beggaring itself in an effort to finish a great undertaking which, in fact, could never be completed without the co-operation of the unwilling sister province. So long as the two colonies remained divided, their finances would continue unstable and the canalization project would remain incomplete. The Constitutional Act, which had divided the old province of Quebec into Upper and Lower Canada, had proved an impossible

[10] *Journal of the House of Assembly of Upper Canada*, 1835, appendix, vol. I, no. 17.

political vehicle for the commercial state. The energy and extravagance of Upper Canada and the inertia and parsimony of the lower province had been left in isolation, to contradict rather than to modify each other; and both provinces, in their different but equally potent ways, contributed to the gradual unsettlement of the whole political machine.

By 1837, the weaknesses of the Canadian economy, the instability of Canadian public finance, and the clashes among the Canadian people had reached a state of ominous exaggeration and strain. Under the grinding stresses imposed upon it, the whole northern system was visibly disintegrating; and the forces which divided and distracted it were now expressed in militant political parties. The quarrel between feudal and frontier agriculture on the one hand and commerce and bureaucracy on the other approached the final limits of exasperation; and the inexorably approaching crisis was welcomed as much as it was feared. Both parties in both provinces began to declare their anticipation of a civil war; and as the meetings, parades, and disturbances grew in number, as the speeches and riotings increased steadily in violence, each party found in the other's menaces the justification for its own appeal to force.

II

A t this point, when the crisis in the Canadas approached its climax, the financial and commercial panic broke in the British-American world. The Canadian provinces could no more hope to escape the economic influences of Great Britain and the United States than they could expect to avoid the distempers inherent in their own economic and social condition. Canada, a dependent, staple-producing country, tied by innumerable and binding connections to the markets of Great Britain and the United States, had always followed the ups and downs of their trade cycle with submissive fidelity; and in 1836 the British-American business world was travelling through the last erratic stages of a speculative prosperity towards an imminent financial collapse. In Great Britain, the first great railway boom approached its climax. In the United States, the proliferation of banks and the vast expansion of credit had encouraged a quickening activity which invaded every sphere of business life;[11] and the unappeasable demand for canals, banks, railways, and other public improvements goaded the American legislatures into more ambitious projects and more lavish expenditures.[12]

In the Canadas, though the prosperity of the early 1830s followed its usual course, it was checked by the embarrassments peculiar to a staple-producing country. The exports of timber and sawn lumber, encouraged by gradually rising prices in the United Kingdom, had reached a new peak in 1835 and 1836.[13] During the early thirties, the exports of wheat and flour had enormously increased. But in 1834-5 the glut forced down prices; the British corn laws for a while prevented the import of Canadian wheat into the United Kingdom; and the Canadas were forced to turn to their second and inferior market in the other British North American provinces and the West Indies.[14] It was in 1836 that this oversupply was succeeded by a disastrous scarcity which affected the entire continent. The crop failed in Lower Canada, as well as in the northwestern American states; Upper Canada disposed of its supply in the United States, despite the tariff; and before the end of

[11]W. B. Smith and A. H. Cole, *Fluctuations in American Business, 1790-1860* (Cambridge, 1935), sec. 2.

[12]R. C. McGrane, *The Panic of 1837* (Chicago, 1924), pp. 1-42.

[13]*Quebec Gazette*, February 13, 1836; January 25, 1837.

[14]F. W. Burton, "Wheat in Canadian History" (*Canadian Journal of Economics and Political Science*, vol. III, May 1937, pp. 210-7).

the year North America had already begun to import breadstuffs from Europe.[15] Flour, which had opened at 28s. 6d. a barrel in Montreal at the beginning of 1836, reached 42s. 6d. in December and 60s. in February 1837;[16] and the savage bread riots which occurred in New York City were paralleled by the distress and real destitution which visited the French-Canadian parishes on the lower St. Lawrence.[17] The boom still continued, but it had grown excessive, erratic, and onerous. And in these exciting circumstances the Upper Canadian Legislature met during the winter and held one of the last prosperity sessions of that period in North America.

It was at this moment that the financial crisis was precipitated in the United States. For years the Democratic administration under President Jackson had fought the Bank of the United States and had unsettled the money market by the transference of federal banking deposits and the distribution of federal surplus revenues. In the summer of 1836, the administration concluded its long warfare with the bankers and the speculators by issuing the notorious specie circular, which abruptly demanded specie in payment of public lands. In the meantime, decline and retrenchment had already begun in England. The London and Liverpool houses, burdened with vast credits in America, were vulnerable before the demands of the English bankers; and their embarrassments, promptly transferred to their clients in America, helped to upset the toppling speculative prosperity in the United States.[18] In March and April the commercial houses began to fail in New York and Philadelphia; and on May 10, 1837, the New York banks suspended specie payments.

In these spring months of 1837, the crisis in Canadian

[15] *The Constitution*, January 18, 1837.
[16] Ibid., December 19, 1836; February 13, 1837.
[17] Public Archives of Canada, *Series Q*, vol. 237-1, pp. 28-31, Gosford to Glenelg, May 6, 1837.
[18] McGrane, *Panic of 1837*, pp. 40-2.

affairs was set in motion irresistibly. In March, when the financial crash was imminent in the United States, the British Parliament endorsed Lord John Russell's provocative resolutions; and this blunt imperial manifesto broke the political deadlock in the Canadas and blasted the hopes of the Canadian Radicals. By a sinister coincidence, the impact of the American financial panic was timed to accompany the impact of British political interference; and under this combined blow the northern commercial state fell apart into its conflicting interests, its rival groups, its antipathies and fears and hatreds. While in Lower Canada the Radicals organized a new series of protest meetings and denounced the policies of Great Britain in shriller tones, the whole populace of both provinces awaited breathlessly the effects of the financial panic. The bankers feared for the safety of their institutions; the bureaucrats in Upper Canada were worried for the security of their London loans; the merchants in both provinces grew suddenly apprehensive for the continuance of their loans and discounts; and the farmers and mechanics, agitated by the tirades of Mackenzie and the other Radicals, were frantic to exchange their bank notes for coin.

The next few weeks were filled with confused activity and angry agitation. In Lower Canada, the banks could suspend specie payments without forfeiting their charters; and the Montreal bankers, with the complete support of the commercial community, abruptly stopped the payment of gold and silver on May 17.[19] So far as was possible the lower province had avoided a severe contraction of credit; but Upper Canada was faced not only with the problem of financial stringency but also with a probable crisis in provincial finance. Of the loan of £600,000 negotiated in London, £147,000 still remained to the credit of the province.[20] Upper Canada had drawn its bills of exchange for

[19]*Montreal Transcript*, May 18, 1837.
[20]*Q*, vol. 396-4, pp. 567-71, Head to Glenelg, April 23, 1837.

part of the balance; and if the houses of Baring Brothers and Thomas Wilson failed, as so many feared they would, then the protestation of the bills would inevitably entail the bankruptcy of the province. W. H. Draper, a member of the executive, was hurriedly dispatched to England;[21] the receiver-general, J. H. Dunn, followed him at once, gloomily warning the executive to curtail the expenditure for public works as much as possible.[22] The stoppage of the canals on the St. Lawrence was generally expected; it was feared by some that the idle labourers might riot.[23] And in those first anxious days of May, the crisis in public finance created even more consternation than the approaching contraction of credit. No doubt the merchants complacently expected the suspension of specie payments, while the Radicals denounced it in advance. But they made, both of them, a lamentable miscalculation. They had forgotten their unforgettable governor, Sir · Francis Bond Head.

Sir Francis, who had dramatically entered Upper Canadian politics in January 1836, was an operatic character whose chief political attributes were a talent for rhetoric and a relish for grandiloquent gestures and heroic attitudes. In his romantic imagination the quarrel of local interests in Upper Canada had been transformed into a grand conflict of political loyalties and moral principles. He attacked Canadian radicalism like a paladin on a crusade: he won the election of 1836 with the impetuosity of a cavalry leader. And until that fatal May of 1837, the gratitude and admiration of the Tories could scarcely be contained within the straining limits of the English language. It was the banking crisis which disillusioned the merchants. It was then that the governor revealed his purpose

[21]Ibid., pp. 620-3, Head to Glenelg, April 29, 1837.
[22]Public Archives of Canada, *Upper Canada Sundries*, Dunn to civil secretary, May 5, 1837.
[23]Ibid., Macaulay to Hagerman, n.d.

to act in character as an officer and a gentleman with most undiscriminating consistency. He decided the question of specie payments on a point of honour and dismissed the problem of credit on a moral principle. In his opinion, the banks were morally bound to pay out specie on demand, as they had promised to do. "Upper Canada," he declared, "would prefer to lose its specie rather than its character. The principle of Monarchy is honour and from that principle the Lieutenant Governor will never consent to depart."[24]

The Bank of Upper Canada, influenced by these inspiring sentiments as well as by the more mundane consideration of its connection with the government, decided, on May 17, to continue specie payments.[25] For a few days the Tory papers talked admiringly of these decisions; and *The Patriot* asserted that the Bank of Upper Canada's "bold and gallant bearing . . . appeals with irresistible force to all the better feelings of man". But in a few days it began to be appreciated that the continuance of specie payments would in all probability entail a discontinuance of discounts, loans, and "banking accommodation" in general. Sir Francis Bond Head might talk with gentlemanly distaste about "accommodation" as if the term were a kind of deplorable coinage of the American vernacular; but the business of Upper Canada was largely based on credit, and before the end of May the merchants were urging the immediate suspension of specie payments and a special session of the Legislature to deal with the financial crisis.[26]

The governor, whose popularity in commercial circles had descended almost as rapidly as it had risen, yielded uneasily; and towards the end of June the provincial Parliament met. The Assembly, which was dominated by the commercial element, was determined to break the contrac-

[24]*Q*, vol. 397-1, pp. 154-79, Head to Glenelg, May 23, 1837.

[25]*The Patriot*, May 19, 1837.

[26]Ibid., May 30, 1837.

tion of credit; and its plan, as finally drafted in legislation, was to suspend specie payments and make bank notes and provincial debentures legal tender.[27] To the governor it was unthinkable that borrowers should be encouraged at the expense of the honour of monarchy and the character of Upper Canada; and, with the help of the Council, he defeated the Assembly's bill and forced through another which permitted the banks to suspend only at the discretion of the Governor-in-Council.[28] The protests of the dismissed Assembly were followed by a general indignant clamour when Sir Francis published the terms upon which he would permit the banks to suspend; but the governor remained firm, with that steadfastness which invariably afforded him such lively gratification. The Bank of Upper Canada practically gave up its ordinary commercial discounting, abandoned the local shopkeepers to their misfortunes, and waxed fat upon the profitable business of foreign exchange.[29] When the anxious merchants and traders of Upper Canada turned from their own banks to the institutions of the lower province, they were met with adamant, if regretful, refusals. "We all here feel the importance of affording facilities to the purchase of wheat in Up: Can:," wrote Peter McGill of the Montreal Bank to W. H. Merritt, "—but the Banks of L: Can: cannot give them, and but few Individual Houses will be able to supply their Correspondents with the needful from hence, because their Capital is already in Up: Canada Credits, and nothing coming down.—In my day such times have never been experienced."[30]

During that summer and autumn, the financial strin-

[27]Ibid., June 20, 27, 1837.

[28]*Q*, vol. 397-2, pp. 475-9, Head to Glenelg, July 12, 1837.

[29]Adam Shortt, *The History of Canadian Currency, Banking and Exchange*, part 8: *Crisis and Resumption* (Toronto, 1902), pp. 5-8.

[30]Public Archives of Canada, *Merritt Papers*, vol. iv, McGill to Merritt, August 16, 1837.

gency continued to embarrass the ordinary commercial activities of the province and to hold up the ambitious program of public works. Though Messrs. Glyn, Halifax & Co. took up the bills of exchange drawn by Upper Canada upon the bankrupt house of Wilson & Co., there was no more money forthcoming from London at the moment;[31] and during the summer the commissioners for the St. Lawrence Canals struggled on under great difficulties and by September were £10,000 in debt to the contractors.[32] The commercial slump, which throughout the United States had followed swiftly on the heels of the financial panic, was accentuated in Upper Canada by the unrelieved and exceptional contraction of credit; and during the spring and summer the whole carrying trade of the St. Lawrence dried up to a mere lethargic trickle of business. Late in May it was reported in Montreal that business in Upper Canada was almost at a standstill;[33] and for weeks there was little or no produce coming down the river to the ports. "An excessive languor," wrote one reporter in Montreal, "pervades nearly every branch of commerce, and our streets have, so far as relates to business, the appearance they are wont to exhibit on a close holiday or a Sunday."[34] In a long, dull, weary season, which showed only a slight flurry of activity towards the end of September, the volume of the timber trade was alone comparable to that of the previous year. There were no exports of wheat, for Montreal was steadily importing from Europe until late in the autumn; the export of flour had declined by over a half; and the value of free goods and goods paying the general 2½ per cent duty, imported from Great Britain, had fallen off over

[31]Public Archives of Canada, *Series G*, vol. 291, Glenelg to Head, July 22, 1837.
[32]*Journal of the House of Assembly of Upper Canada*, 1837-8, appendix, pp. 154-6.
[33]*Montreal Courier*, quoted in *Quebec Gazette*, May 26, 1837.
[34]*Montreal Transcript*, August 12, 1837.

£500,000 from the high of £1,800,000 established in the previous year.[35]

A winter of high prices and real scarcity, a winter which distressed the villages of Upper Canada and brought some parishes in the lower province to the verge of starvation, was followed by an abrupt financial panic and a commercial slump. The credit with the local shopkeeper, the summer employment on the public works, were more than ever necessary to a frontier population distressed by want and suffering; but the public works were half suspended, the commercial operations of the country were distracted, and, while the two provinces waited anxiously for the harvest, Montreal continued to import expensive European wheat. "During my residence in this province," wrote one observer to Sir Francis Bond Head, "I have not witnessed so much absolute distress at any period as now exists."[36] Mackenzie told the farmers that "the days of brass money and wooden shoes" were returning; and the agricultural and commercial depression was put forward as one of the main reasons for the summoning of the Reform Convention at Toronto.[37] It was in this atmosphere that the crisis in the Canadas reached its paroxysm. It was through these oppressive scenes that the two provinces travelled on the last stages of their journey towards armed revolt.

III

In this explosive coincidence the two crises came together. The quarrel between commerce and agriculture had reached the limits of aggravation at the time of a financial panic and a commercial depression; and at the mo-

[35]*Quebec Gazette*, January 25, 1837; March 20, 1838.
[36]*Upper Canada Sundries*, May 8, 1837.
[37]*The Constitution*, August 9, September 26, October 4, 1837.

ment when Great Britain had exhausted its remedies and its patience, the Canadian Radicals and Loyalists were ready to resort to force. In these last few weeks before the rebellions, when men were actively preparing for a struggle or dubiously regretting its approach, their final decisions, of necessity, were determined by a multitude of factors. The old loyalty to empire, the acceptance of custom, the fear of disorder, and the respect due to the solemn warnings of the Roman Catholic and Methodist Churches—all these served to arrest angry men and to curb disaffected communities. But those who did enter eagerly or drift irresolutely into revolt were moved by the old, simple animosities; and to them it was probably of more importance to right economic wrongs and attain vague social objectives than it was to win political independence from Great Britain. In one important sense the rebellions were simply the final expression of the conflict between agrarianism and commercialism, between feudal and frontier agriculture and the commercial state; and when Mackenzie in the Draft Constitution for the state of Upper Canada outlawed incorporated trading companies and declared that labour was the only means of creating wealth, he expressed, in final theoretical form, the old attack upon the institutions, powers, and privileges of the commercial state.[38]

As the inevitable end approached, the constitutionalists in both provinces were recruited by increasing numbers of neutrals and repentant Reformers; but to the end it was the magistrates, bureaucrats, and merchants who were the most determined defenders of the existing order. The towns were the strongholds of the governing class; the most powerful and unified of its various divisions was the commercial group; and it was, appropriately enough, in

[38]R. A. MacKay, "The Political Ideas of William Lyon Mackenzie" (*Canadian Journal of Economics and Political Science*, vol. III, February 1937, pp. 1-22).

Montreal, the focus of the whole trading system of the St. Lawrence, that Toryism found its most provocative and violent expression.[39] Even in the countryside, as Mackenzie found in his famous crusade "north of the ridges", the local shopkeepers were active and their influence apparent. "It is most provoking," wrote Mackenzie, "to see the Storekeepers continually against Reform. . . . At Equesing who were more indefatigable in raising recruits to put down the voice of the town and its 5,000 inhabitants than Squires O'Reilly, Brown, Chalmers, and Chisholm, and Mr. Salisbury, all Merchants? So it was in Caledon, Albion, and Chinquacousy."[40]

In the end the rebellions were precipitated by the riot in Montreal, which occurred on November 6.[41] In the fighting which raged up and down the city streets, the *Patriotes* were defeated. Their hold upon the town was broken; their leaders were forced from it in retreat. And when the executive, misinterpreting their equivocal movements, sought to effect the arrest of the principal Radical leaders, the countryside was driven to resistance and the resistance swelled into armed revolt. It was a rebellion without a plan of operations and without a chance of success. Disorganized, sporadic, hopeless, the *jacqueries* drew towards their inevitable conclusion; and the defeat of the Lower Canadian peasantry was the prelude to the defeat of the frontiersmen in the west. Though there were Reformers in Toronto, they were not prepared to test their strength in the city as the *Patriotes* of Montreal had done. The rebellion was directed, as it had to be, from the countryside against the town. It was Mackenzie, Lount, Matthews, Anderson, and the farmers from "north of the ridges" who

[39]*Quebec Gazette*, October 25, 1837; *Montreal Herald*, quoted in *The Patriot*, November 7, 1837.

[40]*The Constitution*, August 16, 1837.

[41]*Q*, vol. 239-2, p. 372, Wetherall to Gosford, n.d.; *The Patriot*, November 14, 1837.

made the last effort of that protest movement which had always been so largely agrarian in character. And in the mistakes and absurdities of the revolt can be seen the tragic inexpertness of a farming population which had little but its angry sense of injustice to sustain it.

Economic Nationalism
and Confederation

Confed - part
of industrialization
process

- ecw nat.
- pol nat.

I T SHOULD BE emphasized at once that in this paper I
make no attempt to supply what might be called an
"economic interpretation" of Confederation. The effort to explain one group of phenomena supposedly "political" in character by reference to another group of phenomena supposedly "economic" in character seems to me
as mechanical and unreal as the historical dichotomy upon
which it is based. I am interested, not in seeking such
simple causal connections, but in exploring some small
part of the enormously complicated relationships of industrialism and nationality in the nineteenth century. In the
British Empire, Germany, and the United States, the rise
of the new industry and the new transport was accompanied by a strong tendency towards territorial expansion
and by an equally marked impulse towards political union
and centralization. It seems to me that the foundation and
early growth of the Dominion of Canada affords a small
but fairly typical example of this complex politico-economic process. Within the short space of less than fifteen
years, the British North American provinces reached four
major decisions: they decided upon political union, westward expansion, transcontinental railways, and a protective tariff. The coincidence of these decisions was surely
not accidental: they were all products of a vast complex
system of related forces which were continually acting and
reacting upon each other. It is this process of interaction

First read at a joint meeting of the Canadian Historical Association
and the Canadian Political Science Association in June 1942 and
published in the C.H.A. *Report*, 1942, p. 44.

that I propose to explore—in a very general fashion—this afternoon. And I shall focus attention upon only one of these four decisions—the determination to establish a protective tariff—in an endeavour to trace its origins and estimate its significance in the general historical process.

In the middle 1840s, the point at which this analysis must begin, the great triumphs of industrialism and nationality were still in the future. Except in England, the broad general interests of agriculture and commerce still dominated affairs. The economic order was characterized by wooden shipping, wind- and water-power, and ocean and river transport. The relatively tranquil world of politics was made up of little states, small provinces, unconsolidated federations, and sprawling, decentralized empires. The provinces of British North America had grown up in this world and they were fairly happily adjusted to it. Their economies were based upon the St. Lawrence River and the Atlantic Ocean; agriculture, lumbering, and fishing were their staple industries; and they had put their money into canals to improve the inland waterways and into wooden ships to peddle their goods around the world. It was their settled habit to think in terms of remote markets, of commercial systems which extended far beyond their narrow boundaries and vastly transcended their parochial interests. They were members—and fairly satisfied members—of the low-tariff British mercantile system; and the idea of reciprocity, of interchange of privileges, of economic and political give-and-take, was familiar and acceptable to them. Their trade relations with each other were almost negligible; they had no political link besides their common allegiance to Great Britain; and nobody had yet conceived the idea of a transcontinental British North American union. There was little interest in the remote west, little conception of the future of railways, and little appreciation of the vast potentialities of the tariff.

This innocent and idyllic world of our great-grandfathers must have appeared to possess a most comforting sub-stantiality. But in actual fact it was already ominously threatened with approaching dissolution. The first major shock which fell upon it came, appropriately enough, from the original industrialist country, Great Britain. In Great Britain, as in Germany, the United States, and British North America, the problem of commercial policy in general and of the tariff in particular was of essential importance in this period of rapid economic and political change. There were few measures which summed up the interests and expressed the philosophy of the new industrialism and the new nationality more completely and effectively than the repeal of the Corn Laws. To John Bright and the other reforming manufacturers, who somehow contrived to suggest that they ran their mills as unimportant side-shows to the main business of professional moralizing, the principle of free trade was a timeless truth of universal validity. It was not only economic orthodoxy: it was certainly Christian morality; there were even inspired moments when it seemed to take on the awful grandeur of divine revelation. In the light of these heavenly intimations it was easy for the free traders to convince themselves—and very nearly to convince posterity—that they acted in a spirit of cosmic altruism. Obsessed with the elevation of humanity in general, they drove straight towards the goal of national self-interest. In the main, the Anti-Corn Law League was an association of British manufacturers who preferred, with natural Christian humility, to conceal their real identity; and the repeal of the Corn Laws was just as strictly and exclusively a policy of economic nationalism as the tallest tariff on earth. In the interest of industrial specialization at home, and world trade abroad, the free traders had sacrificed both the agriculture of Great Britain and the commerce of British North America. "Blessed are the free in trade," ran the new British industrial beatitude, "for they shall inherit the earth." This terrestrial paradise of world commerce glimmered radiantly in the distance; but to win it, to make oneself worthy of it, it was first necessary to cast off the fleshly trammels of the old British Empire. For Great Britain the new nationality was at first inevitably written as "Little Englandism". It meant the withdrawal of colonial preferences, the recall of colonial troops, the abandonment of colonial obligations. Just as Prussia was forced to break up the ramshackle Germanic Confederation before she could achieve the consolidated German Empire, so Great Britain had to shake herself free from the Old Colonial System before she could begin to realize the world empire of free trade.

This sudden assertion of British national independence was the first formidable impact of the new order on British North America. It was followed almost immediately by another shock, the direct introduction of the new technology. The repeal of the Corn Laws compelled the provinces to grope their way towards a new commercial policy: the construction of the first railways equipped them with the rudiments of the new industrial system. In Great Britain, the first rapid growth of machine manufacture had preceded the construction of railways; but in North America—and for obvious reasons—this order was almost exactly reversed. In the new continent the railway was the first great embodiment of the age of iron and steam; and the construction of the Grand Trunk and the other railways of the 1850s formed the first stage of the slow industrialization of British North America. From that time onward, the development of the provinces was guided by the compulsion of two forces, one external and one native to the provinces themselves. The external pressure was to come from those two great industrialized nationalities, Great Britain and the United States: the internal pressure was to originate in the movement towards industrialism and nationhood within British North America. Each of these influences was driving the provinces towards a new policy, political and commercial. And in time it was to be discovered that the goal of both was one and the same.

II

There was, however, nothing very novel in the first British North American reaction to the new world order. The original responses ran along safely traditional lines. Flung rudely out of the shelter of the Old Colonial System, the provinces could not believe themselves capable of enduring what the British industrial monopolists could complacently refer to as the "bracing atmosphere" of free trade; and except for a moment, during the deep depression of 1849, there was not much serious discussion of a protective tariff. In fact, the provinces had not the slightest intention of taking any action which, in the elephantine language of modern diplomacy, could be described as unilateral. Through long membership in the British Empire, they were accustomed to the idea of an interchange of privileges, of a rough balance of benefits and concessions. And when Great Britain had summarily and forcibly ejected them from their first commercial association, they turned naturally to that other imperialist power, the United States. In 1854 they concluded with the American Republic a treaty of reciprocity, which established a series of reciprocal preferences and concessions, more systematic certainly than anything the provinces had known before, but roughly on the same lines as the old imperial system.

Within the comforting protection of these new fiscal arrangements, the provinces intended to carry on pretty much as they had done before. They were still largely absorbed in commerce, not manufacturing. They still thought, not in terms of a British North American economy, but in terms of great international commercial systems based on the ocean and the continental rivers. Even though they now began to use the new technology of steam and iron, they used it instinctively to buttress and strengthen commercial empires which had been built up long before in the pre-industrial age. It was significant that the Intercolonial, the one serious railway project which was intended to link the Maritimes with the Province of Canada, was taken up by governments rather than by private capitalists; and it was significant also that all the governments concerned, at one time or another, extricated themselves from agreements for its construction with the most surprising agility. The Grand Trunk, which was by far the biggest British American railway enterprise of the period, was obviously planned to strengthen the old international trading system of the St. Lawrence. It was intended, like the St. Lawrence canals before it, to capture the trade of the American Middle West.

All this implied—or seemed to imply—merely a slight modification of the old objectives and methods. The revised arrangement looked durable; but there were elements of disturbance within it. And of these variables perhaps the most important was the ominously uncertain condition of the United States. The Reciprocity Treaty—and it is essential to remember this—was negotiated *before* the triumph of industrialism and coercive centralized nationality in the United States. It was a typical product of the period when the agrarianism and commercialism of the South still struggled against the encroaching industrialism of the North. The South had taught the continent its ideas of equalitarian democracy, preached the principle of local autonomy for the benefit of little states and provinces, and struggled to defend a rough balance of agricultural, commercial, and industrial interests within the republic. The Reciprocity Treaty was in part injurious to Southern interests; but the South supported it precisely because it believed that the arrangement would satisfy the British provinces and prevent or delay their annexation to the United States. The passage of the Reciprocity Treaty was, in fact, one of the last efforts of the South to preserve the economic and political balance of power on the continent, to save

North America from what Parrington has called "an un-
questioning and uncritical consolidation". It was one of
the South's last successes. For the Treaty was accepted in
the year that witnessed the enactment of the Kansas-Neb-
raska Bill, which in effect destroyed the Missouri Compromise. From that moment the struggle between North
and South for the control of the western domain approached its final paroxysm. And the new Republican
party, which represented big business, coercive centralization, and truculent imperialism, adopted a protectionist
creed which was to make such arrangements as the Reciprocity Treaty an idle dream for the next half-century.

But the approaching crisis, which was to transform the
United States into an industrial and centralized nation,
had not yet actually arrived. In the meantime, while North
and South were slowly marshalling their forces for the
conflict, the first results of railway building began to show
themselves in British North America. One at least of these
consequences might have been anticipated with tolerable
certainty. From the earliest times, the governments of
North America, including those of the northern British
provinces, had been compelled to make one peculiar and
significant modification in the doctrine of the *laissez-faire*,
non-interventionist state. They had been compelled to accept the idea that the state in North America must clear
and prepare the way for the beneficent operations of the
capitalist. In the past this had meant the lavish construction of roads and canals; and now it came to imply substantial contributions to railways. In the Maritimes, partly
through choice and partly through necessity, the state itself
frankly undertook the construction and management of its
new transport system. In the Province of Canada, where
the Northern, the Great Western, and the Grand Trunk
Railway companies were supposedly independent commercial concerns, the state subsidized, rehabilitated, and revived these enterprises with a frequency which almost

earned it the title of ownership. All this involved what to British North America was a new and alarming drain upon the treasury; and when the capital imports incidental to railway building had ceased, and the depression of 1857 had descended, the customs revenue dwindled alarmingly. The province, as its financier Galt explained, had cheapened the cost of British manufactures in Canada, and enhanced the value of Canadian products in England, by its expenditures on canals and railways. The traffic therefore could very well bear an increased toll. The government needed the money. And, to make a long story short, it proposed to raise the tariff.

Thus the Cayley-Galt tariff of 1858-9 was one of the first results of the railway construction program. But there was, in addition, another important consequence which perhaps had not been anticipated by even the most hard-headed of the farmers and merchants who had wanted the railways in the first place. The railway boom provided the basis for the new industrialism in British North America. It brought, in volume and numbers such as had never been seen before, the new industrial materials, the new industrial techniques, the new industrial labourers. There was a widening of the economic horizon, a quickening of the tempo of economic life; and the little provincial foundries and manufactories profited from the better markets of the period, and also from the high prices which were partly a result of the Crimean War and partly of the railway boom itself. The little colonial establishments profited; but not, unhappily, as much as they could have wished. Even while the boom was at its height, they were astonished and outraged to discover how much of the profits of Canadian railway construction was going into the pockets of American manufacturers. "The very spades and shovels, axes and hammers used by the workmen and labourers were of American make," wrote one contemporary with indignation. As Galt had intimated, the Canadian canals and the American and Canadian railways were already removing the natural shelter of the northern manufacturers. Their situation had been annoying enough during the boom; it was far worse when the depression of 1857 brought a collapse of prices. They suffered; but this time they suffered in highly important company, for their distress coincided with the financial embarrassment of the government. They desired a higher tariff for protection: the government desired it for increased revenue. And the result of this happy union of sentiments was the Cayley-Galt customs duties of 1858-9. Thus, on the eve of the American Civil War, an important qualification had already been introduced into the traditional commercial policy of British North America. The provinces stood committed to a system of low tariffs and reciprocal preferences. But Canada had abruptly increased her duties with protectionist approval, though ostensibly for revenue purposes. This discrepancy was immediately detected in the United States. And disagreements might have followed this discovery, if all such problems had not been momentarily engulfed in the torrent of hatred unloosed by the American Civil War.

III

For the next fifteen years, the American Civil War and its consequences constituted perhaps the dominant factor in British North American affairs. Nothing is more obvious now than that the new order of nationality and industrialism meant war; and nothing is more ironical than the conviction of its apologists that it meant peace. John Bright stood for pacification with the same moral earnestness that he opposed factory acts and denounced colonies. To these middle-class reformers war was unthinkable

precisely because they had just succeeded in raising politics to such a high moral plane. As Mr. Gladstone said rever-
ently of John Bright, he had "elevated political life to a
higher elevation and to a loftier standard". The Manchester School introduced moral earnestness into English
politics: the American Slavery Abolitionists introduced
moral indignation into North American affairs. Surely this
ought to have improved human conduct; but the strange
fact was that human conduct remained obstinately un-
regenerate. Far from becoming better, it seemed to be getting steadily worse. The aristocratic intriguers who met at
the Congress of Vienna had given Great Britain nearly
forty years of peace. But the ushering in of the Manchester
men's millennium was followed almost immediately by the
Crimean War; and the great humanitarian crusade of the
Abolitionists ended in a bloody civil conflict. From 1854
to 1878, the bulk of the period covered by this paper, there
were few years indeed which did not see armed struggle
among the great powers of Europe and America.

In many ways, which cannot be examined here, the
American Civil War was destined to affect the development of British America. Its influence, for example, on the
formation of commercial policy was decisive in the end. So
far as the Province of Canada was concerned, it helped
from the start to promote the industrial growth which had
begun during the previous decade. "I trust," said James
Watson, President of the Manufacturers' Association of
Ontario at a special meeting held in 1875, "that it will be
borne in mind that the rapid development of manufacturing [in this country] during the past few years is almost
entirely due to the peculiar position of the United States
from the commencement of the late civil war." Inevitably
the war and the economic dislocation resulting from it fo-
cused the manufacturing industry of the United States
upon the home market and limited its export trade. In all
probability there were a good many Canadian manufac-

turers like Edward Gurney of the Gurney Stove Company, who declared in 1876 that his business had quadrupled since 1861 and that, in effect, it was the wartime rise in values in the United States which had sufficed to give him the home market.

Thus one result of the war was to increase the number of people in the Province of Canada who were likely in future to want a protective tariff. Its far more important consequence, however, was to complete the supremacy of those interests in the United States which would never again submit to such a measure as the Reciprocity Treaty. The war was a struggle between an awakening industrial society and a planter community, a struggle for nationality against local independence. And its result, as Parrington has said, was to throw "the coercive powers of a centralizing state into the hands of the new industrialism". The men who stood for transcontinental railways, large-scale manufacture, and western exploitation were to determine, in large measure, the pattern of future American development. They represented unification and expansion within the country and imperialism without. The purchase of Alaska, the freely expressed desire for the annexation of British North America, are evidences of this renewed impulse towards territorial aggrandizement. The establishment of a passport system for the first time against the northern provinces, the threat to repeal the Rush-Bagot Treaty limiting naval armaments on the Great Lakes, the proposal to stop the bonding privileges for trade through United States territory—all illustrate a new truculence of tone.

Again, as in the case of England, commercial policy summed up and expressed the character of the new America which arose from the wreckage of the Civil War. Before the conflict began, the new Republican party had declared in favour of a protective tariff. The financial necessities of the war brought an enormous increase in the customs

duties; and the need for wartime goods and services gave
an immense impetus to manufacturing. When the war was
over, the tariff was unquestioningly continued as one of
the sacred institutions of the unified continental state. In
home affairs, it expressed the victory of the industrial
North over the agrarian South: in external relations, it
signified the triumph of national exclusiveness over international co-operation. In such circumstances as these
the Reciprocity Treaty had inevitably to disappear. In the
winter of 1866, when the British Americans journeyed
down to Washington, in the vain hope of negotiating a
new agreement, Mr. Morrill, the principal author of the
new American tariff, had only a very singular proposal to
make to them. He proposed that, in return for the inshore
fisheries and the navigation of the St. Lawrence and its canals, the United States would consider reciprocal free trade
in five articles of great commercial importance. These articles were unfinished millstones and grindstones, gyp-
sum, firewood, and rags.

The tremendous alteration in the whole position of
British North America had now been brought to an end.
The change had begun with the downfall of the Old Colonial System of Great Britain: it had been completed by
the wreck of the old federal system of the United States.
The insignificant northern provinces were now flanked by
two reorganized consolidated nationalities, heavily industrialized, each of which had adopted a realistic political
and commercial policy in its own exclusive interest. In the
complete absence and apparent impossibility of those reciprocal preferences which had supported the St. Lawrence
route in the past, what hope was there for an international
commercial system based upon it? Even under the favourable circumstances of the past, the St. Lawrence had never
really won the trade of the American Middle West; and
there was all the more reason now why it could never do
so. This collapse of the old hopes in the wreckage of the

old world of trade and politics brought the provinces to the threshold of economic and political nationalism. In the light of the successful examples around them, they saw now how they could use the new concepts of union and expansion as the United States had adapted them for the North American continent. They decided upon a strongly centralized federal union: they determined upon transcontinental railways and the opening of the west. All this was pretty strictly in accordance with the program which had been developed in the United States during and after the Civil War. But there was one significant difference. There was no lofty protective tariff. In Canada, the decisive change in commercial policy had yet to come.

The fact was that for a decade longer the new federation still clung obstinately to the old economic notions which had been the stand-by of the provinces. The interests of the state, and the interests of the principal groups composing it, seemed still to be satisfied with a moderate commercial policy. In the Maritimes, the financial pressure of railways and railway commitments might have forced up the customs duties; and actually, just before Confederation, the tariff in New Brunswick was probably the highest in British North America. But, on the other hand, the revenue position in the Province of Canada was easier; and in 1866, as a pre-Confederation concession to opinion in the Maritimes, it lowered the level of the old Cayley-Galt duties. The manufacturers of Canada strongly protested this reduction; but in general the agricultural, commercial, and railway interests were stronger; and both in Canada and the Maritimes they still wanted what Galt called "modified free trade". They put their hopes in the free-trade area of four million people which Confederation would create. They expected that they could make arrangements for preferential exchange of goods with the West Indies and South America. And, of course, they obstinately continued to believe that in the end they would yet get a new Reciprocity Treaty with the United States.

eco nationalism

Yet twelve years after Confederation the National Policy was an established fact. The twin pressures, internal and external, continued to act in unison; and together they were driving the new Dominion towards the complete American variant of economic nationalism. Gradually the hope of a Reciprocity Treaty with the United States was crushed out of existence by repeated disappointments. Macdonald failed to obtain a new arrangement at the time of the Washington Treaty; George Brown was unsuccessful in the negotiations of 1874. While the prospect of these international agreements faded, the idea of national exclusiveness had already begun to grow. The phrase "a national policy for Canada" appears as early as 1869. By the next year it has become definitely associated with the tariff. In the election of 1872 Macdonald made an open appeal to manufacturers and workingmen with a proposal to support domestic industry with a protective tariff. In the Maritimes, and in old commercial towns like Montreal, the trading interests were strongly entrenched and resisted stoutly; but Hamilton, Toronto, and the other industrial centres of the future were already converted or half-converted to the new views. All this had occurred while prosperity still ruled and while American manufactures had yet to enter the Canadian market in volume. After 1873 the drift towards protection became accelerated and irresistible. The situation was in many respects analogous to that which had existed in the Province of Canada in 1857-9 when the first Canadian protective tariff had come into being. Again depression had exposed the weaknesses of Canadian industry; again the mass-production American manufacturers had invaded the northern market; and again the Canadian government was badly in need of funds. There was one major difference, however—a difference which aggravated rather than alleviated the problem in the 1870s. In 1857-9, British North America had enjoyed a reciprocal commercial agreement with the United States. Now there was no Reciprocity Treaty and no prospect of one. The forces of industrialism and nationality, internal and external to British North America, had finished their work. And the Dominion of Canada completed its program of national unification with the National Policy of Protection.

The Victorians and
the Empire

IN THEIR imperial aspect, the opening and the closing years of Queen Victoria's reign were deceptively similar. The first and the last decades were marked by crises in the colonies overseas and by concern for the colonies at home. And the apparent importance of colonial questions in both the 1830s and the 1890s is attested by the preoccupation of ranking British statesmen in imperial affairs. The reign began with rebellions in the Canadas; it ended with the war in South Africa. Within a year of the accession, Lord Durham, the radical Whig, had been appointed high commissioner to British North America; and when the reign closed, Joseph Chamberlain, the hope of radical liberalism, was in command of the colonial office. These somewhat superficial analogies at least suggest an uninterrupted development of the empire and a continuous interest in imperial affairs. But in fact, of course, the empire which Queen Victoria bequeathed to her successor differed in kind from that which she had inherited; and the colonialism of the early Victorian period is essentially unlike the imperialism of the nineties. In between lies a long period of decadence and growth; and this process, like so many others in Victoria's reign, has its culmination in the early seventies of the century. Before that lies the slow, sombre decline of the second empire; and after that comes the rapid, hectic growth of the third.

First read as a lecture in the series "University College Lectures" in autumn 1937 and published in the *Canadian Historical Review*, vol. 19 (2), June 1938, p. 138.

The difference between these two periods and these two attitudes can be suggested in a number of ways; and since historians, like economists, have an incurable tendency towards moralizing, it has been often presented as a contrast between disinterested liberalism and ruthless acquisitiveness. There is revealed, on the one hand, the good imperialism of the 1840s which we are expected to venerate, and, on the other, the bad imperialism of the 1890s which we are required to deplore. The early Victorian period is made bright with the mild radiance of such liberal colonial reformers as Lord Durham, Charles Buller, Lord Elgin, and Lord Grey; and the late Victorian era is darkened by the sinister presence of such imperialists and capitalists as Disraeli, Chamberlain, and Cecil Rhodes. On the one hand is a disinterested colonial statesmanship manifesting itself in the grant of responsible government and the concession of fiscal autonomy; and on the other is a greedy urge for exploitation revealing itself in the purchase of the Suez canal shares, the penetration of Egypt, the partition of Africa, and the assault on the Boers.

The Victorians themselves—at least the greater part of them—remained happily in ignorance of their descent from righteousness into moral turpitude. And we might possibly profit by copying their attitude, though with a difference. Anti-imperialists and imperialists followed each other in two great assaulting armies through Victorian England; but the one thing common to both the pros and the antis, and indeed to all Englishmen in their political capacity, is the undeviating consistency with which they invariably acted upon the strictest moral principles. When it was the fashion to cut colonial connections, British statesmen were concerned above all else to promote the manly independence of the colonists. When, on the contrary, it became the habit to acquire colonies, British statesmen became acutely sensible of their duty to assist the development of backward peoples. The Victorians claimed by implication a consistency which their liberal and radical historians are not prepared to concede them. But it is possible that the contemporaries have more justification than has posterity. It is the motives of the Victorians, and not the consistency with which they upheld them, which can be called in question. Englishmen were accustomed to explain that they acted for the welfare of the colonists, when what they really and very sensibly did was to act in the interests of Englishmen. They destroyed the second empire and built up the third for mainly the same reason—because they wanted to.

II

The first half of Queen Victoria's reign—the years from the coronation to the early seventies —was the period of lack of faith in the empire, lack of belief in its value, and lack of interest in its continuance. It saw the virtually complete destruction of the old colonial system: it left mainly those sentimental ties and connections which in fact were felt chiefly by the colonies and which could therefore be regarded with complacent indulgence by British statesmen trained in the Manchester school. The work of destruction was only finished in 1870; but in fact, of course, it had begun almost a century before, far back in the days of the American Revolution. For the second empire, the empire which survived the American War of Independence, was cursed from its birth. It was but a contemptible fragment of the first empire and like the first empire it was everywhere supposed to be destined for independence. But in the meantime it was the feeble basis of a great imperial system, both political and economic, which its unimportance and its impermanence alike made ridiculous. The colonies consumed endless time, occasioned ceaseless

trouble, and created uninterrupted expense. And in return they gave nothing which could not be got more copiously, and far more cheaply, from free countries like the
United States.

It was not, however, the colonies but the mother
country which plunged the second empire into disrepute.
It was not the defects of the colonies which were responsible; it was rather the new virtues of the British which enabled them to view these defects with a more coldly critical
eye. From the beginning, the second empire was certainly
a feeble, ill-conditioned youngling in comparison with the
brave fellow who had run away from home. But, what was
even more important, he was compelled to grow up in the
uncongenial home atmosphere of British industrial capitalism and his whole life was made miserable by the un-
feeling discipline of the classical economists from Adam
Smith down to John Stuart Mill. The century which followed the end of the American Revolution witnessed the
rise and splendid maturity of British industrialism, based
on the realities of coal and iron, and of British world commerce, based on the theory of free trade. This system,
sprung upon an unsuspecting world, which was incapable
of serious competition, reaped its gaudiest rewards in the
decades after 1850; but it had other and more consoling
justifications than that of mere material success. There are
always plenty of economists, and there are invariably
hordes of economic vulgarizers, who are ready and willing
to exalt the conditions peculiar to their age or the convictions personal to themselves, into economic and social dog-
mas, absolute, incontestible, and eternal. But it may be
doubted whether even the Marxists afford a more brilliant
example of this truth than do the classical economists of
Great Britain. In the pages of Malthus, McCulloch, and
Mill the principles of political economy became fixed and
unchanging rules which one could only discuss in detail
and which one could never refute in essence. In the

mouths of Cobden, Bright, and other middle-class reformers, these rules became moral principles, which grew ever
more sacrosanct and which took on by degrees the character of divine injunctions. It was intellectually criminal to
refute these rules; it was profane and impious to flout
them. And it is probable that one would have to go back to
James I and the scholars and doctors who developed the
theory of the divine right of kings to discover a more curious union of dogmatism and moral unction, or a more interesting mingling of the divine and the mundane.

For the second empire, the meaning of the new industrialism and the new political economy was all too clear. It
was not that the English had unselfishly abandoned the
urge for empire: it was simply that they had substituted
the new, divinely inspired imperialism for the old, simple-
minded, sinful imperialism of the first empire. They
looked beyond the limits of their stunted, contemptible
little colonies to the trade and the economic domination of
the world. Of what use were colonies, when the special economic privileges which they demanded conflicted with the
mission of the English to sell cottons to the entire globe?
Of what value were the discredited practices of the mercantile system when its errors had been exposed and refuted
by the theorists of free trade? In this atmosphere, which
was the air that everybody breathed and the air through
which all problems of the age were visualized, the burdens
laid upon Great Britain by the second empire began to assume enormous proportions, and the benefits which it conferred to contract within infinitesimal limits. It was these
considerations which helped largely to persuade the British to assume their own major role in the dissolution of the
second empire. It was these considerations which induced
them to give only a half-hearted opposition to the efforts
by which the colonies assisted in the breakdown. "One
thing," wrote Carlyle in 1850, "strikes a remote spectator
in these colonial questions: the singular placidity with

which British statesmen at this time, backed by M'Croudy and the British moneyed classes, is prepared to surrender whatsoever interest Britain might pretend to have in the decision. 'If you want to go from us, go: we by no means want you to stay; you cost us money yearly, which is scarce; desperate quantities of trouble too; why not go, if you wish it?' Such is the humour of British statesmen at this time."

It is distinctly to the credit of the British that they half persuaded themselves and wholly convinced posterity that this was not an imperial dissolution, but a grand imperial reform. The whole series of changes, which completely altered the structure of the second empire, has often been presented as if it were the work of a few disinterested liberal imperialists, acting in a kind of a vacuum created by their own idealism and their devotion to the empire. Attention has been concentrated, not upon the breaches in the imperial system which the British made in despite of colonial protest, but upon the few concessions which they granted in response to colonial importunities. The work of statesmen who were prepared to anticipate the break-up of the empire with equanimity, if not with enthusiasm, has been dignified as colonial reform; and almost any politician who was willing to give up imperial controls, upon which he placed no value, in order to be rid of imperial burdens which he desired to escape, can qualify for the title of colonial reformer. The truth is that, if the British had believed in their empire, they would have fought for it, as they fought in 1775. But since they were non-believers, they were prepared for capitulation; and since they were Victorians, they contrived to invest their surrender with an air of dignified and impressive liberalism.

There were, of course, a few genuine colonial reformers at the beginning of Victoria's reign—men, that is, who understood reform to be something a little superior to the gentlemanly huckstering by which one surrendered privileges in exchange for the cancellation of burdens. Lord

Durham, Charles Buller, Gibbon Wakefield, and William
Molesworth were members of this group; but by the
middle of the nineteenth century their day was definitely
over. A faint air of disrepute hung over them. They were
young, or they were politically unmanageable, or they had
become regrettably involved in marital difficulties; and
concern for the colonies was thus vaguely associated with
political instability and moral error. Finally, the colonial
reformers committed the great mistake of dying early.
Charles Buller, the man who wrote *Responsible government for colonies*, died when he was barely forty; but William Ewart Gladstone, the alleged colonial reformer who
recalled the imperial troops at the moment when New Zealand was threatened with a Maori war, lived stoutly on to
become the very personification of enlightened Victorian
statesmanship.

The ideas of the colonial reformers found echoes in a
few curious places, but perhaps not altogether unexpectedly from Thomas Carlyle. Carlyle has even been called
the father of modern imperialism; he will certainly be
called the father of modern fascism by his next biog-
rapher; and the first description is just about as instructive as the second. Like the colonial reformers, Carlyle believed that emigration to the colonies might be the means
of allaying the social evils in the mother country; but
though he took a practical interest in the colonies as a possible solution for what he used to call the "Sallow or Yel-
low Emancipation" question, he frequently conceived of
them in a more grandiosely romantic fashion. He expa-
tiated proudly upon their vast spaces, their splendid future, and the blood and treasure and bravery which had
been expended in their conquest. Finally, the colonies,
like every other society in which Carlyle was interested, appeared an eminently suitable place for the beneficent operations of the Carlylean hero. Totally rejecting the reformers' idea of responsible government, Carlyle insisted

that the queen should select "some gallant-minded, stout, well-gifted cadet" as the typical governor. To him she was to say: "See, I have scores and scores of 'Colonies', all ungoverned, and nine tenths of them full of jungles, boa-constrictors, rattlesnakes, Parliamentary Eloquences, and Emancipated Niggers, ripening towards nothing but destruction; one of these you shall have, you as Vice-King; . . . go you and buckle with it, in the name of heaven; and let us see what you will build it to."

These odd, unimportant discordant protests were the only thing that broke the silence of indifference or interrupted the steady, peevish whine of belittlement. Colonial historians are naturally though erroneously accustomed to evaluate British interest in the colonies on the basis of the reams of paper which were consumed in the writing of colonial dispatches. It may be observed that, in general, colonial officials wrote dispatches because they were paid to do so; and being normal men, they took a normal interest in doing a good job. But their activities could, and sometimes did, have about as little significance for the mass of their fellow-countrymen as do the operations of the Indian department for the population of Canada. It was in parliament itself, as well as in the country in general, that the attitude of the English people to colonies was plainly revealed. The colonial portfolio was itself regarded as of secondary importance in the cabinet. It was looked upon either as a brief stopping-place for some gifted politician on the make or as a somnolent sinecure for someone who had lost his ambition or his party usefulness. And often it was very hard to fill. "Well, I'll take the office myself," Lord Palmerston is alleged to have said to a permanent official on one occasion. "Just come upstairs and show me on the map where these damned places are." Even as late as the nineties, it was a matter of some small wonderment that Joseph Chamberlain, of whom one naturally expected better things, should actually prefer to take the colonial portfolio.

The mere mention of things colonial was usually sufficient to clear the House of Commons of all but the most obstinate parliamentarians; and the opening sentences of the colonial secretary were lost in the noise of members departing for the more intellectual atmosphere of the lobbies or neighbouring chop-houses. The few members who watched the British North America Act of 1867 in its speedy passage through parliament could scarcely conceal their excruciating boredom; and after the ordeal was over, they turned with lively zeal and manifest relief to the great national problem of the tax on dogs. Most of the permanent under-secretaries for the colonies during the early decades of Queen Victoria's reign subscribed to what may be called the pomological view of colonies—the view, that is, that all colonies, like ripe apples, were destined inevitably to drop off the parent tree. They and their contemporaries showed little disposition to arrest the fall. There was scarcely a front-rank statesman in early Victorian England who was not prepared to view the departure of the colonies with cheerfulness decorously mingled with resignation. And Lord John Russell, Gladstone, and Disraeli were all at times jarred out of their habitual polite indifference into positive and indignant denunciations of the imperial tie.

The heart of the whole movement was Manchester— Manchester, the centre of the new imperialism masquerading in a sober anti-imperialist disguise. It was Manchester's machinery and capital which destroyed the second empire; it was Manchester's prophets and priests who justified the destruction to an impressed and attentive populace. The Manchester school produced Goldwin Smith, who throughout a long life devoted himself to the task of assisting nature in breaking up the second empire; and although Messrs. Cobden and Bright could give only intermittent attention to the imperial problem, their whole philosophy was the sufficient basis for the anti-imperialist attack. As fanatically righteous free-traders, they abhorred the whole tangle of tariffs, preferences, and shipping regulations which made up the old colonial system. As professional anti-militarists, they deplored the awful business of colonial defence. Their tone, the whole character of their argument, was such a pleasantly acceptable mixture of practicality and unction, of pecuniary considerations and moral earnestness, that it commanded devout and grateful respect.

Under the inspired leadership of the Manchester school, the whole political and economic world of Great Britain made a determined assault upon the second empire. In the period between 1840 and 1870, it was systematically destroyed, in all aspects, economic, political, and military. Great Britain repealed the corn laws, the timber duties, and the navigation laws, and thereby destroyed at a blow the whole system of imperial preferences and shipping monopolies upon which the colonies had built up their economic existence. But when the colonies, emulating Great Britain's exclusive concern for her own material interests, sought to build up their puny national economies by means of tariffs, there was a great wail of shocked surprise from the mother country. None of the alleged colonial reformers would listen for a moment to the absurd argument that if it was permissible for Great Britain to destroy tariffs in what Englishmen considered to be the national interest, then it was equally permissible for the colonies to establish tariffs in what the colonists considered to be their national interest. The reason for this distinction was transparently clear. Free trade was not an advantage to England; it was a principle of political economy; and Mr. Cobden, who knew all about these matters, was aware that it had the sanction of the deity. Protection could never be an advantage to any state, for it was founded on economic error and was *prima facie* evidence of moral turpitude. Great Britain had embraced free trade merely because she had seen the light; the colonies hankered after protection merely because they had an incurable tendency to sin. This point was beautifully put by Goldwin Smith, in a passage which combined intellectual and moral arrogance in nicely graduated quantities: "The colonies have a strong propensity to the commercial vice of Protectionism. . . . Protection is the natural resort of ignorant cupidity, and ignorant cupidity is the besetting sin of communities intensely commercial and wanting in education."

It was, however, upon the question of imperial defence that the Cobdenites trained their heaviest artillery. Dislike of the garrisons, which Great Britain maintained in the colonies for their protection, was strengthened by Cobden's desire for what he called retrenchment and by Bright's love of peace; and the opposition to imperial militarism evoked all the exquisite talent for moral argumentation which the reformers had developed in their other humanitarian crusades. Messrs. Cobden and Bright, as is well known, opposed the ten-hours' day for industry in England; but they did so, not merely out of preoccupation with the pecuniary interests of the employer, but also out of deep concern for the moral fibre of the labourers. Cobden, as he was careful to point out, was one of labour's sincerest friends; but he deplored what he called "a spurious humanity" or "a morbid sympathy" with labour's woes; and he greatly preferred a "masculine species of charity" which would encourage among workmen an independence, a self-respect, and a disdain of being patronized and petted. This argument, which had served so well in the relations between capitalist and employee, was used unaltered to elucidate the proper relations between the colonies and England; and in this case, of course, the thoughtful capitalist was the mother country, and the workmen lacking moral fibre were the colonies. If Great Britain were to withdraw her troops from the empire, it would be admittedly a financial advantage to England; but it would also be—and was not this the real point?—a moral gain for the colonies. "If," said John Bright, "they are to be constantly applying to us for guarantees for railways, and for grants for fortresses, and for works of defence . . . then I think it would be far better for them and for us—cheaper for us, and less demoralizing for them—that they should become an independent State. . . ." It was, in fact, a matter of great consolation for the Victorian imperial reformers to realize how invariably the pecuniary advantage of England coincided with the moral betterment of the colonies.

British statesmen could take an unprejudiced and manly stand in the subject of imperial defence, for, of course, nobody expected that the colonies would ever move to the assistance of the mother country. Great Britain had no desire to aid the colonies; and she naturally assumed that the colonies, acting on correct Manchester principles, would never have any intention of aiding her. The few people who discussed the bare possibility of colonial assistance did so merely with the obvious intention of being humorous. Sir Charles Dilke, who made a tour of the English-speaking world in 1866 and wrote a book called *Greater Britain*, could wax very indignant over the spectacle of "Dorsetshire agricultural labourers paying the cost of defending New Zealand colonists in Maori wars", for the simple reason that he had not the faintest expectation that New Zealanders would ever come in scores of thousands from the other side of the world to fight for Great Britain in Belgium. "It is not likely, nowadays," he wrote, "that our colonists would, for any long stretch of time, engage to aid us in our purely European wars. Australia would scarcely feel herself deeply interested in the guarantee of Luxembourg, nor Canada in the affairs of Servia." This peculiarly unfortunate prophecy was the calm assumption of all who were concerned at home in the empire's affairs. And in 1869-71, the Gladstone government recalled the troops, despite the bitter protests of New Zealanders that they were left de-

fenceless in the probable event of a Maori war. The Gladstone government, adopting a tone which they might have
employed in addressing a tenth-rate foreign power, replied
to these protests with long, hectoring lectures. The evacua-
tion of the troops went on all over the empire; and when
in November 1871 the last imperial soldiers marched
down the streets of Quebec singing "Auld Lang Syne", the
second empire of Great Britain was ended forever.

III

At almost exactly the same moment the change began.
The death of the old empire coincided almost exactly
with the birth of the new imperialism. The very country
which had dropped a few of its possessions and had considered dropping a lot more now became curiously interested
in acquiring new colonies. The very people who had derided the sentimental affection by which the colonists had
kept the empire together now began to develop imperial
emotions of their own. The Royal Colonial Institute was
founded in 1868: the recall of the troops from New Zeal-
and aroused a sudden curious burst of imperial sentiment.
In 1872 the incredible Disraeli—the man who had talked
angrily a few years before of the "colonial deadweights"—
informed an impressed audience at the Crystal Palace that
the preservation of the empire was one of the three great
objectives of the Conservative party. In 1875 that un-
repentant spendthrift, the Khedive Ismail of Egypt,
brought his shares in the Suez canal to market; and Disraeli, prompted no doubt by that oriental imagination of
which disapproving English historians make so much,
overcame the opposition of the cabinet and used the
Rothschild money to purchase the Khedive's interest.
Moreover, he created that strangely un-English title "The

Empress of India" to the immense gratification of the queen and to the embarrassment, disapproval, or amusement of his colleagues. The Indian empire was new only in name; but the adventure into Egypt was a real, if apparently a modest, novelty. And it had been preceded, a few years before, by the even more inconspicuous beginning to an even wilder series of imperial adventures. In 1868 a Boer farmer in South Africa purchased a small stone from a native witch-doctor. He paid everything he had for it— 500 sheep, 10 oxen, and a horse. But he sold it to a trader for £11,000; and the trader resold it for £25,000. The stone weighed 83 carats and it came to be called the Star of South Africa. Two years later, in 1870, diamonds were discovered in considerable quantities at Kimberley. And in the same year, by one of those beautiful coincidences of history, Cecil John Rhodes landed in South Africa.

The change from the commercial cosmopolitanism of the Cobdenites to the territorial imperialism of the later Victorians is one of the most fascinating and the most difficult problems of the nineteenth century. But in the main the change was due, not to the altered stature of the colonies, but to the disturbed state of Europe in general and England in particular. It was not the novel importance of the colonies which created the new imperialism any more than it was their previous insignificance which had precipitated the collapse of the second empire; in the second case, as in the first, it was British interests and British necessities which dictated the change. It was obvious, of course, even to the Victorians, that the empire was changing in character. Few people, except freaks like Carlyle, had predicted that the settlement colonies would ever amount to anything. But the plain fact seemed to be that they were progressing; and there were even a few daring Englishmen who were willing to prophesy that in the remote future they might be of some slight consequence in world affairs. It came home to the Victorians with a great shock of surprise that other European powers—powers who were fortunately bereft of colonies—seemed actually to be making very strenuous efforts to acquire some. Could it be that the British had underestimated their overseas possessions? The idea was, of course, nonsensical and anyway it could never be publicly acknowledged. But might there not be in it an infinitesimal grain of truth?

It was, in short, the changed economic and political balance of power in the world at large, rather than the growing consequence of the settlement colonies, which gave impetus to the new imperialism. The year 1870 lifted the curtain on a new and vaguely disturbing scene. The world was suddenly crowded—overcrowded—with great hulking and ambitious national states. Italy was no longer a congeries of petty principalities: it was a nation. The Civil War and reconstruction had created a new United States. The German empire had sprung into being. These great national states were destroying the early Victorian ideal of peaceful commercial cosmopolitanism. They were violating the principle of free trade which had been the basic theory of Manchester; they were breaking up the economic unity of the globe which had been Manchester's material objective. The new world was evincing a disappointing disinclination to remain an economic unit—open and passively ready for the exploitation of the British. France and Germany and the United States were intent on tariffs— and the magisterial rebukes of Earl Grey and William Ewart Gladstone were even more ineffectual here than they had been in the case of the colonies. Moreover—alarming thought—the great national states began to manufacture, and on a large scale. They developed technical skills and superior technical education. And in the last crucial test, the test of world trade, the results of this revolution were manifest. Great Britain lost that position of uncontested and commanding superiority which had been hers since the beginning of the industrial revolution and which she had accepted complacently as the rightful reward of her pious adherence to the inspired doctrines of political economy. The new national states began to invade the markets of the world. They began to pre-empt these markets as colonies or as spheres of influence.

Urged on by the pressure of these material factors and goaded by her capitalists and publicists, Great Britain entered the race for empire once more. The new imperialism was not, of course, a really novel apparition; it was simply the older and even more arrogant imperialism of the Cobdenites, suitably altered to meet the changing conditions; but its spirit, its methods, and its territorial interests were profoundly different. The older settlement colonies—Canada, Australia, New Zealand, as well as the empire of India—were all swept into the movement and sometimes occupied a central position in it; but it was not those places which kept the interest of capitalists and aroused the imagination of the people: it was Afghanistan, Egypt, and above all Africa. The drama of the new empire was played out against a gaudy backdrop of tropical forests, and great sluggish rivers, and empty veldt and sand, and terrible mountain passes. It has its triumphs and its heroic tragedies. There was that lost hundred soldiers at Rorke's drift, nearly half of them ill and fevered, who fought all night against the massed thousands of Zulus. There was that mere handful of men—Alan Wilson's patrol—who were surrounded by the Matabele army and fired their last round of ammunition, and stood up, the few survivors, and sang "God Save the Queen" and fell where they stood. These deeds of simple and outrageous bravery were followed and preceded by other acts, some of unremitting devotion, others of greed, cunning, and unprovoked violence. Livingstone plunged into the depths of central Africa; but in other remote and barbaric places, such as old King Lobengula's court in Matabeleland, concession hunters, with tired, anxious, predatory faces, intrigued among themselves and imposed on native credulity to win the contract which would give them the right to dig for imagined gold. The period has its heroes—simple, fearless soldiers like Kitchener and Gordon: it had its capitalists and picturesque adventurers like Beit, and Barney Barnato of Kimberley. And among these last was Dr. Leander Starr Jameson, the hero or the villain of the raid into the Transvaal, with his "I-suppose-I-must-do-this" expression and his "I-know-I-will-do-this" mind.

Of them, but above them all, was Rhodes. He summed up the entire new empire—he personified it—its diverse and contradictory characteristics are united and reconciled in the elemental fact of his personality. He was at once an absurd romantic and a cool and cynical realist. There is both a massiveness and a childish naïveté in his designs. He was a portent of those forces, both material and moral, which are even now effecting the transformation of modern politics. In a document which he wrote in 1877, when he was twenty-four, he declared that he would work "for the furtherance of the British Empire, for the bringing of the whole civilized world under British rule, for the recovery of the United States, for the making of the Anglo-Saxon race into one Empire". He was a visionary who dreamed dreams; but he was also a capitalist who kept his eye unerringly fixed on realities; and the grandiose clauses of the various wills by which he bequeathed his fortune for the spread of Britain's empire are paralleled by the cool, laconic phrases in which he described the brute facts of his time. "Cobden," said Rhodes tersely, "had his idea of Free Trade for all the world, but that idea has not been realized. The question of the day is the tariff question, and no one tells the people anything about it. . . . These islands can only support six millions out of their thirty-six millions. . . . We cannot afford to part with an inch of the world's surface which affords a free and open market to the manufactures of our countrymen. . . . It must be brought home to you that your trade is the world, and your life is the world, and not England. That is why you must deal with these questions of expansion and retention of the world." Rhodes, in short, aspired simply to win a universal empire for England; and to himself, as the first task, he allotted Africa. And he was in a hurry—in a desperate hurry. For beyond the Cape Colony were the Orange Free State, the Transvaal, Bechuanaland, Matebeleland, and the whole north—"My North", Rhodes used to call it.

In the meantime, while the soldiers and promoters and speculators were founding the new empire overseas, there was an increasing boom in imperialism at home. The imperialists began to get into the newspapers and periodicals: they started to hold conferences. J. A. Froude founded the school of philosophy which was to supersede Manchesterism, and in 1883 Seeley published *The expansion of England*. The change was observable, however, not merely in these new voices, but also in the strangely novel accents of the old. Charles Dilke, the man who had written *Greater Britain*—of which he evidently considered the United States to be the most important part—published a new treatise entitled *Problems of Greater Britain*; and to the altered Sir Charles the chief problem appeared to be, not the task of expediting imperial separation, but the labour of promoting imperial unity. Tennyson's *Hands all round*, when it was first published in 1852, was chiefly made up of a denunciation of France and an offer of friendship to America. But the laureate, in imperial matters as in so many others, moved resolutely with the times; and when *Hands all round* reappeared in 1882, it was found to contain a great hymn to empire, with Canada, Australia, and India all mentioned in terms of respectful admiration. With a rapidity which left the colonies dizzy and breathless, Great Britain passed from the novel conviction that she must keep her surviving colonies to the inspired reflection that she could federate the entire empire.

The colonies, which had barely ceased to fear imperial dismemberment, were suddenly invited to declare their views on imperial federation. They were haled forth, blinking, into the sunshine of Britannic favour; they were invited to sit in colonial congresses and to participate in the colour and splendour of the jubilees.

The movement for closer imperial unity, which reached and passed its height in the last two decades of the century, travelled the old and difficult paths towards the old and almost forgotten objectives. The early Victorians, who had recalled the legions, broken the mercantile system, and conceded responsible government, were now succeeded by the late Victorians, who hoped to establish a common system of imperial defence and to tighten the commercial relations and the political unity of the empire. The work of imperial unification was undertaken in the same disinterested and liberal spirit in which the process of imperial decentralization had been carried through; and it was assumed that, in some unexplained and not entirely explicable fashion, imperial federation would be a great concession to the older settlement colonies. It was a concession whose merits were more adequately appreciated in Great Britain than in the colonies; but even in Great Britain it encountered resistance from the established policies of the past. The new British imperialism was in large measure the response of the British national state to the new national state system of Europe; and it was not unfitting that the movement for imperial federation should be blocked by those very national forces which had helped to set it in motion. Great Britain was just as unwilling to surrender the remnants of imperial control as were the colonies to abandon their newly won political autonomy. Preferential tariffs were just as objectionable to free-trade England as were imperial *zollvereins* to protectionist colonies. The Imperial Federation League, which had tried vainly to reconcile these conflicting interests, wound up its affairs in

1893; and the imperial conference of 1897 dispelled some of the great dreams of formal reorganization upon which Victorian imperialism had fed for the last two decades.

It was the war in South Africa and not the achievement of imperial federation which was to form the not inappropriate climax of the new Victorian imperialism. The issue of preferential trade remained and was to divide the British Unionist party in the near future; but the exponents of closer political unity had failed to find their formula and the new imperial association assumed the vaguer title of British Empire League. As its theories were tacitly abandoned, British imperialism took on a more cloudy grandeur; and, as the Boer War drew steadily closer, it acquired a kind of exalted truculence of tone. It was this spirit, disseminated unconsciously and deliberately through various channels to the receptive peoples of the empire, which decided one of the great questions which the imperial conference of 1897 had left unresolved. The words of Reid, of New South Wales, at the imperial conference were prophetic. "The great test of our relations . . . ," he said, "will be the next war in which England is engaged . . . That feeling of patriotism, we may call it—it would flame out just as practically in the Colonies, in the hour of danger, as in England; but it is only in those moments that you can make the people one in the sense of sacrifice." It was not through the grant of political and economic concessions, but through the sense of sacrifice in a great imperial effort, that the empire of the Victorians was united at the last; and the very consciousness of colonial nationalism which had checked the invasions of autonomy now encouraged the colonies to take the important place to which they felt entitled in the great affairs of an empire of which they were morally a part. It was a tribute to the potency of the new imperialism that, thirty years after Great Britain had withdrawn the garrisons from the colonies, the colonial contingents should be fighting in their first imperialist war.

The Decline and Fall
of the Empire
of the St. Lawrence

THE PHRASE "the Empire of the St. Lawrence" made its first public appearance in the autumn of 1937 when the first edition of my book *The Empire of the St. Lawrence* was published. The phrase is thus only a little over thirty years old; but already, somewhat to the surprise of its inventor, it has acquired a symbolic and legendary significance. It has been regarded as the inspiration, at least in part, of a new school of Canadian historians and as the genesis of a new historical doctrine, the Laurentian interpretation of Canadian history. Its origins, now buried in a past which may seem virtually prehistoric to most of you, have been explained by several curious myths and legends. At moments, I have been visited by the thought that I have apparently founded a new religion; and this, to a person who has all his life been a highly sceptical anticlerical, is not an entirely agreeable reflection. At the same time, I have no wish to disavow the parentage of an idea. And I thought that I could not do better today than to talk to you for a while about the Empire of the St. Lawrence. I shall try, very briefly, to explain the origins of my first book and to indicate what I think the Empire of the St. Lawrence meant for Canada in the days of its greatness. Finally, I should like to suggest, at somewhat greater length, why I believe we are now witnessing the lamentable spectacle of its decline and fall.

First delivered at a meeting of the Canadian Historical Association at York University on 5 June 1969 and published in the C.H.A. *Report*, 1969.

The Empire of the St. Lawrence, it is sometimes confidently asserted, was the fruit of my friendship with Harold Innis; it was a typical example of the preoccupation of Canadian historians, in the 1930s, with economic themes, in reaction against the political and constitutional studies of the previous decade. These explanations, like most simple generalizations, happen to be wrong; the truth is more complicated and also, I feel, somewhat more interesting. At the risk of boring those among you who may be only too familiar with the facts, I ought to begin by saying that I never intended to be an historian of Canada. My ambition, on the contrary, was to do work in the history of Europe, preferably on some phase of the French Revolution; but this meant long years of research overseas, and at that time, the late 1920s, there were no fellowships, grants, or any kind of financial assistance for scholarship in the humanities and social sciences. Out of my annual salary of $1,800, I was able, though with difficulty, to finance a summer's work at the Archives and the National Library in Paris; but the effort left me completely broke, and I realized that it would be utterly impossible for me to carry on sustained historical studies in Europe or Great Britain. Yet I earnestly wanted to write history, and to begin at once. There was only one choice left, though it was a bad second or third choice—the history of my own country.

I went off to Ottawa in the summer of 1930—it was my first visit to the capital—with a definite subject in mind. It was suggested, not by Harold Innis, whom I barely knew at the time, but by W. P. M. Kennedy, the Professor of Law at the University of Toronto, whose work had been done, not in Canadian economic, but in Canadian constitutional, history. He proposed that I should do a biographical study of Lord Dalhousie, Governor-in-Chief of Canada from 1819 to 1828, whose papers had just been acquired by the Public Archives. These papers turned out to be very official and impersonal, and I soon lost interest in

Dalhousie the man; but I could see possibilities in the quarrel which he and his supporters in the Executive and Legislative Councils were continually carrying on with the Assembly. I realized that I was committing myself to a fairly familiar story, the political conflict in Lower Canada which culminated in the Rebellion of 1837; and I decided that I must adopt a new approach to this more than twice-told tale. In the past, it had been viewed chiefly from the point of view of the *Patriotes* in the Assembly. I came to the conclusion that in order to get a novel and interesting subject, I must take the Conservatives in the Councils, the so-called Château Clique.

For some time I was very unhappy about my choice. I had always been told that the quarrel in Lower Canada was a constitutional dispute, envenomed by ethnic difference; but, on closer examination, this traditional explanation did not appear entirely satisfactory. It soon became obvious that a good many members of the Château Clique were merchants, or landowners and professional men who were closely connected with Montreal's staple trades. They did not seem to be very much concerned about language, religion, or British constitutional principles; but they hardly ever stopped talking about canals, river improvements, tariffs, imperial preferences, markets, and sources of supply. The evidence I was laboriously accumulating left me very dissatisfied, and I was occasionally tempted to throw up the whole enterprise; but I persevered, if only because I was determined to realize something out of my long months of effort. It was not, I think, until the winter of 1931-2, that I began to understand that I had unwittingly got hold of a good, and even a great, subject. If ever an historian was reluctantly convinced by the weight of his own evidence, it was I.

The defeat of the St. Lawrence system in 1849 was the conclusion of my first book; but it did not seem to me to be the end of my theme. I determined to carry it forward to some undetermined date in the future; but for some time I could see no suitable approach to this second phase of my subject. The protagonist of the Empire of the St. Lawrence was the River itself; but it was obvious that the River could not play the same dominating role in the period after 1850. The Pacific railway, which had always interested me deeply, was a possible alternative; but, unlike the St. Lawrence, the railway was not, it seemed to me, a sufficiently comprehensive and unifying theme. It was not until several years later that I was attracted by the idea of writing a biography of John A. Macdonald. I began this work without properly appreciating its connection with my first book; but later I gradually came to believe that, in selecting Macdonald, I had stumbled upon the only satisfactory method of writing the second phase of the history of the Empire of the St. Lawrence. What I had written, if the word is not too pompous, was a trilogy on one theme.

II

This Laurentian theme has its basis in the fact that the St. Lawrence is the one great river system that leads from the Atlantic seaboard to the heart of the continent of North America. Its owners, the Canadians, have held in it a unique possession; and the realization of its potentialities has been one of the most persistent and compelling aims of their existence as a people. The river has inspired generations of Canadians to build a great territorial empire, both commercial and political, in the western interior of the continent. The prime feature of this imperial drive is therefore western expansion—expansion across the continent to the Pacific Ocean. At first, during the French régime and the early days of British rule, the undivided west was sought as a whole; but after the Treaty of 1783 had drawn an unnatural and unhistorical boundary line across the middle of the continent, the Canadians were faced with a choice between two alternatives and two quite different kinds of western expansion. They could seek to gain either an international commercial empire on both sides of the new boundary or a commercial and political empire to the north of it.

For three generations after 1783 the international commercial empire was the preferred alternative of Canadians. The fur traders of the eighteenth century tried to hold the trade south of the Great Lakes. The millers and merchants of the nineteenth century hoped to monopolize the traffic of the new American Middle West. With the aid of canals, river improvements, imperial preferences, and appropriate shipping regulations, they struggled to make the St. Lawrence the main commercial channel between Great Britain and the agricultural west of North America. In the end all these efforts proved vain. By the middle of the nineteenth century it was clear that the millers and merchants had failed, just as the fur traders had failed more than thirty years earlier. The international commercial empire had been lost; but beyond the international boundary, safely protected as British territory, lay another great empire, the British northwest. The fur traders had turned to it as a valuable alternative; and their successors, the Canadians of the mid nineteenth century, swerved northward in exactly the same fashion. The first object of Confederation was the preservation of a separate British America in the new continent; the second aim was the acquisition of the whole of British America's patrimony in the northwest. The west, it was believed, would make Canada a nation, and the east-west axis would be its backbone.

Western expansion was thus the prime urge, and the main theme, of the Empire of the St. Lawrence; but two other themes, of only slightly less importance, had from the first been closely associated with it. In their struggle for western empire, the Canadians soon discovered that they were confronted by formidable rivals and needed the support of powerful friends. The rivals were the Thirteen Colonies, soon to become the United States, a far more powerful nation than British America, with western aims as vast as those of the St. Lawrence. The ally was Great Britain, whose assistance could alone redress the dangerous imbalance of power on the North American continent. British military power had enabled British America to survive the American War of Independence and the War of 1812. The Old Colonial System, with its tariff preferences and shipping monopolies, had been the chief support of Montreal in its battle with New York for the trade of the new west. By itself the St. Lawrence system was doomed to defeat; even with British help, it had twice failed to gain its international commercial empire. But in the northwest, in acknowledged British territory, and with British assistance, it could make good its claim to the dominion it had inherited; and with British capital, British markets, and British immigrants, it could settle and develop it.

The Anglo-Canadian alliance, which was the substantial reality beneath the formality of the imperial connection, was essential to the St. Lawrence system. But the Canadians realized that they must have self-help as well as the assistance of others and that they must maximize their own strength in the unequal struggle for survival. The impulse towards unity in the interests of strength and expansion is one of the oldest and most powerful tendencies in the history of the Empire of the St. Lawrence. The merchants of the eighteenth and early nineteenth centuries struggled to prevent the partition of their empire by either provincial or international boundaries. They were the first to denounce the division of the old Province of Quebec into Upper and Lower Canada, and the first to propose its reunion in the Province of Canada. The Fathers of Confederation took over unaltered the old aim of unity for strength and expansion. Their principal leaders, Macdonald and Tupper for example, would have preferred a complete or legislative union for British America; but, since this was impossible, they tried to make the new Canada the most strongly centralized union that was possible under federal forms.

The primary purpose of Confederation was political: the creation of a new nationality. The union was the result of a political agreement among several provinces, not of a cultural compact between two cultural groups, English and French. At the Quebec Conference, the Fathers of Confederation acknowledged the presence of French Canada and provided certain safeguards for its continuance; but the resolutions on ethnic and cultural matters were few, precise in their wording, and limited in their scope. The distinctive cultural features of French Canada were confirmed in those parts of the new Dominion in which they had become established; but they were not extended farther territorially, and they were not intended to restrict the federal authority in directing national expansion and growth. In 1864-5, the memory of the long struggle between the merchants of Lower Canada and the French-Canadian *Patriotes* in the Assembly over the commercial development of the Province was still vividly present in the minds of the Fathers of Confederation. And there is no more significant episode in the long debate on the Quebec Resolutions in the Canadian legislature than the passage in which Cartier repudiated Papineau's opposition to economic change, and assured the English-speaking citizens of the future Province of Quebec that they need have no fear of Confederation, since their major interest, the economic progress of the nation, would lie in exclusive federal control.

III

In my view, these are the four principal features or characteristics of the Empire of the St. Lawrence and of its subsequent political embodiment, the Canadian nation. At Confederation and for a long time afterward, the permanence and the importance of these distinctive features seemed assured. They lasted, in fact, for another sixty years after Confederation, and it was not until the decade of the 1920s that signs began to multiply that they were losing their force. From then on, the familiar distinguishing characteristics of the Canadian nation began to weaken; and the historic themes of its history lost their old dominance. Up until the beginning of the Second World War the decline was gradual and slow; from that time it has hurried forward, with steadily increasing rapidity, towards what now looks like its inevitable and final fall. What has happened to Canada? Why did it change direction so decisively? And where is it now bound?

The first object of the Empire of the St. Lawrence was western expansion; the first aim of Confederation was the settlement and development of the northwest. The northwest was the common patrimony, and its occupation the joint endeavour, of all Canadians. The country, with the assistance of the national policies of immigration, railways, and tariffs, was organized on an east-west axis. The prairie wheatlands were linked with Canada's commercial and industrial base in the east, and with its overseas markets in the United Kingdom; and for more than half a century the main thrust of Canadian economic activity was transcontinental and transatlantic. The climax of this whole phase of our existence came in the great prosperity of the first decade of the twentieth century and its conclusion in the First World War. In many important respects, the First World War is the great divide in Canadian history, the great watershed of time from which Canadians can enjoy their last clear, spacious view of the Empire of the St. Lawrence. After the War, wheat, the great single export staple, gradually lost its unifying influence on the Canadian economy. In the 1920s, the grain trade fell deeply into trouble. During the depression, prairie agriculture collapsed, its people reduced to beggary and much of its land in desolation.

The old, original Canadian west, the west of wheat fields and grain growers, never completely recovered from this disaster; and nothing has ever since replaced it as the great national enterprise and common interest of all Canadians. In the 1920s, the focus of economic attention shifted from the west to the north, to the water-power, minerals, and pulpwood forests of the Precambrian Shield. But these new export specialties were not national properties as the Dominion Lands in the west had been. They were provincial natural resources whose benefits accrued mainly to the capitalists and public treasuries of the province in which they lay. At first it seemed likely that the lion's share of the new riches would go to the central provinces, which occupied most of the Precambrian Shield; but the discovery of oil in Alberta proved that the northern extension of the great central plains concealed treasures perhaps equally valuable. Alberta became the second province of the new west, the west independent of wheat. The first original province of the separate western economy was British Columbia, which had always felt detached from the prairie provinces, and increasingly found the outlets for its energies apart from the national transcontinental system.

The market for most of these new export staples was not the British Isles, but the continent of North America and chiefly the United States. The main direction of Canadian trade was shifting slowly but surely from east to south. Exports to the United States first began seriously to rival the value of exports to the United Kingdom after the First

World War; after the Second, the dominance of the American market in Canadian trade became more solidly established every year. The east-west axis, transcontinental and transatlantic, had ceased to be the main line of Canadian endeavour; and while Vancouver, Edmonton, Calgary, and Toronto, the cities close to the new economic activities, prospered mightily, the old capitals of the Empire of the St. Lawrence languished in decline. Winnipeg, the hub of the grain trade, had failed to become the metropolis of the west. Montreal, the old commercial centre from which capital, if it could get away, was fleeing, sank slowly into depression.

Along with the increasing weakness of the historic east-west axis there went a corresponding decline in the old Anglo-Canadian alliance. This second great change in the character of the Empire of the St. Lawrence first manifested itself in the 1920s, that crucial decade significantly dominated by Mackenzie King. Up to that point, the old alliance had flourished; and during the First World War it had been put to new uses and had provided new outlets for Canada's expanding interests and energies. In the nineteenth century, the British Empire had ensured Canada's survival and growth in a continent dominated by the United States. In the first two decades of the twentieth century the British Commonwealth provided an opportunity for Canada, along with the other Dominions, to share the influence and take part in the decisions of a world power. Borden proposed contributions to imperial defence in exchange for a voice in the determination of imperial foreign policy; and this formula for an effective co-operative Commonwealth was realized during and after the First World War in such bodies as the Imperial War Cabinet and the Prime Ministers' Conference of 1921. There Canada was able to play a part in world politics such as she had never done before and would never do again.

All this was changed in the 1920s; and the change has

been interpreted as the liberation of Canadian nationality from the hideous toils of British imperialism. Mackenzie King, already a stocky, barrel-like figure, with an audible wheeze when in full voice, is cast in the appealing role of a bulky St. George confronting a slavering imperial dragon. He is deified as the great Canadian nationalist, the legitimate heir of that other great Canadian nationalist, Wilfrid Laurier. In reality, of course, neither was a nationalist at all. Laurier was a neo-colonial who hoped that, with the help of both the Monroe Doctrine and the Britannic Peace, he would be kept in comfortable colonial security and go on building political railways for the rest of his life. King was not so much a Canadian citizen as a citizen of North America. The most important part of his academic training had been gained in the United States, and he spent five formative years as professional adviser in labour relations to the Rockefeller Corporation and other large American firms. Laurier, the neo-colonial, had simply tried to resist the development of the co-operative Commonwealth; King determined to destroy it. In Canadian politics his work is purely negative and destructive. He broke up the Britannic union without even attempting to devise policies for a separate and independent Canada. In effect, he prepared her for eventual absorption into the United States.

The Second World War offered a last chance for a revival of the Anglo-Canadian alliance, a last chance to return to the co-operative Commonwealth of the First World War; but it was a chance that neither Churchill nor King had the slightest intention of grasping. For eighteen months the war was fought by the Commonwealth alone; but King saw the dreadful spectre of imperial centralization in every proposal that Canada should take part in its direction. Churchill, who could hardly have cared less for the old Commonwealth of the settlement Dominions, was intent upon a virtual dictatorship in his own cabinet and was not in the least inclined to share his authority with Dominion Prime Ministers. Lloyd George's aim had been to satisfy the legitimate aspirations of the Dominions; Churchill's aim was to propitiate the United States. His central object, from the first, was to win the moral and material support of the American Republic, and if possible, to get it into the war. When this was successfully accomplished, he never gave another thought to the Dominions; they were useful to him only as a collective makeweight against the preponderating power of the United States. Together Churchill and Roosevelt exercised complete and exclusive control over the forces and policies of the Commonwealth and the Republic. Canada had become an autonomous Dominion during the First World War; she reverted to the status of a dependent colony during the Second.

The post-war dissolution of the British Empire utterly changed the character of the Commonwealth. Its old military power was gone for ever; but as a link between East and West, a bridge between different races and contrasting ideologies, it might have had a considerable moral influence in international affairs. The Colombo Conference implied as much; but the promise of the Colombo Conference was never fully realized. Canada first betrayed its hopes by failing to follow the rest of the Commonwealth in the recognition of the People's Republic of China. The Korean War widened the division between the eastern successor states on the one hand and Britain and the older Dominions on the other; and the Suez crisis dealt the Commonwealth a heavy blow from which it has never really recovered. Today, the new African nations, who exercise with complete impunity their family privilege of pouring abuse on the Mother Country, are the only delegations that get much satisfaction out of the proceedings of a Commonwealth Conference. Britain views the old institution with obvious boredom and irritation. Her own course, oscillating uneasily between the security of her "special relationship" with United States and the attractions of the European Common Market, is highly uncertain. If she can save herself, which is doubtful, she can certainly give no help to Canada.

IV

Canada now stands alone. She has stood alone, in reality, ever since the beginning of the Second World War. And the fate that overtook the Empire of the St. Lawrence in both its fur-trading and grain-trading days has now overtaken Canada, the Empire's residuary legatee. Since 1940, Canada has been exposed to the irresistible penetrative power of American economic and military imperialism. The process by which the Dominion became a branch-plant dependency and a military satellite of the American Republic began with the Ogdensburg Agreement of 1940; and since then Canada's subordination to American foreign policy and American capital has continued progressively with scarcely a serious interruption. Canada joined NATO largely because the United States was certain to do so. Canada was taken in by the confidence trick which President Truman and his aides practised on the United Nations in 1950 and, like Britain, agreed to accept American leadership in the Korean War. Canada consented to the American fortification of her northland, and thus implicitly permitted her defence policy to be determined by the anti-Communist mania that swept over the United States in the 1950s. In the meantime, under the benevolent supervision of C. D. Howe, the economic continentalist who was King's perfect associate, American ownership of Canadian industry grew apace.

This whole trend is now probably irreversible. At any

rate, the experience of the last dozen years goes far to prove that it cannot be easily changed. It is now more than twelve years since the pipeline debate first revealed the deep anxiety of the Canadian people over the prospect of American domination; but since that time they have never agreed on a method of resistance. No political party has ever drawn up a comprehensive program for the defence of Canadian economic and political independence; and only a few individuals—a Governor of the Bank of Canada, a Conservative Prime Minister, a Liberal Minister of Finance, and a few university professors—have ever urged that there was a real danger which must be met, if Canada wished to survive. The fate of these separate protests has been monotonously unvarying. Dismissal, enforced resignation, defeat at the polls have been the results for the politicians and civil servants. The urgings of the professors have been either ignored, or read and forgotten in daily newspapers, or embalmed in government reports.

Canadians are held back from any determined action on their own behalf both by their own fears and inhibitions and by the bluffs and threats of Americans and their government. Bruce Hutchison, that Doric pillar of the Liberal establishment in Canada, threatens massive American retaliation if Canada withdraws from NATO. There are always anonymous American imperialists in high places who are eager to bluff and threaten; but, in addition, as Walter Gordon has recently been pointing out, the American State Department is prepared to go into instant action whenever some important American interest, such as the journalistic empire of the late Henry R. Luce or the National City Bank of New York, seems endangered by Canadian policy. In 1963, at the height of the Bomarc crisis, it was not merely the American State Department but the entire American executive that intervened directly in Canadian politics. The real leader of the Liberal party in the winter and spring of 1963 was not Lester B. Pearson but

John F. Kennedy; and it was press interviews by the American commander of NATO, press handouts by the American Secretary of State, and public opinion analyses by an American presidential adviser, who, with Kennedy's blessing, was sent up to Canada to work for the Liberals in the election, which probably contributed most to the downfall of Diefenbaker. About the only manifestation of American power which was spared Canada in the crisis was the sight of American tanks rumbling up Parliament Hill in Ottawa. But the Canadians, unlike the Czechs, who are a brave and independent people, do not need tanks to coerce them. All they require is the instructions of an American President, an American Secretary of State, and an American general as to where their best interests lie. Then, dutifully, they act accordingly.

One of the main reasons why the Canadians have surrendered so easily is that the primitive Canadian belief in unity for strength in defence has been so seriously undermined. A debilitating weakness has spread over the fourth and last of the main features of the Empire of the St. Lawrence. The Fathers of Confederation tried to establish a strongly centralized union; but their purpose has been defeated in the first place by the chain of legal decisions in the Judicial Committee of the Privy Council. By the early 1920s—again the crucial decade in Canadian history— these decisions reduced the federal government's residuary authority to an emergency power, exercisable normally in crises such as war. In an age of social welfare and economic regulation, these strangling legal limitations were likely to confine the federal government within very narrow bounds. Before the war both Bennett and King tried in vain to break through these barriers; after the war was over, King and St. Laurent renewed the attempt to take the initiative in a national program of social security and economic growth. This effort was maintained, with small results, for about a decade. Then it was abandoned; and, at the béginning of the 1960s, the federal government found itself on the defensive. It was not long before it began a retreat which now threatens to end in a rout.

The reason for this drastic decline in the confidence and prestige of the government of Canada is, at bottom, fairly simple. It arose out of a profound and revolutionary change in the way in which the Canadian people looked at their federal union. For the first time in the hundred years of their history, a large and influential number of Canadians were induced to accept the idea that what were now called "ethnic and cultural values" were, and ought to be accepted as, the fundamental values in Canadian federalism. The most important thing about Canada was not its economic growth, its constitutional viability, its political independence and freedom from external control, but simply and solely its cultural duality. Confederation had failed to satisfy French-Canadian cultural needs and fulfil French-Canadian cultural aspirations; for a hundred years French Canadians had been reduced to a second-class citizenship, not by their own church, or their own educational system, or their own government, or their own timid capitalists, but by the English-speaking majority, and its instruments, the federal government and the British North America Act. To remedy these hideous injustices, one, or both, of two remedies were proposed. Bilingualism must be officially recognized and, as far as possible, protected and promoted throughout the whole of Canada; and Quebec must be recognized as essentially different from the other provinces and given a special position distinct and largely detached from the rest of Canada.

These ideas, the dominant ideas in Canada today, are in effect, a repudiation of the intentions of the Fathers of Confederation; and, in the decade that is now ending, they have led to a steady demolition of the structure the Fathers built. Quebec, granted exemption from federal programs without losing the accompanying federal revenues, began effectively to gain the special position she had claimed; but these concessions did not satisfy her demand for complete and exclusive control over virtually the whole range of the economic and social life of her citizens. Backed by Ontario, which now revived the Toronto-Quebec axis, Quebec pressed the case for more drastic change; and finally the federal government sponsored a general and fundamental revision of the constitution. The progress of this revision so far is not likely to renew the confidence or even win the respect of Canadians. The priority which the federal government has given to fundamental rights and governmental institutions reveals a continued obsession with ethnic and cultural values, and an astonishing ignorance of parliamentary government. The provinces, secure in the possession of their present legislative powers, have declined to follow the federal lead and instead demanded a reallocation of the sources of revenue. Nobody has yet been willing, or has yet dared, to breathe a word about the subject which logically comes first, the division of powers. If that subject is ever seriously considered, there is no guarantee that the federal government will gain any essential power. In the present state of Canadian opinion on federalism, it may suffer substantial losses. And thus Canada may very well enter the final struggle of its existence as a united and separate nation without the means of ensuring its own survival.

Part III
Sir John A. Macdonald

George Brown,
Sir John Macdonald,
and the "Workingman"

O N THE north side of King Street, Toronto, a short distance east from Yonge, there stood in 1872 the offices of the Globe Printing Company. It was the sixth building which had been occupied by the *Globe* since its establishment back in 1844; and the solid opulence of its construction reflected the prosperity, the popularity, and the enormous influence which the newspaper had gradually come to enjoy. Built of white brick, faced with imported stone, and lighted by the tall, narrow windows which were characteristic of the period, the building provided the ample accommodation of three spacious storeys.[1] The first floor was occupied by the counting house and the big printing presses; the third was taken up with editorial offices and newsrooms; and in between, oc-

First published in the *Canadian Historical Review*, vol. 24 (4), December 1943, p. 362.

[1]J. Timperlake, *Illustrated Toronto, Past and Present* (Toronto, 1877), pp. 205-8.

cupying the whole front of the second storey and overlooking the noisy activity of King Street, was the editorial
sanctum of the proprietor and editor, George Brown. Here
was the source and centre of Brown's authority and
influence. Here, for the last fifteen years of his life, he did
his best work as critic, promoter, and crusader; and here
also, at half past four on the afternoon of March 25, 1880,
George Bennett, the employee discharged for "intemperance", fired the shot that brought an end to the dynamic
and assertive labours of the journalist's career.

In 1872 this last grotesque tragedy was still eight years
away. George Brown was only fifty-four years old. For
twenty years he had played a part of central importance in
Canadian politics; and there seemed no good reason why
he should not continue to play it with equal ability for
another twenty years. It was true that in 1867, in the
first election for the federal House of Commons, he had
been defeated in the constituency of South Ontario; and it
was well known that he had unregretfully accepted this defeat as his release from active parliamentary life. For most
men such a retirement would have brought political
death; but in Brown's case it resulted merely in a more effective concentration of political activity. As a politician,
the editor of the *Globe* had always been inhibited and
frustrated by a naïve maladroitness, an uncompromising
sincerity, an intractable spirit of independence; but as a
journalist, his vigour, his enthusiasm, and his assurance
had brought him unbroken and increasing success. It was
still his fixed determination "to see the Liberal party re-
united and in the ascendant"; and in the early months of
1872 it almost seemed as if his hopes were soon to be realized to the full. Already, in December 1871, the Liberals
under Edward Blake had driven the John Sandfield Macdonald government from office in the province of Ontario;
and, in the federal general election which was inescapably
approaching in 1872, it seemed highly probable that the

Liberals might dislodge the John Alexander Macdonald administration from power in the Dominion. The campaign neared its climax; the issue promised to be wholly favourable; and George Brown, with all his stormy energy and his confident dogmatism, grasped the initiative and pressed the offensive against his enemies.

It was at this point that something occurred which altered the whole face of the struggle. Superficially the affair was not an important one. It was, in fact, a printers' strike in the city of Toronto, without, apparently, any political implications whatever. There was no obvious reason why it should be avoided. On the contrary, by its very nature it insistently invited the interference of the editor and proprietor of the *Globe*. The printing and publishing business was surely alone involved; and however much he might be inclined to admit his failure as a politician, Brown was justifiably convinced that as a journalist he was a complete and unqualified success. He knew all about the printing and publishing business; he wielded an authority in the newspaper world which was surely the rightful prerogative of his enterprise and his success. The strike annoyed him as a journalist, exasperated him as a proprietor, outraged him as a stout believer in the Cobdenite philosophy of free enterprise and *laissez-faire*. And once his own shop became involved, he acted with more than usual of his truculent abruptness and overbearing confidence. He was blind to the political perils involved. His character, his training, and his interests alike unfitted him to appreciate the significance of the labour movement and the importance of the industrial revolution which lay back of it.

Yet the labour movement, pushed forward by the spread of industrialism and the recurrence of good times, was now reaching significant proportions. In both Great Britain and the United States, the two countries with which British North America had been most closely associated in the past, and by which the Dominion of Canada was to be most deeply influenced in the future, the cause of organized labour had advanced rapidly in the 1850s and 1860s.[2] In both countries the trade unions had created new forms of organization, developed new programs and objectives, acquired a new position of greater prestige and security within the community as a whole. The growth of national unions and the spread of urban trade councils or assemblies were prominent features of the movement in both the old world and the new; and the common urge toward some kind of centralized union had come to be embodied in such temporary and imperfect forms as the "Junta" of England and the National Labor Union of the United States. Political and social reforms, as well as industrial protection and mutual benefits, were all included in the varied programs of these working-class organizations. At times their plans might seem vague and over-ambitious; but, on the other hand, they had set their hopes also on certain practical objectives of vital and immense importance. The agitation for the eight-hour day had started in the United States as early as 1864; the great struggle for the nine-hour day got under way in England in 1871. In England, moreover, the unions had just completed the first round of their long fight to win the security of legal status. Under prolonged and insistent pressure the Gladstone government had at length consented in 1871 to enact the Trade Union Bill, which freed the unions from the old common-law restrictions as combinations in restraint of trade. It was a great concession; but it was not granted without conditions by any means. In the same year the government also passed the Criminal Law Amendment Act, which subjected the newly legalized unions to penalties for picketing and other forms of "molestation" and

[2]See G. D. H. Cole, *A Short History of the British Working Class Movement, 1789-1937* (London, 1937); J. R. Commons *et al.*, *History of Labour in the United States* (New York, 1918), ii; N. J. Ware, *The Labour Movement in the United States, 1860-1895* (New York and London, 1929).

"intimidation". It was an ambiguous conclusion to the first stage of the struggle for legal status. The round was over; but it was not yet very certain which of the two contestants had won it.

This was the atmosphere of tension and excitement, the spirit of effort and accomplishment, which at that time pervaded the working-class movements of the English-speaking world. Two decades—even a single decade—before, the tiny isolated unions of British North America would have remained unaffected by these controversies and, indeed, largely ignorant of their existence; but in the meantime a rapid and drastic change of circumstances had brought Canadian labour out of its old isolation and into sensitive communication with the trade union movements of the outside world. The railway had brought the industrial revolution to British North America; the Crimean War and the American Civil War had given British North American manufacturers an exceptional opportunity to exploit their own home market; and, as Canadian industry expanded, as boom periods succeeded each other in rapid succession, the ranks of Canadian labour began steadily to expand. Powerful and aggressive trade unions crossed the ocean from England, and the border from the United States, to establish locals in different parts of the Dominion; and in active manufacturing centres such as Toronto and Hamilton, central trade assemblies on the English and American models were formed to bring the different unions and workers' societies of these cities together. By 1870 the fifty thousand industrial labourers of Canada had developed many more habits of co-operation among themselves and many more means of communication with the outside world than they had ever possessed in the past.[3]

Prominent—perhaps even foremost—among these new Canadian working-class organizations were the Typograph-

[3]H. A. Logan, *The History of Trade Union Organization in Canada* (Chicago, 1928).

ical Societies, or printers' unions. In all probability the Typographical Society of Quebec City should be regarded as the first Canadian union; and the Toronto Typographical Society, only slightly younger than its French-Canadian associate, had had an unbroken existence which dated back as far as 1844. In the 1860s and early 1870s the new International Typographical Union, with headquarters in the United States, began to bring into its ranks the already existing Canadian societies and to establish new locals in different parts of Canada. In 1866, some time after it had first been invited, the Toronto Society joined the International Union as Local No. 91; and for the next few years, under a number of able and vigorous leaders, its growth was rapid and promising. Obviously the printers' union was one of the most active and progressive in the city; and in 1871, when the first Canadian "city central", the Toronto Trades Assembly, was established in the provincial capital, J. S. Williams of the Toronto Typographical Union was made its first president. The printers were ready and waiting for the struggles of the future. And already they had been tried and nerved by the conflicts of the past. It was, moreover, during these early controversies of the 1850s that they had first made a remarkable discovery—a discovery of which they were to be sharply reminded in the very near future. They had found in George Brown of the *Globe* their most obstinate and resourceful opponent in the city of Toronto.

It was almost certain, therefore, when the decade of the 1870s opened, that Canadian labour would take its own small place in the working-class crusades of the period. It was almost equally certain that the Toronto Typographical Union would be in the forefront of any Canadian labour controversy that might break out. In 1871, when the agitation for the shorter working day was at its height in Great Britain and the United States, the new Nine Hours League in Hamilton and the Trades Assembly in

Toronto began to press vigorously for a reduction of hours. On March 15, 1872, in the Toronto Music Hall, Richard Trevellick, a prominent American labour leader and one of the officials in the newly formed National Labor Union in the United States, addressed a large and enthusiastic working-class audience in support of the nine-hour movement.[4] For days the town buzzed with debate over Trevellick's claim that the workingman had a "natural right" to the nine-hour day for education and improvement. But, while most people talked and argued, the Toronto printers, in characteristic fashion, had been proceeding rapidly from negotiations with their employers to direct action against them. The dispute, like most labour disputes before and since, was a complicated one; but, broadly speaking, the printers demanded the fifty-four-hour week without reduction of pay. On March 13 they issued their ultimatum to the master printers. On March 19 the master printers emphatically rejected it; and six days later the members of the Toronto Typographical Union walked out on strike.

II

This was the peremptory challenge which George Brown had to meet. He responded to it with the greatest possible energy and conviction. From the start he took a prominent place in the employers' committee which fought the strike. The great editorial office overlooking King Street became the appointed rendezvous for conclaves of furious master printers; and the columns of the *Globe* continued, almost without interruption, to record the astonishment, the outraged pride, and the rising moral indignation of its proprietor. In George Brown's convic-

[4]The Toronto *Leader*, March 16, 1872.

tion the Canadian nine-hour movement was both questionable in its associations and unsound in its principles.
It had been imported from the United States (the *Globe*
persistently refused to recognize the specifically English origin of the nine-hour agitation) by a few professional agita-
tors of whom Trevellick was the chief. And the resulting
conflict, arbitrarily aroused in the peaceful setting of Canadian society, could only be regarded as profoundly incongruous, factious, and unnatural. "We have no such class as
those styled capitalists in other countries," declared the
Globe roundly. "The whole people are the capitalists of
Canada. . . . We have no Rothschilds in Canada, no Jacob
Astors, no Vanderbilts, no Tweeds, no Goulds, no Jim
Fisks. . . . We all work. We all began with nothing. We
have all got by hard work all we own—and the richest
among us work on still and like to do it."[5] There could be,
therefore, no such thing as a class struggle in Canada; but
there could be—and would be—the very real struggle of
the capitalists of Canada, of the people of Canada, that is,
with George Brown at their head, against the insolent des-
potism of a few demagogues from the United States. "At
whatever cost," declared the *Globe*, speaking in the name
of the Toronto newspaper proprietors, "they are determined to be masters of their own offices. They have submitted long enough to the insolent dictation of a few reck-
less lads who have managed to control the action of the Society—but they will do so no longer."[6]

These were brave words, spoken with all Brown's usual
aggressive confidence. And yet, at the very moment when
they were uttered, the first signs of trouble, of future political embarrassment, had already appeared. The regrettable fact was that the master printers of Toronto were not
completely united on the subject of the strike. It was true
that the group which met in Brown's office was certainly a

[5]The Toronto *Globe*, March 23, 1872.
[6]The *Globe*, March 22, 1872.

numerous and imposing one. There were John Ross Robertson of the *Daily Telegraph*, James Moylan of the *Canadian Freeman*, J. B. Cook of the *Express*, and E. R. Stinson of the *Christian Herald*. The representatives of Hunter, Rose and Company, Copp, Clark and Company, the Methodist Book Room, and the other printing establishments of the city were all present, at least at the opening meetings. In fact, at the beginning there was only one important empty place—one solitary but highly significant absentee. It was James Beaty, a Conservative politician of some standing and the proprietor and editor of one of the local daily papers, the Toronto *Leader*. Actually, at the moment when the strike broke out, the *Leader* was apparently a journal of decreasing circulation and declining influence. It was regarded none too favourably, even by the Conservatives themselves. In fact, a movement in which Sir John Macdonald and other prominent Tories participated had already begun to establish a new Conservative newspaper with able editorship and sound financial backing to carry the fight forward more successfully against the *Globe*; and later on in that very year these plans resulted in the publication of the Toronto *Mail*. But at the moment, James Beaty's *Leader*, however ineffective and moribund, was the leading Conservative paper; and James Beaty alone of all the newspaper proprietors in the city graciously and unreservedly conceded the demands of the Toronto Typographical Union. He did even more. He wrote editorials in defence of the printers, published long and favourable news accounts of their proceedings, printed their advertisements and threw open his correspondence columns to the angry letters of the strikers and their wives. Having made his decision, he proceeded to extract from it the utmost amount of capital for the benefit of his newspaper, his own political career, and the fortunes of the Conservative party. He was invited to labour meetings; the working-class circulation of the *Leader* began to go up. An impression rapidly pervaded the city that the Liberals were hand in glove with the capitalists and that the Conservatives were the true friends of the workingman.

All this, however, did not deter the majority of the master printers from their policy of resistance. In particular the popularity of James Beaty had no effect whatever upon the conviction of George Brown. Brown was flushed and excited by the just anger of a righteous cause. He was both cunning in defence and aggressive in attack. On the one hand he brought country printers to Toronto and continued triumphantly to issue the *Globe*; and on the other hand he and his fellow proprietors spied upon the members of the Typographical Union and did everything in their power to impede and harass their activities. In the eyes of these master printers, a combination of capitalists, united to impose a uniform set of hours and wages, was entirely lawful; but a combination of workmen, united to maintain another and slightly different system of hours and wages, was entirely illegitimate. As early as March 28, the *Leader* asserted that the master printers had tried to have the strikers arrested on charges of vagrancy;[7] and the very next day, in a threatening editorial, the *Globe* revealed that urgent efforts were in fact being made to combat the "bribery" and "intimidation" by which the strikers sought to induce the scabs to leave their new employment.[8] "This can, however, no longer be submitted to," the *Globe* declared, "and steps have been taken for the detection and prompt prosecution of all guilty of indictable offences." Among the steps taken was the employment of a private detective from Ottawa who prowled about the city streets seeking evidence against the union members. Everything looked as if the master printers were preparing a major attack; and two weeks later the blow fell. On April 16—the day after the united workingmen of Toronto had

[7]The *Leader*, March 28, 1872.
[8]The *Globe*, March 29, 1872.

held a great demonstration in Queen's Park in favour of the nine-hour day—Magistrate Macnabb issued warrants for the arrest of twenty-three printers, the members of the "Vigilance Committee" of the Toronto Typographical Union, on charges of conspiracy.

Two days later, on April 18, the trial of the arrested printers began before Magistrate Macnabb.[9] The issue was of crucial importance for the entire future of organized labour in Canada, and the Toronto Typographical Union was acutely aware of the fact that its whole strength must be flung into the struggle. It selected D'Arcy Boulton, A. W. Lauder, and Dr. C. McMichael as chief counsel; and these men brought considerable resources of knowledge, experience, and ability to the defence. From the start they did their clever best; but it soon became apparent that they were struggling against forces which were very potent and might prove irresistible. At the very beginning the magistrate showed himself irascible and unsympathetic. A cheer was raised when the prisoners first appeared. Macnabb instantly cleared the court; and it remained unopened during the entire course of the first hearing. It was a bad beginning. The magistrate's testiness was unfortunate; but more serious were the dogmatic convictions which he gradually revealed, and more disastrous still was the unreformed state of the Canadian law upon which these convictions were founded.

There was only one line of attack open to Messrs. Lauder, Boulton, and McMichael. They took it and tried hard to establish a conspiracy on the employers' side. Witnesses were asked to reveal who had requested them to give evidence. E. J. O'Neil, the detective sent from Ottawa, was pressed to explain who had hired his services in Toronto. Again and again the defence lawyers manoeuvred for a renewal of this flank attack; and again and again the magistrate headed them off in disorder.

[9]See the *Globe*, April 19, May 7, 1872, for detailed accounts of the trial.

"We want to prove a conspiracy on the other side," said Lauder frankly.

"But," declared Macnabb, "you cannot bring it in as a set-off."

On this point the magistrate remained adamant. He would not accept such evidence as material; and he refused to compel witnesses to give it.

"You need not answer that," he abruptly told one man whom D'Arcy Boulton was cross-questioning.

"I decline to answer that question," said the witness.

Boulton was visibly annoyed.

"We will have you in a place shortly," he told the witness with evident fury, "where we will make you answer."

It was inevitable, however, that the chief efforts of Boulton and his associates should be defensive in character. They argued that the Toronto Typographical Union was a combination which sought to benefit its own members and not to injure others; that it had been tacitly accepted as a legitimate institution in the community for over a quarter-century; and that the master printers had themselves negotiated with it and on several occasions at least had acceded to its demands.

"Does that make it legal?" interposed Macnabb.

"We want to show the custom," replied Lauder.

"If a man meets you on the street and demands your watch," said Macnabb impatiently, "does your giving it to him make it legal? Here is an illegal act shown and you say because the other party acceded to it, it is not illegal."

"But," Lauder shot back, "we say it is not illegal."

Macnabb became more annoyed and more dogmatic.

"By law," he declared with assurance, "it is illegal to combine for certain purposes."

"We say that has to be proved," said Lauder stoutly.

The magistrate was plainly exasperated.

"There is no need to prove the law," he said with heat. "It is not a foreign law, it is the law of the land."

The trouble was, as Lauder himself tacitly admitted on one occasion, that there was a large element of truth in what Macnabb said. It had to be admitted that Canadian unions enjoyed no statutory protection at all. The legislatures of Canada had evidently never dealt with the subject of unions and combinations; and of course the British statutes relating to the matter did not extend to North America. Canadian unions had never been harassed by Pitt's Anti-Combination Laws of 1799; but on the other hand they had never been able to profit by the Francis Place statutes of 1824 and 1825; and—which was even more important—they could not now derive any advantage from Gladstone's Trade Union Act of 1871. As the Crown lawyers pointed out on more than one occasion, the only law governing the whole matter in Canada was the common law; and under the common law successful prosecutions had sometimes been launched in England in the first part of the century against workmen who combined and struck. It was in the light of these precedents that Macnabb stopped the first day's hearing abruptly, when only a few witnesses had been heard. A continuation of the proceedings was, he declared, "entirely useless". A combination had been proved and the strike was an admitted fact. For a few moments it seemed as if the whole matter would be settled summarily, on the spot.

In actual fact the defence lawyers were able to get first one, and then a second, adjournment. These delays were helpful; but it seemed scarcely possible that they could alter the ultimate issue of the case. So far as the magistrate's court at least was concerned, the outcome appeared absolutely certain. The master printers had triumphed—triumphed easily. In fact, had they not triumphed too easily—so easily that their success scarcely looked like a triumph at all? They had been required to prove virtually nothing. The court had not even given them the chance to establish those scandalous overt acts of "intimidation" and "molestation" on the part of the strikers which had so horrified George Brown.

"From my recollection of the law," Macnabb had declared to the Crown lawyers, "combinations of this kind are illegal. You have proved that there has been and is a combination, and that there was a strike, and that these men are members."

"If your Honour is satisfied of that," answered Mackenzie, who was chief counsel for the prosecution, "we will only call one or two witnesses to prove certain very gross overt acts."

"These," said the magistrate simply, "are separate offences."

In other words, any union or society of workmen which went on strike in Canada in 1872 was an illegal combination. The working-class movement stood in a more vulnerable position in the Dominion than in either Great Britain or the United States. Canadian labour was governed by a set of antiquated common-law decisions; and it was on the basis of these outworn precedents that the masterprinters were certain to win their facile and almost empty victory. Certainly they had prepared for a much more difficult contest. They had hoped to brand the strikers with the stigma of a most reprehensible series of crimes. As the *Globe* confessed ruefully in an editorial of April 19, over twenty witnesses had waited vainly in court to testify to various acts of intimidation, coercion, bribery, and personal violence on the part of the strikers. They all remained unheard and unneeded. Even the energetic Mr. O'Neil might just as well have stayed in Ottawa. And the strange and awkward result was that really nothing at all had been proved against the striking printers. They ought to have looked like convicted malefactors when they left the court; but in actual fact they began to take on the unmistakable appearance of injured innocents. The prosecution, which ought to have ruined the Typographical Union, had suddenly and unexpectedly recoiled on the master printers. In the public eye they had been convicted of using an outworn, unreformed law to take an unfair advantage of their opponents. In the public eye, moreover, George Brown was the centre and inspiration of this "conspiracy". As A. W. Lauder said at the first court hearing, "there was no doubt George Brown was at the bottom of the whole thing."

III

In the meantime, from his post of vantage in Ottawa, Sir John Macdonald, the Prime Minister of Canada, was watching the controversy in Toronto with steadily rising interest. It was, of course, his business to be concerned with such matters; but at the moment his curiosity was perhaps even more thoroughly awakened than would have been normally the case. The term of the first parliament of the Dominion of Canada was inexorably approaching; and he was watching eagerly for any political advantage—any political opportunity—that fortune might fling in his way. He was only too well aware that his government had been weakened by the Riel controversies and the Washington Treaty. He had only too much cause to fear that the defeat of the Sandfield Macdonald administration was simply the ominous prelude to the downfall of his own cabinet in Ottawa. Unquestionably he was disturbed. The last few months had been passed in uneasy preparation for the approaching election. He had made a visit of personal reconnaissance to western Ontario; he had discussed Conservative policy in long letters to his correspondents; he had taken an active part in the founding of the Toronto *Mail*.

It was at this point that the printers' strike broke out in Toronto. Almost from the start Macdonald was quick to see, and to exploit, its possibilities. In part, of course, he was influenced—and, indeed, committed—by the actions of James Beaty. But the Tory press and the Tory politicians of Toronto had little to teach him about the importance of the labour movement in particular and industrial affairs in general. He had far fewer direct contacts than Brown with the growing manufacturing system of the country; but he had a far greater instinctive appreciation of its social—and, above all, of its political—significance. A lawyer himself, an amateur in finance and economics who had always rather ostentatiously effaced himself in the presence of Galt and Hincks and Tilley, Macdonald nevertheless showed an extremely sensitive awareness of the economic and social developments in the Dominion. He was not unlike Disraeli in this, as in a number of other ways. Appropriately enough, at the very moment when the nine-hour movement was reaching its climax in Toronto, Hamilton, and the other manufacturing towns, he had been anxiously debating the commercial policy—the tariff policy—of the Conservative party. He had been interested in industry; now he saw that he must also devote himself to labour.

Fortune favoured him. As things stood now, this slight change in strategy had become almost ridiculously easy. He had been presented, as if by magic, with a policy which would at once gratify the workingmen and discomfit the Liberals. He had merely to re-enact, with suitable modifications, the two British statutes—the Trade Union Act and the Criminal Law Amendment Act of 1871; and the unimpeachable orthodoxy of Gladstonian legislation would remove all doubts and silence all criticisms. The situation must have amused Macdonald immensely. To confound George Brown with William Ewart Gladstone, to silence the disciple with the latest revelation from the master—this was a most gratifying manoeuvre; and he set about it with enthusiasm and speed. On May 7, the very day on which the second hearing in the printers' trial was held before Magistrate Macnabb, he introduced his Trade Union Bills in Parliament; and early in June, with virtually no opposition from the Liberals, they became law. The two measures were frankly based upon the British legislation of the previous year. On the one hand they freed Canadian unions from the antiquated limitations of the common law; but on the other hand they subjected them to new statutory penalties for "molestation" and "intimidation". The *Globe*, indeed, tried heroically but vainly to convince its readers that the Crown's case against the arrested printers was just as valid under the new law as it had been under the old common-law cases. The argument was by no means absurd; but, unfortunately for the *Globe*, a serious flaw appeared in it almost immediately. The prosecution of the printers was not continued and completed. In fact it was abruptly dropped. And thus the populace was confirmed in its original impression that the early triumph of the master printers was based merely on their unscrupulous use of an antiquated and half-forgotten law.

Sir John Macdonald stood forth as the friend and saviour of the workingman. Without hesitation, and in his usual accomplished manner, he had confirmed and generalized James Beaty's stand; and thus the Liberal-Conservative party appeared suddenly as a new colonial embodiment of Disraeli's Tory Democracy. On June 19 John Hewitt, corresponding secretary of the Toronto Trades Assembly, wrote to Macdonald informing him that the Canadian unions would like the privilege of making a presentation to Lady Macdonald "as a slight token of our appreciation of your timely efforts in the interests of the operatives of this Dominion."[10] On the night of July 11 a great crowd of working-class people assembled in the Toronto Music Hall. A jewelled gold casket was presented to Lady Macdonald by J. S. Williams, president of both the Toronto Trades Assembly and the Toronto Typographical Union;

[10]Public Archives of Canada, Macdonald Papers, General Letters, 1872.

and Sir John, who spoke in reply on behalf of his wife, took advantage of the occasion to make a direct and forceful appeal to Canadian labour. He told them how glad he had been to prevent "the barbarous resurrection of a disgraceful old law"; he invited their suggestions and advice in the further improvement of the Canadian labour statutes; and he ended by emphasizing, in his own characteristic facetious fashion, the association which had come into being between the working-class and himself. "I ought to have a special interest in this subject," he told them, "because I am a workingman myself. I know that I work more than nine hours every day, and then I think I am a practical mechanic. If you look at the Confederation Act, in the framing of which I had some hand, you will admit that I am a pretty good joiner; and as for cabinet-making, I have had as much experience as Jacques & Hay themselves."[11]

All this was highly satisfactory. Yet the labour laws were not the only, nor perhaps the most important, inducement in the new Conservative appeal to the industrial population of Canada. An even greater change in the fiscal policies of the party was actually impending. All that winter Macdonald had been deeply preoccupied with the party platform. The whole matter of policy had come up with the founding of the *Mail*; and Sir John had given the subject his unremitting attention. He had come back from his tour in the "West" (western Ontario) with the firm conviction that tariff protection would be a popular policy to advocate. "It is really astonishing," he told George Stephen, the future president of the Canadian Pacific Railway, "the feeling that has grown up in the West in favour of the encouragement of home manufactures. I am sure to be able to make considerable capital out of this next summer."[12]

---

[11]The Toronto *Mail*, July 12, 1872. Jacques and Hay were a large firm of furniture manufacturers in Toronto.

[12]Macdonald Papers, Letterbook 17, Macdonald to Stephen, February 20, 1872.

Many of the party stalwarts were dubious, but Sir John was full of confidence. "The paper must go in for a National policy in Tariff matters," he told T. C. Patteson, the first editor of the *Mail*, "and while avoiding the word 'protection' must advocate a readjustment of the Tariff in such a manner as incidentally to aid our manufacturing and industrial interests."[13] On July 13, at Hamilton, in the first great public meeting of the campaign, Macdonald and Hincks announced the new party platform of "incidental protection to home industry".[14] The election of 1872—not that of 1878—was the first election in which the Conservatives went to the country on the basis of the National Policy.

In history, of course, the election of 1872 is famous for another and very different reason. It is famous—and indeed notorious—as the election which was disfigured by the Pacific Scandal. This was, in the end, its most obvious, its most glaring, distinction; but not, perhaps, its most important one. Until everything else was forgotten in the excitement aroused by L. S. Huntington's charges concerning the Conservative campaign funds, contemporaries saw a very different meaning in the political battle of 1872. For them it was the first election in which the industrial classes of Canada had been the chief centre of interest and the industrial future of the Dominion the main question at issue. In their eyes it had been made memorable by workingmen candidates and great labour rallies; and it had been won by the party which most successfully united in its own favour the twin interests of labour and capital. The money contributions of the Canadian Pacific Railway may have helped to save Sir John Macdonald from defeat; but there were also other and more legitimate sources of

[13]Macdonald Papers, Letterbook 17, Macdonald to Patteson, February 24, 1872.
[14]The *Mail*, July 15, 1872.

strength at his disposal. He was supported by the growth of industry and the rise of the nine-hour movement, by the Toronto printers' strike, and by the National Policy of protection.

Macdonald and
Canadian Historians

JOHN ALEXANDER MACDONALD was born on January 11, 1815, and died on June 6, 1891. Of the seventy-six years of his long life, well over half—forty-seven in all—were passed amid the agitations of Canadian politics. He was elected to Parliament in 1844, when he was not yet thirty; he became a minister of the Crown in 1847, when he had just turned thirty-two. For over ten years under the system of the dual premiership which obtained in the old Province of Canada, he was one of the two principal leaders of government; and for nineteen years he was prime minister of the new Dominion. It is an astonishing record—astonishing, and, as a whole, unique. It is true that Mr. Mackenzie King has been prime minister of the Dominion of Canada for a longer period than Sir John Macdonald. But Macdonald's career of leadership stretches back beyond Confederation; and his record as a whole, in both the Province and the Dominion, is unsurpassed and probably unsurpassable.

The very length and variety of a career which spanned so much of Canada's history and touched so many of its activities poses a question which is, perhaps, of general interest to Canadian historians. What have we done with the man who lived at the centre of Canada's political affairs for nearly fifty years and who dominated them for over twenty-five? What have we done with the five hundred volumes of

First given as a paper to the Graduate History Club at the University of Toronto in autumn 1947 and published in the *Canadian Historical Review*, vol. 29 (1), March 1948.

his papers which lie in the Archives at Ottawa, with the monumental mass of government documents, parliamentary debates, newspapers, periodicals, pamphlets, memoirs, and autobiographies which record his multifarious activities in neutral, complimentary, or abusive terms? It seems a fair question to ask—a reasonable test to apply to Canadian historiography. How do Canadian historians measure up to it? It may be that, in an effort to answer this question, we shall come upon certain qualities, or characteristic features, of Canadian historical writing which are worthy of critical reflection.

There are, to begin with, two curious and unexpected facts to be noticed about the biographical literature on Macdonald. In the first place, there is not very much of it; and in the second place, what there is is not new, but relatively old. In the years immediately preceding and following Macdonald's death, when his career was at its end and his reputation at its apogee, there appeared several biographies of him, written with little concern for form and in a spirit of uncritical laudation, of which the best, by long odds, because at least it was based upon the documents, was Sir Joseph Pope's two-volume study. These were followed, after a long interval, by Sir George Parkin's volume in the original "Makers of Canada" series, and, after a further and longer interval, by Mr. W. S. Wallace's short biographical sketch. There the procession ended. It ended, curiously and incomprehensibly, in the middle nineteen-twenties, at the very moment when historical scholarship in Canada was already launched upon a sustained and comprehensive attack on the problems of Canadian history. And it has not been resumed. The thirty years from 1918 to 1948 have witnessed a minor revolution in the study of Canadian history; but they have added very little to the biographical literature on Sir John Macdonald.

This is not to say, of course, that the work of these years

has contributed nothing to our knowledge of Macdonald's career, or to our understanding of his personality. Within limits, it has done both. During the last twenty years the Macdonald Papers in Ottawa have been raided by a small company of scholars for all sorts of purposes, and in pursuit of all kinds of themes—national and regional, political, constitutional, military, and economic. But the interest of these scholars in Macdonald has been secondary, not primary, and sometimes even accidental. They have, so to speak, walked all round Macdonald without troubling to look at him. They have taken him for granted, mainly because they were preoccupied with other matters, partly because they assumed that they knew all about him anyway. Almost nothing has been done to examine, correct, or justify the traditional picture of Macdonald—the picture, half legend and folklore, of the easy-going, pleasure-loving, and none too scrupulous opportunist, who survived a half-century of political conflict by means of a dubious series of compromises, appeasements, and reconciliations.

Now there may be a single, simple, and sufficient explanation for these calm assumptions and this evident neglect. Canadian history, even when it is regarded as a part of the history of either the British Empire or the North American continent, is possibly a parochial, not to say limited, theme. It attracts a few enthusiastic scholars; but their number will never be very large; and, though their work has acquired a certain popularity at the present moment, both publishers and public have not shown a great deal of interest in it in the past, and may possibly show as little in the future. All this may be enough, and more than enough, to account for the slow and uneven progress of Canadian historical research, for the unaccountable gaps and lamentable omissions in Canadian historical literature. Possibly. And yet the explanation seems somehow unsatisfactory. It explains too much or too little. It has little light to throw upon the direction and the character of the work which has actually been produced. Perhaps it is worth while to pursue the matter a little further, to approach a little more closely the problem of Canadian history and Canadian historical biography in general, and of the biography of Macdonald in particular.

II

Biography is a distinct and special branch of historical writing. Of all branches it is perhaps most closely related to the art of the novel, and this in both a legitimate and an illegitimate sense. In a biography, as in a novel, the phases of historical development and the conflict of historical forces are seen, not in generalities and abstractions, but concretely, in terms of a central, main character, a set of subordinate characters, and a series of particular situations. A biography may achieve the vividness and actuality of a novel; but, with even greater ease and frequency, it may degenerate into the trivial or dull improbability of fiction and propaganda. The complex facts may be cheerfully disregarded for the sake of dramatic simplicity, or they may be deliberately perverted for the purpose of political justification. And all too frequently, therefore, historical characters come to be divided into two broad classes: those who look like appropriate figures for melodrama, and those who appear to be required subjects for political panegyric. On the one hand there is the light-hearted, fictional biography with its gaudy jacket which has been written with a keen eye, not so much for facts as for sales; and on the other there is the solemn work of commemoration, usually in two fat funereal volumes, which looks, as Lytton Strachey observed, as if it had been composed by the un-

dertaker, as the final item of his job. These are the two ex-
tremes of historical biography in English; and in the late
nineteenth and twentieth centuries fashionable practice
has tended to alternate between them in certain fairly well-
marked cycles or periods.

Canada has never passed through these alternating
phases. It would have been better if it had. But in this, as
in so many other aspects of our literary development, our
experience has been almost entirely vicarious. It may be,
of course, that we have derived some indirect profit from
the more daring experiments of others. We may perhaps
no longer act the part of historical undertakers in quite the
same obvious way as when Alexander Mackenzie wrote his
life of George Brown, or Joseph Pope composed his biography of Sir John Macdonald. But we still seem to lack what
the fictional biography might at least have taught us—a
lively interest in character and personality. Canadian biographies have a formal, official air, as if they had been written out of the materials of a newspaper morgue, or from
the resources of a library largely composed of Blue Books
and Sessional Papers. In all too many cases, the subject
remains an important Public Personage—in capitals—
dwarfed by the circumstances of his "Times", which are
portrayed in great chunks of descriptive material, pitilessly
detailed, and among which he drags out an embarrassed
and attenuated documentary existence, like an unsubstantial papier-mâché figure made up of old dispatches
and newspaper files. It seems difficult for us even to make
our characters recognizably different; and as one reads
through a small shelf-full of Canadian biographies, one is
aware of a growing and uncomfortable sensation that one
is reading about one and the same man. Is it possible that,
even in Canada, people can actually be so indistin-
guishably alike? Is there really only one Canadian statesman, whose metamorphoses have merely involved a change

of name? Or are all Canadian statesmen simply members of the same family, a spiritual family at any rate, with certain persistent and unchangeable family characteristics, and a distinguished hyphenated surname? Are there really biographies of Baldwin, Hincks, and Laurier, or are these merely lives of Robert Responsible-Government, and Francis Responsible-Government, and Wilfrid Responsible-Government?

Now this abstract and inhuman method of presentation, which may be called the Procedure Appropriate for the Portrayal of Public Personages, is damaging enough to most historical characters, but completely fatal to Macdonald. It is a nineteenth- and twentieth-century historical technique; and Macdonald, though his entire political career lies within the reign of Queen Victoria, was never an exemplary and typical Victorian statesman. In some important ways at least, his affinities seem to lie rather with the eighteenth and early nineteenth century than with his own age; and, at any rate, the materials which he left behind him are not, in many cases, easily susceptible of manipulation by the methods of the standard biography. He could, and did, make some great speeches; but in both the earliest and the latest periods of his career he was often a casual and indifferent speaker. The great state papers of his career were often written by others, notably by A. T. Galt; and, even more important, some of his most characteristic habits of thought and methods of action are tradeable through the stray hints and oblique references of his private letters, or through other still more scattered and fugitive evidence. It is difficult to make a standard biography of his life; Pope's effort proved that; and, therefore, perhaps the first reason for the failure to grapple efficiently with Macdonald's career lies in a certain immaturity of craftsmanship, which is as much literary as historical.

III

A second reason is to be found surely in the strong partisan tone of a good deal of Canadian historical writing. Macdonald was a Conservative; and throughout Canadian historiography there is easily discernible a stiff strain of Liberalism with a capital L. It would not be very difficult, and it might be amusing, to compile a list of Canadian historians and political scientists who have been editors of Liberal newspapers, cabinet ministers in Liberal administrations, deputy ministers, heads of boards, and members of Royal Commissions appointed by Liberal governments. In respect of the last of these gentlemen, it is not necessarily implied that appointment, in their case, was a kind of public recognition of strict party fidelity; but, in the state in which Canadian politics were and perhaps still are, the evidence is, to say the least, suggestive. The list would not be a very short one; and it might be supplemented by a further list of historians and political scientists who have, so to speak, shared the Liberal ethic and contributed to the growth of the Liberal interpretation of Canadian history.

This interpretation has, in the first place, its solemn side, its aspect heroic and almost sacred, with prophets such as Baldwin, wise kings such as Lord Elgin, great moments of deliverance from bondage as with the formation of the Reform Ministry in 1848, and terrible plagues and tribulations as when Metcalfe and Head were sent to smite the chosen people. It has also its familiar and popular side; and it is to be hoped that what might be called the Liberal folklore of Canadian history will some day be investigated scientifically, as has already been done with the rhymes of Mother Goose. But these sagas and fairy tales are not the whole of the Grit interpretation of Canadian history; much of it is straightforward, hard-hitting journalism. There are moments when almost any book on Canadian affairs during the nineteenth century begins to sound like a string of *Globe* editorials; there are times when every treatise on external relations during the twentieth century begins to echo the confident ring of the leaders in the *Winnipeg Free Press*. The tone is unmistakably journalistic; and yet, curiously enough, it is perhaps the journalists—and particularly J. S. Willison—who have kept the greatest measure of detachment. And there are few more diverting passages in Canadian historical writing than the paragraphs in which journalists Willison and Dafoe rebuke the insinuations and correct the errors of that eminent scholar Dr. Oscar Douglas Skelton, Ph.D.

Every historian must have a point of view; but it will be valuable to his readers precisely to the extent to which it escapes from the parochial and transitory. If it is based upon some general view of man and society, if it is built up in accordance with the rules of independent craftsmanship, if it is shaped by a strict theory of art, then it may be an inextinguishable source of illumination and delight. Gibbon took his stand upon the broad, substantial ground of the eighteenth century, upon its values—moral, intellectual, and artistic—of scepticism and urbanity, of moderation and harmony, of symmetry and balance. Macaulay's point of vantage was at once more exiguous and more impermanent. He was a complacent child of early nineteenth-century Whig politics and the early nineteenth-century Industrial Revolution. He was a Philistine, a materialist, a bigoted partisan, with an overemphatic, debating style. As a political and social philosopher, he was damned; but what saved him was his high conception of the historian's vocation and his unflagging devotion to the art of narrative prose.

Canadian historians, in all too many cases, commit Macaulay's mistakes, without the excuse of his virtues. Rarely does one feel that they have taken their stand upon a broad, general philosophy and within the framework of a great literary tradition. They are apt to be parochial, contemporary, and argumentative. Even the buttresses of modern scholarship do not seem to have made it a great deal easier for them to maintain their critical judgment or their independence of spirit. Their values often seem to have a disturbingly close approximation to the planks of one of the party platforms of their period of study. And to view Canadian history through mass-produced spectacles such as these is simply a bore. Canadian affairs in the nineteenth century, like English affairs in the seventeenth and eighteenth, are interesting because they concern human beings confronted with human situations and human problems of permanent and universal importance. But to watch this varied and changing spectacle from one side or other of the House of Commons at Ottawa, with somebody nudging you in the ribs every second moment, is to undergo an experience of colossal tedium.

This tradition of partisanship in its narrowest sense may derive, in part, from the relative unimportance of universities in Canada during the nineteenth century, and from the dominance of journalism and politics in Canada's intellectual life. Nobody in the nineteenth century seemed to be able to do much to check this prevailing tendency; and one man who might have flung the whole weight of his considerable influence against it failed miserably and completely to do so. This was Goldwin Smith. Smith, who had been professor of history at Oxford, enjoyed a high prestige at the moment when he arrived in Canada in the early eighteen-seventies. He possessed a genuinely lively mind, a wide range of knowledge, a rich experience of men and affairs, and a fluent and pointed style. In that atmosphere of agitated and unreasoning prejudice which was Canada in the eighteen-seventies and eighties, he might have stood up for the values of detachment, urbanity, and moderation. He might, if he willed, have represented civilization. A following was waiting for him, for a group of young men, the members of the so-called Canada First party, were honestly sick of the malevolence, abuse, and corruption of the politics of the time. But he failed them. It is not too much to say that he disappointed an entire generation of Canadians.

It is true, of course, that he posed as what he might have been, but never was. He kept on signing his little articles with the pseudonym "A Bystander"; and, oddly enough, it is this conception of him which has imposed itself upon posterity. In reality, nobody was ever less a bystander than he. He was an intellectual partisan, a coldly furious intellectual partisan, but a partisan all the same, like everybody else. He was a journalist among other journalists, a propagandist among other propagandists, and not very different from his fellows in either category, except that he had a sharper pen and a longer purse than most. It is true that he quarrelled with both the old parties in turn, and it is possible that his personality was one of the main factors in the disintegration of Canada First. But these successive estrangements by no means implied an attitude of serene and Olympian detachment. They simply meant that Goldwin Smith was a one-man party, that he was the Goldwin Smith party, to which he attached himself with all his petulant vanity and rancorous vindictiveness. Indeed, if he is to be distinguished from his fellows at all, it will probably be not by the deficiency but by the excess of his partisanship. Beneath his restrained and slightly donnish exterior there seethed and bubbled the most extraordinary mixture of venomous resentments and hatreds. Almost invariably—at least when he wrote of Canadian affairs—he was a debater, a debater who composed mainly for definite political occasions and for particular political purposes, a debater who always fought to win. The points of his arguments, like small, flat-headed nails bought by the keg from the parliamentary debating ironmongery, are invariably nailed in with the greatest precision and agility; and the thoughts themselves are often as thin and flat and brittle, as unvarying and invariable, as shingles. Always in reading him one is conscious of the uneasy impression that some large and important consideration has been conveyed away, surreptitiously and with the greatest possible lack of ostentation, under the apparently comfortable assumption that its absence will never be noticed. It is like describing Niagara with the Horseshoe Falls left out, or painting a picture of the Toronto skyline minus the Royal York Hotel.

This ingrained disposition to partisanship has been weakened with time; this hard debating style has been dulled by academic caution, possibly to the disadvantage of Canadian prose style. But the old tradition lasted well into the twentieth century and its effects are not yet entirely dissipated. It would be too much to say that there are no modern biographies of Macdonald because there are too many Grit historians; but there is a small kernel of truth in the remark, and it may stand. The obvious misrepresentation of actions, the easy imputation of unworthy motives, the facile condemnation based on scarcely concealed political preferences—these transparent manoeuvres we have learnt largely, if not entirely, to avoid. But back of these particular biases lay a far more general and fundamental prepossession—a prepossession which, if it did not impel us to misrepresent, at least prevented us from understanding. We had ceased, or were ceasing, to be converts to party programs; but we had fallen victims to the nationalist interpretation of Canadian history.

IV

The chief characteristic of nationalist history has been a preoccupation, amounting almost to an obsession, with the twin achievements of Responsible Government and Dominion Status. And it is through this obsession that the concept of Canadian nationality has been largely shaped. The development of Canada's national autonomy has been identified almost exclusively with the process of emancipation from British control, and the process of emancipation itself has been represented, all too often, as a continuous struggle between legitimate colonial demand and obscurantist imperial resistance. These interpretations have both narrowed and distorted our understanding of Canadian national growth; they have virtually eliminated one main theme in the history of that development and they have left the other misshapen and unconvincing. For obviously the reality of Canadian nationality depends as much upon the separateness of Canada in North America as upon its autonomy within the British Empire; and obviously also the winning of autonomy within the Empire has not been a continuous hateful struggle, but a long process of bargaining, adjustment, and reorganization in which, not infrequently, the initiative came from the mother country rather than from the colony. Nationalist history has, on the whole, shown astonishingly little interest in either of these evident facts. The achievement and the maintenance of Canadian separateness in the North American continent have either been neglected or have been represented, in the main, as an easy and perfunctory business, in sharp contrast with the unending and acrimonious conflict by which autonomy within the British Empire has been achieved. Inevitably, therefore, "imperialism" was identified simply and exclusively with British imperialism. Other "imperialisms" were supposititious, and fictitious; British imperialism alone was horribly real.

There can be little doubt that these assumptions were central in the body of popular nationalist thought which was urged so vociferously by politicians and publicists in the period before the war of 1939-45. It is to be hoped that, in the near future, the nationalism of that era will be subjected to a curious and careful scrutiny, for it is an attractive subject, with lots of easily available evidence, since the nationalists spread themselves so copiously and vehemently upon the record. Obviously this analysis cannot be begun here; but it may at least be said that two of the frequent, normal, and almost inevitable ingredients of pre-war nationalism were a lively dislike of Great Britain and the British Empire and a respectful admiration for the institutions and forms of life of the United States. Indeed, it might be suggested that, in certain cases at least, nationalist feeling was not primary at all, but secondary and derivative—that it was, in fact, a function which depended for its value upon two other factors, and was almost invariably expressed in terms of them.

Whatever the ultimate source of their impulses, the nationalists set out, with a fair degree of unanimity, to rescue Canada from the discredit of its all too British past and to rehabilitate it as a decent American community. J. W. Dafoe's *Canada: An American Nation* (the omission of the word "North" is not entirely without significance) is an example of this kind of effort, on a high level; and there were other and lower levels which were successfully reached and plumbed by the books and articles of the period. It began to be popular to portray the English Canadian as a typical North American, virtually indistinguishable from his neighbour to the south, a little stolid perhaps, a little slow—slowness was, indeed, one of his few admitted distinctive characteristics, and it was generally agreed that he was about a quarter-century behind the times—but plodding bravely onward in his great neighbour's wake and determined to realize his personality in his great neighbour's image. It was true, to be sure, that his political institutions were regrettably monarchical; but from the time of the King-Byng controversy, there was an evident inclination, which became at times a determined effort, to republicanize these institutions in the popular imagination. In the autumn of 1945, when Mr. Ilsley attempted to define the constitutional position of the Cabinet to the House of Commons, the resulting general discussion afforded some curious evidence as to just how far this process had gone. Mr. Ilsley's constitutionally correct statement that "the authority of government is received from the Crown" evoked strong criticism, not only from the opposition parties in Parliament, but also from certain Liberal newspapers in the country. This criticism was apparently based upon the assumption that there was some fundamental conflict between the principle that the authority of government is derived from the Crown and the principle that government is responsible to the House of Commons and the electorate; and this, in turn, may very well have had its origin in the more fundamental, if inarticulate, premise that government could not be "democratic" unless it was republican. We have travelled a long distance since 1867. In that year, the Fathers of Confederation struggled to obtain the title "Kingdom of Canada"; and in the decade before the war of 1914-18, this was still the ultimate objective of a man like J. S. Ewart. But nowadays, though many people at Ottawa are obviously tired of the word "Dominion", nobody apparently would dream of applying the word "Kingdom" to a country which is in fact a monarchy.

For historians, the most interesting feature of this whole movement is the effect which it may have had upon Canadian history. Already, of course, Canadian history was reasonably well adjusted to the new nationalist temper. The main staple of that history was the chronicle of the valiant and persistent efforts by which British North America had extracted Responsible Government and Dominion Status from a grudging and resisting Great Britain. This was much; but, in the new frame of mind, it was clearly not enough. Themes more eloquently expressive of Canada's destiny in the new world were required. If the country was to have a typical North American future, then surely it must have had a typical North American past. A normal

American community, virtually indistinguishable from the United States, it must have been moved by the same impulses and governed by the same forces as the American republic; and two countries must have passed through similar tribulations and comparable stages of development. This chain of reasoning may not have been so logically worked out by Canadian historians; they may have been moved merely by a desire to broaden the scope of their research. But, in any case, there can be little doubt as to the new direction which was given to Canadian history. Scholars began to import large chunks of American history into their Canadian historical studies, making comparisons, pointing out resemblances, drawing analogies, and using terminology and concepts derived from American history with the greatest gusto and abandon.

One of the early manifestations of this new movement in Canadian historical thought was the publication in 1927 of W. B. Munro's Marfleet Lectures given at the University of Toronto, *American Influences on Canadian Government*. It became fashionable, in the years that followed, to insist that Canadian politics was a British game played according to American rules, or an American game played according to British rules (I am afraid I have forgotten the exact form the epigram took); but evidently its clear implication was that though the form of the game might be British, its vital reality was American—American in the sense in which the word is used by citizens of the United States. Ideas such as these meant obviously a strong bias towards environmentalism; and environmental notions were still more clearly indicated in the amazingly ubiquitous use of the concept of the frontier. For a time the frontier was dragged in at every opportunity, appropriate or otherwise. It was used to explain almost anything, particularly anything that was new, dynamic, and vaguely forward-looking. It explained Mackenzie, the rebellion, the Clear Grit movement; there were even times when it seemed that it was going to explain the entire course of Canadian Liberalism. As for the Reformers and Liberals, they became practically the same as Jeffersonian and Jacksonian Democrats; while the Conservatives, on their part, were made to appear almost identical with Hamiltonian Federalists or with Republicans. Finally, and this was perhaps the most heroic effort of all, an attempt was occasionally made to prove that Canadian relations with the United States had been fairly amicable throughout, or, at any rate, that the main disagreements between the two countries had been exacerbated out of all recognition by the bunglings of British diplomacy.

It is not likely that we shall ever understand Macdonald or his times through the uncritical use of concepts and methods of this kind. The balance of our historical interpretation, which may have stood in need of rectification a quarter-century ago, has now clearly fallen too far on the other side. The rather simple-minded environmentalism of the past twenty-five years stands in obvious need of a careful re-examination. We should ask ourselves what we mean by treating the North American environment as a solid, undifferentiated bloc; we should pay more attention to the cultural baggage, to the ideas and values, of the people who developed it; and, above all, we should begin to treat those ideas with some respect, without instantly rejecting about one-half of them—usually the half that we do not happen to like—as fraudulent and time-serving. Sir John Macdonald lived, not in the twentieth, but in the nineteenth century; and the English Canada of his days was largely a provincial society, a section of a larger British community which was still in many important ways a unity, culturally and spiritually as well as in the realm of politics, diplomacy, defence, and finance. For Canadians the two capitals of their world were Ottawa and London; these cities were almost equally important to Macdonald and to those with whom he worked. He knew them both—

lived in them both—in London, on one occasion, for several months; and to the end of his days the holiday that he enjoyed most was a trip to the capital of the Empire.

Macdonald and the
Anglo-Canadian Alliance

EVERYONE KNOWS the traditional picture of Sir John Macdonald. It is perhaps the most remarkable achievement of that remarkable creation, the Liberal interpretation of Canadian history. Easy-going, convivial, bibulous, none too scrupulous, Macdonald is presented as the man who, above all others in Canadian politics, made himself master of the dubious arts of political expediency. In his own day, of course, this severe judgment took on a deeper note of moral reprobation. At evening prayers in Liberal households during the 1880s, his dread unuttered name was unquestionably linked with those of Satan's principal associate fallen angels. At tea-time, when Grit families gathered together for instructive conversation and the portrait of George Brown looked down approvingly from the wall, the master of the house could readily find some hideous episode in the career of the Conservative leader to illustrate the moral tale which he was imparting to the horrified little group of earnest Liberal youths and round-eyed Liberal toddlers. In those days and in those circles, Macdonald was quite simply the politician without principles, without scruples, and without remorse. And although those days have long ago vanished, Liberal journalists and Liberal historians—the two groups are not very easily distinguishable—have combined to ensure that this lurid caricature should leave an enduring imprint on the collective memory of Canadians. Macdonald, it came to be assumed, was a supremely adroit politician, with few

First delivered as a lecture at Carleton University in 1957, and published in C. T. Bissell (editor), *Our Living Tradition: Seven Canadians*, Toronto, 1957, under the title "Sir John A. Macdonald".

real purposes and even fewer ideas. He excelled, if he excelled in anything, in postponements, adjustments, reconciliations. He was "Old Tomorrow", "Old Compromise", "Old Appeasement". He was, in short, the "fixer" in politics, elevated—if such a thing were morally conceivable—to a level nearly approaching that of genius. And, like all such time-servers who deal purely in temporary expedients, he could have nothing of any value whatever to say to posterity.

The portrait, of course, is not all wrong. Even a figment of the Grit interpretation of Canadian history can have a few grains of truth in it. There can be not the slightest doubt that Macdonald was a most accomplished master of the craft and mystery of politics. He brought to his chosen art great natural gifts of mind and heart, character and temperament; and he developed and refined them during nearly half a century of active political life. Every device, every ruse, every conceivable subtlety was instantly at his command. And yet he carried out his magical feats in such an easy, jocular fashion that he seemed more like a gifted amateur than a grim professional. There was always time in his crowded schedule for lounging and drinking, for good books, good talk, and good stories, and for quantities of acquaintances and friends. He never seemed to be in any particular hurry about anything. He rarely got excited or angry. He never became morally unctuous or morally indignant. The incredible fact was that he actually appeared to be enjoying life! How could one take such a man seriously? And yet, for some strange unaccountable reason, he *had* to be taken seriously. The solidity of his achievements mocked the facile depreciation of his character. The bibulous party hack became the principal author of the constitution of a great state. The indolent procrastinator created a transcontinental nation in less than a quarter of a century.

The defects and limitations of the popular portrait are obvious. It is not so obvious how they got there; but many of them are ultimately traceable to what may be called the Authorized Version of our nation's story, the Liberal or Grit interpretation of Canadian history. This interpretation, like its more famous prototype, the Whig interpretation of British history, is a curious and complex subject which must be analysed in detail to be understood; and all that can be ventured here are a few very general remarks about its origins and nature. The bases of the theory, which are largely journalistic, were laid during the last third of the nineteenth century; and as a result it has about it to this day a grimly puritanical, unctuously pious air which recalls its mid-Victorian origin. Obviously the preferred politician of the Authorized Version is a sober, earnest, volubly virtuous man, whose generalized features unmistakably suggest the lineaments of William Ewart Gladstone rather than those of Benjamin Disraeli. Liberal politicians, from Baldwin to King—but with, of course, the single great exception of Laurier—have conformed fairly faithfully to this ideal. Laurier, like Macdonald, had style; graces of manner, a gift of eloquence, a flash of wit, were all his. But Baldwin's speaking manner, to judge from the slight extant evidence, was as earnest, as characterless, as humourless as even Mackenzie King's; and Blake, though he had great intellectual power and a real capacity for sardonic humour, could put his own followers to sleep with the tedious prolixity of his speeches. All of them were respectable, serious, weighty men—obviously acceptable provincial Mr. Gladstones. But Macdonald was not. Macdonald was a quite unusual Victorian statesman.

He thus affronted the morality of the Authorized Version of Canadian history. He also was never accepted as a sincere believer in its principal doctrine. That doctrine is concerned, of course, with the central mystery of the emergence of the Canadian nation. Canada, the creed of the Authorized Version declares very firmly, is the outcome of an encounter between the forces of nationality and British imperialism. Great Britain has always been the real opponent of Canadian nationalism. The only serious struggle which Canada has ever had to wage was the struggle to win autonomy inside the British Empire; and the progress of national development can thus be identified simply and exclusively with emancipation from British control. Canadian history therefore becomes the record of the stupendous crusade, mainly constitutional in character, by which Canada has ascended from the degraded status of dependent colonialism to the serene heights of autonomous nationhood. All the great Liberal leaders, from Baldwin to King, have been passionate crusaders in the good cause. Baldwin won responsible government; Blake reduced the powers of the governor-general; Laurier foiled the plots of the Colonial Office; and King effected his people's final deliverance through the Statute of Westminster.

But what of Macdonald? Eyebrows were lifted, lips were pursed. It was plain, according to the Liberal interpretation of Canadian history, that Macdonald was just as badly deficient in faith as he was in good works. He had been heard to say that the maintenance of a separate political existence in a continent dominated by the United States was the most difficult task confronting the Canadian nation. He had gone so far as to imply that it was American imperialism, not British, which constituted the real threat to Canadian autonomy. He had even had the temerity to suggest that the British connection, far from being a constitutional fetter, was a valuable alliance by which Canada could correct the imbalance of power on the North American continent and help to ensure her own survival as a distinct and separate nation. Obviously these were not honest doubts and legitimate questionings. They were appalling heresies; and on their basis he would have to be judged. He was certainly heretical, possibly idolatrous, for he had gone a-whoring after strange gods; and all that could be said for his political immortal soul was that he had shown a certain low cunning as a politician. In the Authorized Version, little space would be given him, little respect would be paid to him. A collection of amusing, slightly bawdy stories, a number of drunken sprees, a few unsavoury scandals, a gerrymander or two, a couple of railway jobs, and a shrewd ability to persuade Orangemen and Ultramontanists to enter the same cabinet—this was Sir John Macdonald.

It takes a good deal of moral courage to question even the smallest part of this judgment. In other countries, the search for historical truth, the process of historical revision, is regarded as an important and laudable activity; but in Canada any irreverent inquiry into the official Liberal interpretation is frowned on very darkly indeed. In Canada, it is not necessarily assumed that historical truth is to be found in a comprehensive and careful investigation of the evidence of archives, libraries, and men's memories. Historical truth is laid up, a priceless and absolutely untouchable deposit, in the private minds of Liberal politicians, Liberal civil servants, Liberal journalists, and Liberal historians. And as the Liberal government of Canada has gone on from strength to strength and decade to decade, the majestic orthodoxy of the Authorized Version has grown. It may even be established, like the Church of England in Queen Elizabeth's day, by act of Parliament. Already a national repository or shrine has been founded in Ottawa at Laurier House; and two eminent scholars have been appointed, whom we have the best of reasons for thinking of as the "historians laureate" of Canada. Should we not crown them, metaphorically at least, with laurel wreaths, as King George crowned Mr. Masefield, the poet laureate of England? They will recite the old, well-loved stories of the Authorized Version. They will tell our children and grandchildren how Edward Blake exposed the serpentine machinations of Sir John Macdonald and how

Mackenzie King finally slew the hideous dragon of British imperialism with the glittering lance of national autonomy.

They will do it admirably, of course. Perhaps this is all we need. Perhaps this is all we ought to get. And yet I venture to ask Canadians to admit the possibility of another version, and to begin their own re-interpretation of the career of Sir John Macdonald. What they discover may not be simply a collection of old stories that amused their grandfathers and great-grandfathers. What they find may be a tract for the times, which will enable the youth of today and tomorrow to make a new Canada.

II

Any attempt at a reassessment of Macdonald's contribution to the national tradition must begin by a swift disposal of the bits of folklore and the worn-down theoretical stereotypes on which the traditional estimate is based. There is no point, either, in going back, as scribes of the Liberal interpretation usually do, to Great Britain for historic definitions of Conservatism, and then, after having proved that Macdonald's program does not exactly meet the standard British requirements, ending up with the sage conclusion that therefore nineteenth-century Canadian Conservatism had no political principles. This kind of doctrinal pedigree-hunting, this form of ideological ancestor worship, is one of the silliest manifestations of the colonial mind. It is not necessary to trace an idea back through Edmund Burke to Charles I in order to prove that it is a Conservative political principle. Nineteenth-century Conservatism in Canada is not what Burke and his successors and commentators thought it ought to be in theory, but what Macdonald and his principal associates made it in practice.

From the beginning Macdonald had never shown himself a very orthodox Tory in the historic British sense. At the start of his career, both his friends and his opponents united in describing him as a moderate or liberal Conservative. He believed firmly in the monarchy, the British connection, the parliamentary system, responsible government, a moderate property franchise, and a life peerage, as he called it, for the upper house or Senate. He was, however, by no means singular in these beliefs, for all his principal Grit opponents cherished almost exactly the same convictions; and the amazing extent of their unanimity is recorded for all time in the Quebec Resolutions, which formed the basis of the British North America Act. The old historic disputes between Whig and Tory, Roundhead and Cavalier, were never serious subjects of controversy in Canada; and the extent of Macdonald's detachment from them is indicated in his attitude to the very name Conservative itself. In 1872, when the first election after Confederation was approaching, he had got to the point of considering a new name for the party, though he realized that the title "Liberal-Conservative" could not be completely dropped. "I think, however," he wrote, "that it should be kept in the background as much as possible, and that our party should be called the 'Union Party'; going in for union with England against all annexationists and independents, and for the union of all the Provinces of British North America, including Prince Edward Island and Newfoundland, against all anti-Confederates. . . . What think you of such a name as 'the Constitutional Union Party'?"

It is this word "Union" which provides the key to the purpose and meaning of Macdonald's grand design for Canada. The basic Conservative belief that the nation transcends the group, class, or section lies back of this idea of national union. It is here, rather than in any other part of his political thought, that Macdonald approaches British Conservatism most closely. It is here also, although he

has been dead well over sixty years, that Macdonald becomes as vividly contemporary as any Canadian politician
now living. The supreme purpose of his existence was the
creation of a great transcontinental British North American nation—a nation separate, distinct, and independent
on the North American continent. He aspired to found it,
expand it, develop it, preserve it, and defend it for British
North Americans and their descendants until the end of
time. Others, of course, had had the same idea. Nova Scotians, Canadians, British statesmen, British North American governors, had suggested it or advocated it in the past
or during Macdonald's own generation; and people like
D'Arcy McGee or Alexander Morris were far more elo-
quent prophets of Confederation than he could ever hope
to be. But that is not the point. The point is that Confederation was a political achievement, and that until a responsible ministry in Canada, which was the strongest of
all the British North American provinces, adopted Confederation as a plank in its political platform, the idea of a
general union was bound to remain academic and theoretical. When, therefore, in the summer of 1858, John A. Macdonald and George E. Cartier formally announced a federal scheme as a government measure, they made the plan
of union a political reality for the first time.

At this stage, and until the achievement of Confederation in 1867, the scheme was primarily political in character. It was governed by two main principles, the idea of
comprehension and the idea of strength. The plan of union which Macdonald proposed was intended, from the
first, to embrace not merely all the existing politically organized colonies, Canada, Nova Scotia, New Brunswick,
Prince Edward Island, and Newfoundland, but also the
immense politically unorganized territories of the Hudson's Bay Company. A nation which included the whole of
the still enormous British inheritance in northern North
America would be impressively vast in extent. It was also

intended—and this was the second principle of the plan—to be equally exceptional in strength. Three years before the beginning of the American Civil War, Macdonald, Cartier, and Galt, the principal authors of the proposals of 1858, had drawn what seemed to them to be the only possible constitutional moral from the deepening political schism in the United States. As they saw it, it was states' rights and regional divisions which were dragging the great republic through weakening quarrels towards probable ruin. And they determined to make their projected British North American federation as strong as it was comprehensive. Other people in the colonies, at this time and a little later, were considering regional unions, or decentralized regional federations. Macdonald never showed any interest in either. And in the end he was able to win the support of most of the principal leaders of the period—Cartier, Brown, Tupper, and Tilley—for his plan.

This first, mainly political phase of Macdonald's national plan may be said to have reached its logical conclusion in 1873, with the entrance of Prince Edward Island into Confederation and the realization that union with Newfoundland would probably be indefinitely postponed. The strong federal constitution had been embodied in the British North America Act. The transcontinental nation stretching from Atlantic to Pacific, and from the river unto the ends of the earth, had become a triumphant reality. It remained to discover and bring out as completely as possible the economic and social meaning of this enormous expanse of territory. And this, in several important ways, was an even more difficult task than the political business of constitution-making and territorial acquisition. Half a continent, well over three-quarters empty, would have to be peopled. Its resources would have to be discovered and developed. Its potentialities, about which the bitterest disputes were still raging, would have to be tested and assessed. How was all this to be done? Was it to be left to chance? Or was it to be directed according to some plan? And if a plan, what plan was the new nation to follow?

It was at this point that Macdonald determined upon the general design of the second, or economic, phase of his nation-building. The policies in which the plan was embodied were not all adopted at once, of course. But the development of the scheme as an integrated whole did not occupy a great many years; and by the time of the election of 1878—only a little more than a decade after Confederation—the design was complete. It rested on a single, gigantic assumption. Canada, Macdonald and his advisers assumed in effect, was economically viable in its own right. Canada's economy could be organized, on an east-west basis, as a separate and competitive economy in North America. This was, in several ways, a more imaginative and daring conception than the original idea of the political union of British North America itself. The little northern provinces had had no reason to anticipate such an ambitious, independent, continental future. For generations now, they had existed as simple, staple-producing parts of great commercial systems dominated by metropolitan powers. They had grown up inside the protection of the Old Colonial System of the British Empire, contentedly accepting the benefits of its tariff preferences and shipping monopolies. And when Great Britain declared for free trade, and the Old Colonial System abruptly vanished, British North America sought and found an alternative preferential relationship with the United States, through the Reciprocity Treaty of 1854. In other words, before Macdonald worked out the national economic policies in the 1870s, there had seemed to be only two possible courses for Canada. She had existed in the past as a subordinate, tributary part of the maritime empire of Great Britain. She could continue in the future as a subordinate, tributary part of the continental empire of the United States.

Macdonald rejected both these destinies. He believed in the possibility of a strong, diversified and integrated national economy in Canada. His hopes were based partly upon the known and varied resources of the original eastern and central provinces and also—and much more importantly—upon the enormous potential productive capacity of the northwest. The territories which Canada acquired in 1870 from the Hudson's Bay Company included not only the present prairie provinces, and the existing Northwest Territories, but also vast stretches of what is now northern Ontario and Quebec. This was the empire upon which his hope for the future was based. The northwest, he believed, would in the end make Canada a nation. He clung to this conviction, despite the frustrations of the great depression of the last quarter of the nineteenth century, to the end of his career. It was upon this issue that he fought the last election of his life, the election of 1891, which is probably the most important general election in the whole course of Canadian history. And although he did not live to see the fulfilment of his hopes, the northwest did in the end perform exactly the miracle he had expected. Under Laurier, who in all essentials continued Macdonald's national economic policies, and with the coming of better times, the prairies were occupied at headlong speed and put rapidly into large-scale production. In the first decade of this century, the tide of grain pouring like a golden river out of the west brought prosperity to Canadians and success to the Canadian national economy.

It is this which explains in large measure the extraordinary contemporary revival of interest in Macdonald and in Macdonald's design for Canada. In one very important way, we stand exactly where we did in the early 1900s. "The twentieth century," Laurier declared proudly, "belongs to Canada." There are not many individuals or nations who are given a second great opportunity; but the Canadians, the luckiest people in the world, have been given a second chance to make Laurier's boast come true. The first half of the century opened with all the encouragement of boom times. The second half of the century has commenced in an even greater burst of prosperity. And in both cases Macdonald's northwest, the region upon which he staked his whole tremendous gamble for the future of Canada, has provided the rich sources of national success. Fifty years ago, in the first decade of the century, it was wheat; now it is the new metals, the new fuels, the new sources of energy and power. How shall we use these new-found riches of half a continent? Upon what national plan should we try to develop this second huge bounty of good fortune? These are the questions which should be occupying us to the exclusion of almost everything else. For upon our answers will depend not merely the course of events for the next few years, or for even the quarter-century of Mr. Gordon's report, but, in all probability, the entire future history of Canada.

III

Our interest in Macdonald is an indication of the urgency of our position. And our sense of that urgency grows in part out of an obscure, uneasy realization that we have lost or thrown away for nothing some of the valuable assets which he possessed. We are at once weaker and stronger than he was: stronger largely because we are the heirs of the good fortune which resulted from his imagination and daring; weaker because we have lost either the will or the power to use certain policies which he considered essential for the safety of our inheritance. A dim unhappy awareness of our predicament has been slowly growing in us during the last few years. What, we ask ourselves miserably, can have happened? We were all taught—it was the basic doctrine of the Liberal interpretation—that national progress was to be identified solely with emancipation from British control. We all believed that once the great crusade against British imperialism was won, we would ascend unimpeded to the serene and spacious uplands of nationhood. It has not worked out quite that way. The uplands of nationhood have turned out to be, not serene and spacious, but troubled and restricted. And a whole generation of Canadians has been reaching the angry conclusion that it has been deceived.

Macdonald was not deceived. He realized that the nation which he hoped to create, strong and united both economically and politically, had a double task to perform. There were two goals of nationhood, not one. Canada must, in the first place, maintain a separate political existence on the North American continent; and in the second, she must achieve autonomy inside the British Empire–Commonwealth. Obviously the first national objective was the more basic and therefore the more important. It was also the more difficult to achieve; for the North American continent was dominated by the United States and, of the two imperialisms, American and British, the former was by far the more dangerous. It was upon these broad considerations that Macdonald based his foreign policy. A rough balance of power within the English-speaking world seemed essential to him to ensure Canada's survival. The diplomatic and military support of Great Britain could alone offset the political preponderance of the United States; and Macdonald proposed therefore to bring in the old world to redress the balance of the new. The Anglo-Canadian entente became the foundation of his foreign policy.

It goes without saying that, in the Authorized Version of Canadian history, this policy has been consistently misinterpreted. Macdonald has usually been called "an imperialist"; his party has been described as "the party of fervent imperial loyalty". These words and phrases mean, of course, exactly nothing; they are simply the Canadian equivalent of modern Communist abuse. Macdonald's whole plan for Canada was essentially nationalist; every policy, political or economic, was conceived as a means to the same great nationalist goal. At Halifax, at a dinner held in September 1864, just after the Charlottetown Conference, he spoke of "founding a great British Monarchy" in North America. He tried, in the first Canadian draft of the British North America Act, to name the country he was creating "the Kingdom of Canada". And in later years he repeatedly referred to the Dominion, in language which was unusual for the time, as a separate, "auxiliary" kingdom. His view of the Empire-Commonwealth was instinctively the pluralistic view to which we have become accustomed in modern times. He was convinced, long before Confederation was achieved, that the relationship of Great Britain and Canada was rapidly changing in character. In the past it had been a connection of subordination and dependence. It was becoming an association of equals or near equals. It would be, in his own words, "a healthy and cordial alliance".

It is this word "alliance" which is the key to Macdonald's conception of the Commonwealth relationship. He hoped and believed, with all his heart, that Canada would forever remain a kingdom under the British Crown; but for him the vital reality underlying the formal association of the Empire-Commonwealth was the Anglo-Canadian entente. The word "alliance" was frequently on his lips. He took its terms very seriously. He believed that it should be expressed in fairly definite agreements between the two governments. In 1865, just before Confederation, when the question of British North American defence was up for discussion in England, and again in 1871, when the imperial garrisons were recalled from central Canada, Macdonald obtained pledges from the British government promising military assistance to the limit in support of Canada

in the event of a war with the United States. After-
wards he always referred proudly to these agreements as
"treaties"; and there is no doubt he believed that similar
arrangements or "treaties" must regulate any contribution
that Canada might make in the future to the defence of
British interests overseas. Such a contribution, of course,
was never made during his lifetime. He was convinced
that, while the Dominion was in the formative stages of development, the whole force of the Anglo-Canadian entente
must be placed in support of Canada's weak position in
North America.

It was not until the twentieth century, when his design
for a transcontinental Dominion had become a reality, that
his successor, Sir Robert Borden, felt strong enough to extend the operation of the alliance to Europe. Borden held
fast to Macdonald's conception of the entente. He offered
contributions to Great Britain's European defences in return for a voice in the determination of Commonwealth
foreign policy. And the place which he secured in the Imperial War Cabinet and in the British Empire delegation
to the Peace Conference gave Canada an authority and an
influence in world affairs which was commensurate with
the sacrifices she had made in the First World War. The
ambit of the alliance had been enormously enlarged; but it
had been kept true to the principles that Macdonald had
laid down. It was an alliance of kingdoms, formally expressed in agreements and institutions, with benefits on
each side, and shared responsibility and power. It had begun as an alliance for the defence of Canada in North
America. It had become an alliance for the assertion and
protection of Canadian interests in the world at large.

In the brief space of a quarter-century, this alliance, in
both its European and its North American aspects, was
abandoned by Mackenzie King. King could hardly have
chosen a more inappropriate moment in which to let it go.
The first half of the twentieth century witnessed a persist-

ent decline in the power of Great Britain. It saw an even more impressive and steady rise in the preponderating authority of the United States. The imbalance of power in the English-speaking world, the overwhelming influence of the United States in the Americas, grew increasingly obvious; but King, with an old man's obsession for the now antiquated and meaningless cause of autonomy inside the British Empire, chose this particular time to cut us off from necessary associations with Great Britain and to plunge us deeper and deeper into continental commitments with the United States. If he had wished to do so, he might in 1939 have forced the creation of a Commonwealth Council which would have given Canada a voice in the conduct of the war in Europe and support in defence arrangements with the United States in North America. He repudiated the very idea of such a body. With his mind in the past, he regarded any formal association with Great Britain as "imperial centralization". He preferred to let the United States and Great Britain run the war in Europe. He preferred to do his own negotiating in North America. And whereas Macdonald negotiated from positions of relative strength, King negotiated from positions of serious weakness, and—we are told by those who ought to know best—in a spirit of ready compliance. The result has been the series of discreet, informal bargains with the United States which, since 1940, has been one of the most distinctive features of Canadian foreign policy.

It is this which has filled the Canadian people with misgiving and apprehension. It is this which has awakened a new interest in Macdonald and his national Canadian design. Macdonald's prime purpose was to found a transcontinental nation which would have a separate and autonomous existence in North America. His fundamental aim was to protect Canada from the dangers of continentalism; and it is the dangers of continentalism, economic, political, and military, which now seem to be pressing in upon us steadily and from every side. We are worried today, as we never were before, about the ownership of our strategic raw materials, our metals, our new sources of fuel and power. We have a resentful feeling that we are overpersuaded into an unwelcome arrangement about the St. Lawrence Seaway, which we are now trying to rectify by additional expenditures of our own; and we have an uneasy suspicion that the unpublicized negotiations which are going forward about the Columbia River will end in some serious reduction or abandonment of our unquestionable rights. Under persuasion which may very well be heavy pressure, are we being fitted smoothly and permanently into a continental capitalist organization, a continental power grid, a continental defence system? In Europe, NATO is a collective defensive enterprise; but in North America it is a two-power organization in which Canada can accept only the assistance, and the direction, of the United States. In the north, Americans build and man our radar installations; and in the east, in Newfoundland and Labrador, they hold and occupy military bases. The foreigner sits firmly astride the eastern approaches to our country; and the base, a primitive form of military imperialism, grimly questions Canada's claim to control her own destiny.

It is this sense of the danger overshadowing the main purpose of our existence which has brought Canadians back with interest and with almost the excitement of rediscovery to Sir John Macdonald. Perhaps the concern of these anxious Canadians is justified; but they should realize that, in the eyes of the teachers of the Authorized Version, they have behaved deplorably in yielding to it. The *Winnipeg Free Press* is an august guardian of the Liberal interpretations of Canadian history; and one of its reviewers has recently and magisterially denounced what he calls "the vain and blundering attempts of some Canadians" to convert Macdonald's life into a tract for the times. It is all right, he implies, for us to remember "the meddlesome arrogance of the British government"; but it is very naughty indeed to dwell upon Sir John Macdonald's diplomatic battles with the United States. We should expunge from our books and our minds "these old unlovely quarrels which belong to a vanished past". And in the space left vacant by the simple process of historical rubbing-out, we should put—what? Why, of course, we should put "a few more picturesque anecdotes of Sir John and his wayward greatness".

And so we can end, as befits loyal Canadian citizens, with a lesson from the Authorized Version, appointed to be read in all histories, articles, and speeches. We must never take Macdonald seriously. A few more whimsical stories about his weaknesses—that is what history should provide for Canadians as they enter the most exciting and dangerous period in their political existence.

Macdonald, Confederation,
and the West

TODAY, JANUARY 11, 1967, is the 152nd anniversary of the birth of John A. Macdonald; the centenary of Confederation is less than six months away; and in only three years from now the province of Manitoba will be a hundred years old. It is appropriate for students of history to re-examine these major events of the past; and it is particularly important to do so at the present moment, for we are now confronted by a radically new interpretation of their meaning. Historians, of course, are always busy revising and modifying the accepted historical record; but I am not thinking of such minor changes in detail or emphasis. The version of Confederation which has become current during the past few years is much more than this. It amounts, in fact, to a new theory of Canadian federalism, a theory which rests on the basic assumption that ethnic and cultural values are and ought to be recognized as fundamental in the life of the Canadian nation. The real essence of the Canadian federal union is thus the cultural duality of Canada. And Confederation becomes a compact between two cultures, two nations, English and French.

This interpretation, I have already suggested, is fairly new. The point deserves to be emphasized. In fact, the new version has been given expression mainly during the last six or, at most, the last ten years. Its increasing popularity among historians, writers, and journalists may, of course, be attributed in part to the interest in Canadian federal-

First given as a paper at a meeting of the Manitoba Historical Society on 11 January 1967 and published in the Historical and Scientific Society of Manitoba *Transactions*, 1966-7.

ism which has been growing steadily as the centenary of Confederation approached. But though the Centennial would naturally have revived an interest in Confederation, it would not necessarily have inspired a radical new interpretation of it. The real origins of the new theory are political; they lie in the rapid rise of French-Canadian nationalism which has come about since Jean Lesage in 1960 assumed power in Quebec. For the last half-dozen years a group of politicians, lawyers, historians, and journalists, mainly French Canadian but with some English-Canadian associates, have been disseminating a radically new view of Confederation and of French Canada's place in it. Their aims are varied and in some degree contradictory. On the one hand they have tried to improve the status and enlarge the rights of French Canadians in the nation as a whole; on the other, they have sought to emphasize the separateness and strengthen the autonomy of the Province of Quebec. At one and the same time they seem to believe in a bilingual, bicultural but united Canada, and a virtually independent Quebec, which, if it decides to remain in Confederation at all, will have to be given a "special position" and may even become an "associate state".

Obviously, the realization of either or both of these aims would mean a revolution in the present structure of Confederation. But Confederation, embodied in the law and custom of the constitution, is an inheritance from the past; and inevitably, therefore, the French-Canadian nationalists and their English-Canadian associates have had to cope with the intractable problem of history. Like everybody who desires social and political change, or is merely interested in its possibility, they had to make up their minds about the past. Revolutionaries have realized this necessity long ago and they have evolved two different, and indeed quite contradictory, methods of coming to terms with history. The "quiet revolutionaries" of Quebec appropriated both. The first method is to dismiss the past as irrelevant and meaningless for the present; the second is to identify the past with the revolutionary aims of the present. In other words, history can be rejected as a useless obstacle to the revolutionary program; or it can be re-interpreted to provide a justification for it.

The case for the dismissal of the past is not our business tonight. But the historical re-interpretation of Confederation which the Quebec nationalists have been so persistently offering for the last six years is certainly worth examining. This is an historical society and I am an historian; and we are—or should be—interested in the use, or misuse, of history. Revolutionary re-interpretations of the past usually have a purpose. In this case, the object of the "quiet revolutionaries" was to back up a political program with a new theory of federalism. The old view of Confederation as a political union of several provinces must be broken down and discredited; and the conception of Canada as a cultural duality, as a partnership of two different cultures or "nations", must be established in its place. The fiction of duality was to be substituted for the fact of plurality. The true meaning of Confederation, the French-Canadian nationalists argued, has been misunderstood and its essential spirit forgotten. Only on the surface can it be regarded as an agreement among several provinces; in reality it was a compact between the two cultures, the two nations, English and French, of Canada.

There is very little aid or comfort for the believers of this theory in what we know of the aims and intentions of the Fathers of Confederation. There is no support for it at all in the lean, spare phrases of the Quebec Resolutions or the British North America Act. It is obvious that the last thing the Fathers of Confederation wanted to do was to perpetuate duality; they hoped, through Confederation, to escape from it for ever. They had seen enough, and more than enough, of duality in the old Province of Canada. There it had paralysed governments and prevented progress for a quarter of a century. The new Dominion of Canada was to be organized, as the arrangements for the

Senate make quite clear, not as a duality but as a trium-virate of three divisions: Quebec, Ontario, and the Atlantic provinces as a group. The distinctive cultural features of French Canada—its language, civil code, and educational system—were confirmed in those parts of Canada in which they had already become established by law or custom. But that was all. They were not extended in their application to Ontario or to the Maritime provinces. There was nothing in the Quebec Resolutions or the British North America Act which remotely approached a general declaration of principle that Canada was to be a bilingual or bicultural nation.

The evidence against the two-nation theory of Confederation is so overwhelming that some of its advocates have been driven back upon a secondary line of defence. The bicultural compact, they admit, was only a "tacit" or "implicit" agreement, or a "moral" commitment, when the British North America Act was framed. But later, when Canada expanded westward and the Hudson's Bay Company territories were taken over, the Fathers of Confederation honoured the moral commitments and took care to provide that the new western domain should become the joint possession, on equal terms, of both English- and French-speaking Canadians. The first Conservative government after Confederation established separate schools and gave legal status to the French language in Manitoba. The first Liberal government after Confederation did exactly the same for the Northwest Territories. It was a basic national policy, deliberately adopted, carefully carried out, concurred in by both parties.

This, in short, is the theory of Confederation as a bicultural compact applied to Manitoba and the Northwest Territories. What is its truth when tested by the actual events of the time? This is the problem which I should like to examine with you tonight.

II

John A. Macdonald was above everything else a nation-builder. The union of the original British North American colonies was the first of his two greatest achievements; the expansion and integration of the new Dominion on a continental scale was the second. He was an expansionist; but he was also a realist. His purpose was to ensure that Canada would not be despoiled of her great territorial inheritance on the North American continent; he was absolutely determined that, as he himself put it, "the United States should not get behind us by right or by force and intercept the route to the Pacific". In his mind there was no doubt about Canada's ultimate destiny; but at the same time he was equally convinced that Canada should assume its great heritage slowly and prudently, a step at a time, by one firm stage after another. Even as late as March 1865 he would have preferred to see Rupert's Land and the Northwest Territories remain a Crown colony under imperial control. He soon realized, however, that the march of events could not be so deliberate as he had hoped. Great Britain's urge to withdraw from her North American commitments, the British government's desire that Canada should take over its responsibilities in the northwest, and the threat of American northward expansion all helped to convince him that there could be no more delay. In the spring of 1869 the bargain with the Hudson's Bay Company was finally concluded and Canada prepared to assume the assets and liabilities of its new western Dominion.

At this point it should be emphasized that Macdonald was still trying to hold fast, as far as he was able, to his original policy respecting the northwest. He had been compelled, far earlier than he had wanted to, to assume responsibility for Rupert's Land and the Territories; but he knew very well that the problem of their government and future development was a difficult one and he had no intention of risking a hasty solution to it. The bill which he introduced in the Canadian House of Commons late in May 1869 was characteristically entitled "For the Temporary Government of Rupert's Land". It deserves far more attention than it has yet received. It is the only document that embodies the Conservative cabinet's original policy respecting the northwest; it expresses Macdonald's original intentions, his first tentative provisional plans. And it is obvious from its few brief clauses that he was trying to keep as closely as possible to the idea of a Crown colony, the idea which he had proposed as little as four years before. The northwest was to be governed not as a province, but as a territory, by a lieutenant-governor and a small nominated council. The existing laws were to continue until altered; the public officers were to retain their posts until it was ordered otherwise. Nothing was to be changed in a hurry. Nothing new was to be introduced at once. There was no mention of either schools or languages.

Now it is usually assumed that this whole provincial plan of government was invalidated by the Red River Rising of 1869-70. It is also usually taken for granted—even less justifiably, it seems to me—that the Manitoba Act of 1870 was the only natural result, the logical and inevitable constitutional consequence, of the rising. Both these assumptions, I am convinced, badly need a critical examination; and the examination ought to begin by making a clear distinction between the Red River community on the one hand and the military dictatorship of Louis Riel on the other. There is no doubt whatever about the kind of government which the Red River community would have liked to see established in the northwest. Their wishes were democratically determined in the debates of the Convention which met at Fort Garry in mid winter

1870; and the results were embodied in the resolutions of the second "List of Rights". If this second list—the one document in which the constitutional preferences of the whole Red River community are faithfully recorded—had formed the basis of the negotiations at Ottawa, the Manitoba Act of 1870 would have been a very different statute. The Convention, against the opposition and to the intense indignation of Riel, decided against provincial status, at least for the time being. It requested equality for the English and French languages in the legislature and the courts; but it made no mention of separate or confessional schools. If the wishes of the Convention and the terms of the second "List of Rights" had been followed in drafting the Manitoba Act, there would have been no very serious departure from Macdonald's Act for the Temporary Government of Rupert's Land of the previous year.

But this moderate and sensible constitutional settlement was not to be. Riel was determined to prevent it. An adroit and ruthless dictator, he had no intention of permitting democracy to have its own way at Red River. His terms for the union with Canada had been openly and emphatically rejected by the Convention; but at the same time, as a final reluctant concession in the interest of political conciliation in the Settlement, the Convention had confirmed the provisional government and elected Riel as its president. At once and with purposeful energy he took over control of the negotiations with Canada. He quickly nominated Ritchot and Alfred Scott, who, he felt confident, would support his own private plans for the future of the north-west; and he persuaded the reluctant Convention to accept them as two of the three emissaries to the Canadian government. He then proceeded to make short work of the Convention's "List of Rights". The wishes of the Red River community where they differed from his claims for his own people, the *Métis*, meant nothing whatever to him. In two quite new and increasingly detailed "Lists of Rights", drawn up in private by Riel and his lay and clerical advisers, the delegates sent to Ottawa were instructed to insist that the Northwest should enter Confederation, not as a territory, but as a province. It must have, they demanded, an elaborate provincial constitution with an absurdly top-heavy bi-cameral legislature, including a little senate on the model of Quebec. It must also have a system of sectarian or confessional schools, again on the Quebec model. This, if you like, was a demand that biculturalism should prevail on the prairies and that French and English institutions should be combined in the government of the northwest; but it was neither a demand that was made by the community at Red River nor a plan proposed by the government at Ottawa. It was a claim exacted by Riel's dictatorship.

Why did Macdonald accept it? Why did he consent to impose such an elaborate constitution upon such an immature colony? How was he persuaded to settle all the basic institutions of a community which had not yet had time to develop its real and permanent character? The answers to these questions can never be absolutely certain, for the conclusive evidence is lacking; but the probabilities at all events are very clear. The pressures in favour of a quick settlement in the northwest were inescapable and compelling. Macdonald's foremost aim was to ensure, at almost any cost, Canada's continental destiny, her unobstructed expansion from the Atlantic to the Pacific Ocean. His greatest fear was that the United States, by deliberate policy or tragic accident, might prevent the achievement of these natural limits. He knew only too well that the acrimonious disputes which had arisen between Great Britain and the United States during the American Civil War had not yet been settled. There was evidence that both President Grant and Secretary of State Hamilton Fish were annexationists, prepared to use any method short of war to acquire all or part of British America. And finally it was clear from the beginning that the American expansionists at St. Paul, Minnesota—the "Yankee Wire-pullers", Macdonald called them—were eager to exploit the rising at Red River, and that American citizens in the settlement were deep in Riel's councils. So long as the provisional government continued, so long as the future of the British American northwest remained uncertain and Confederation was still incomplete, the threat of American intervention hung over Canada's future.

A quick settlement was urgently necessary. And its character by this time was fixed and virtually unalterable. Appeasement on any terms meant in fact appeasement on the terms demanded by the fanatical emissaries from Red River, backed up by Cartier and his French-Canadian "Bleu" followers, and supported by Sir Clinton Murdoch of the British Colonial Office. It is true, of course, that the Canadian government refused to yield to Riel's vainglorious and incredible demand that the entire northwest enter Confederation as a single province; and it is also true that the request for provincial control of public lands was likewise rejected. Macdonald could limit boundaries and withhold lands, but within the restricted area of the new province of Manitoba he had to accept a bilingual and bicultural system of rights and institutions. "The French," Sir Stafford Northcote observed, "are earnestly bent upon the establishment of a French and Catholic power in the North-West to counteract the great preponderance of Ontario." Their purpose was to fix the character and institutions of the new province at a time when French-speaking Roman Catholics formed a large part of its population, and therefore at the most favourable moment for preparing defences against the approaching influx of Protestant, English-speaking settlers.

III

The Manitoba Act did not represent the carrying-out of a solemn commitment to biculturalism which had been made at Confederation. It was not drafted in fulfilment of an ideal conception of what Canada should be; it was, to a very large extent, imposed simply by the force of circumstance. In 1869-70 a particular set of circumstances, including some very frightening external circumstances, had practically dictated a hasty policy of appeasement. But these circumstances were exceptional and transitory; they did not reappear in quite the same powerful combination; and as a result the main argument in favour of biculturalism lost most of its force. This would not have mattered, of course, if the Fathers of Confederation had really felt morally committed to the ideal of a bilingual and bicultural Canada, to the conception of two nations in the Canadian national state. But the simple truth is that they did not. The French language and French-Canadian institutions had not been given legal status in any province of the original union outside Quebec; and no attempt was made to establish the equality of the two cultures in any of the provinces that entered Confederation after Manitoba. The Manitoba Act did not lay down a national bicultural pattern which was solemnly confirmed and carefully followed thereafter. When British Columbia and Prince Edward Island joined the union, nobody so much as mentioned the great moral commitment to biculturalism.

The exception to this consistent record is, of course, the Northwest Territories. And it is a very dubious exception which effectively proves the rule. It was not until the session of 1875, nearly five years after the passage of the Manitoba Act, that the Parliament of Canada finally got around to setting up a system of organized government in the western territory beyond the new province of Manitoba. The main feature of the Northwest Territories bill, which the new Prime Minister Alexander Mackenzie introduced in the Commons, was a rather complicated set of clauses providing for the gradual introduction of elected members in the North-West Council as the population of the region increased. The bill contained no reference to separate or confessional schools, and no provision for the French language. If this silence could have been made to appear as a betrayal of a recognized bicultural compact, it is obvious that the Conservative opposition, in which several of the Fathers of Confederation were sitting, would have been quick to grasp the opportunity of so doing. But the Conservative members sat silent. And it was left to Edward Blake, who was not a Father of Confederation and knew nothing whatever at first hand of its purposes or principles, to move, in amendment, that separate or confessional schools should be established in the territories.

Why did Blake take up the cause of what he called "religious instruction" in the northwest? On the record, there was no reason to expect him to show any particular sympathy for the Roman Catholic *Métis* of the prairies; on the contrary, he was thought to share the critical views of *Canada First* and its representatives at Red River, Mair and Schultz. In 1871, when he had been leader of the opposition in the Ontario legislature, Blake had moved a resolution demanding that the "murderer" Riel should be brought to justice; and in the following year, after he had formed the first Liberal government in Ontario, he introduced a similar resolution offering a five-thousand-dollar reward for the arrest and conviction of the "murderers" of Thomas Scott. Undoubtedly he had gained a good deal of political capital from these astute moves; and political capital may well have been what he was after in the session of 1875. He was not a member of Mackenzie's government; he had been angling deviously for Mackenzie's post as Prime

Minister; he was critical of Mackenzie's policies and determined to block his railway bill; and he was embarrassing
him at every turn.

It was in this curious way, and with this unexpected
sponsorship, that separate schools found their way into the
North-West Territories Act of 1875. The grant of legal
status to the French language, which was made when the
statute was amended in 1877, came about in an even stran-
ger and more accidental fashion. It was not a government
amendment at all; it was proposed by a private member in
the Senate. And the speech with which David Mills, the
Minister of the Interior, greeted this amendment when it
was brought down to the Commons effectively destroys the
odd notion that the promotion of biculturalism on the
prairies was the settled policy of Liberal as well as Conservative governments. Mills reminded the members that
the dominant language of the region was Cree; he thought
the North-West Council was the only body that could properly settle the question of official languages. He regretted
the Senate amendment; and he reluctantly accepted it because otherwise it would be impossible to get the revised
statute through Parliament before the end of the session.

We are now in a position, it seems to me, to come to certain conclusions. The bicultural compact theory of Confederation as applied to Manitoba and the Northwest Territories cannot be sustained. The idea of a solemn commitment to biculturalism, accepted in principle and deliberately implemented by both parties, is simply not borne out
by the facts. The west did not get its institutions in accordance with the provisions of some long-range plan; on the
contrary, the process was characterized throughout by accident and improvisation. The pressure of circumstances,
the influence of certain powerful political interests, and
the ambition of a few key personalities all combined to
force a series of hasty and ill-considered decisions; and the
result was the abandonment of Macdonald's plan for the

gradual development of government in the northwest and the premature establishment of an elaborate and cumbrous constitution. This attempt to fix the political institutions of the west before immigration and the growth of population had determined its true and permanent character was a mistake for which the whole of Canada paid dearly. By 1890—only twenty years after the Manitoba Act and fifteen years after the North-West Territories Act— the west had outgrown the inappropriate constitutions that had been imposed upon it. It began suddenly and uncompromisingly to change the status of the French language and the character of its schools. The violent controversy that followed lasted for more than a quarter of a century; and it ended in the virtual extinction of biculturalism in the Canadian west.

This is an episode in our history which should not be forgotten. We should all remember it when we come to read the forthcoming report of the Royal Commission on Bilingualism and Biculturalism. The commission may possibly recommend constitutional changes designed to improve the position of the French language and of French-Canadian culture throughout the nation, including the west. These proposals should be judged critically in the light of history; and with the aid of the same clear light, westerners should examine the historical theory by which these proposals will probably be justified. The idea of a bicultural compact, of the two nation state, has got much of its currency and its vogue during a period of profound revolution in Quebec; and this very fact ought to make it suspect. New historical interpretations which make their appearance in revolutionary times are usually the result, not of the search for truth, but of the need for historical justification. They are invented—or partly invented—to supply historical authority for a program of radical changes. Canadians on the whole are badly equipped to protect themselves against this kind of propaganda. For

they are not as historically minded as the English, and, unlike the Americans, they have not been brought up in a
thorough knowledge of their own history. They cling to
old myths, and are easily sold new and spurious inven-
tions. It would be a tragedy if, at this most critical period
of their history, they were led to damage their future ir-
retrievably through a serious misunderstanding of their
past.

Part IV
Continentalism and Biculturalism

Canada and the Cold War

THE FIRST THING that Canadians must try to do, before we attempt to decide whether our country has or has not played a role commensurate with its strength, is to make up our own minds about the goals which we wish to attain in international affairs. It is hard enough for us to make up our own minds about domestic issues. It is even harder for us to begin the difficult business of independent thinking on foreign affairs. In our climb to nationhood, foreign affairs was the last subject in which we claimed and won the right to formulate our own policies; and even yet there exists among us the tacit assumption that in these matters it is something of an impertinence for a Canadian to hold any independent opinions at all. In a past now growing remote, we used to look up trustingly to Great Britain for leadership in world affairs. But shortly after the War of 1914-18—in a shift that was, to a considerable extent, the personal accomplishment of Mr. Mackenzie King—we began to transfer our intellectual subservience to the United States. We have been wait-

Read at the Couchiching Conference in August 1954 and broadcast on C.B.C. radio under the title "Canada in World Affairs". Published here for the first time.

ing humbly upon American guidance ever since.

It is only natural that our picture of the world should be shot from American cameras. The Canadian Broadcasting Corporation and the Canadian Press provide us with some independent comment and some independently gathered information. A Canadian correspondent is sent off every once in a while by some large metropolitan newspaper to report on the fortunes of a war or the doings of an international conference. But these are plainly exceptions to a general rule—brief intervals of home cooking in a very steady diet of imports supplied by the great American press associations, and by columnists and news commentators who are citizens of the United States. Every minute of every day Canadians are reading or listening to words which have been written by Americans for American audiences, and almost exclusively in terms of American national interests, purposes, and ambitions.

The results are interesting. Canadians get rapidly to the point of assuming that opinions expressed in the United States alone have any value and decisions taken in Washington alone have any significance. A while ago, when the Congress of the United States decided at the last minute to thrust its way into the St. Lawrence Seaway project with a contribution which it had not even troubled to discuss with the Canadian government, many Canadian journalists seemed quite incapable of containing their rapturous excitement. On the editorial pages, it is true, the leaderwriters frequently gave the shabby, self-interested proposal a very frigid welcome; but on the front pages of the newspapers, there was almost unqualified jubilation. The United States had spoken! Let the great waterway roll through its new bed! Let every Canadian attempt to express his almost unutterable sense of gratitude. It was only subsequently, and rather less conspicuously revealed, that the Canadian government was not prepared instantly to get down on its knees and accept this American offer in a proper spirit of abject humility.

In other matters, in which we are much less directly concerned, Canadians are even more disposed to accept the latest advices from Washington as the modern equivalent of divine revelation. For the past eight years the nation which virtually invented modern advertising has been engaged in what can only be described as the greatest sales campaign in its history, the campaign to sell the Cold War, in an exclusive American package, to the rest of the Western world. Canada, which was treated as an adjunct of the domestic market, received the full impact of this promotion. To put it in commercial terms, which are in reality the most appropriate, American-packaged Cold War was outselling every other brand of packaged Cold War ten to one in the Canadian market. The policies and opinions of other Western countries were given prominence chiefly when they agreed with those of the United States; and the contradictory decisions or views of such countries as Great Britain, France, and India were depicted as unsound, mischievous, doubtfully loyal, or Communist-inspired.

II

It is under the influence of these pressures, of whose existence we have now almost ceased to be conscious, that we tend inevitably to think of foreign affairs. We are in danger of accepting uncritically a North American view of the world, mass-produced in the United States. We run the grave risk of adopting ends and means, purposes and methods, which are not necessarily ours at all, and of judging our own conduct by standards which we have had very little part in setting. We must scrutinize these standards before we make any important judgments based on them. Upon what assumptions, expressed or inarticulate, are they based? What habits of thought and feeling in North America help to give them their strength and popularity?

The first and basic assumption, which has been tirelessly promoted in North America, is that the Cold War is essentially a conflict of rival ideologies. Every college football team in Canada and the United States has a yell, a song, a set of colours, and, of course, a college spirit second to none on the continent. If the Communists have got what they call an ideology, then of course we must have an ideology also; and, equally inevitably, our ideology must be a lot better than theirs. We are all perfectly sure about this; but we are a good deal less certain about the nature of the faith which binds the peoples of the West together in their holy alliance. Is its first principle Christianity? If so, what are we going to do about the Mohammedans, Jews, and Buddhists whose support or sympathy we hope for? Is the basic principle democracy? Then how do we explain the presence in our ranks of Spain, the Argentine, and that new military régime in Guatemala whose establishment we were invited so peremptorily to applaud a few weeks ago? Is the basic principle, as the Americans are always loudly insisting, private enterprise? Then are we to expel from our society the Communist-controlled Yugoslavia, the welfare state of Great Britain, and our own province of Saskatchewan, not to mention the large Communist or Socialist minorities in Europe and the Commonwealth? If our quarrel is really with Communists as such, then we ought logically to begin by exterminating the several million professed Communists in France and Italy. But, oddly enough, not even Mr. Dulles has suggested that we set about doing this.

No, the notion that the West has a single ideology is quite simply false, in any absolute and unqualified sense; and it is dangerous for Canadians to permit themselves to be deluded into believing that it is true. If the Cold War is regarded as a conflict of fundamental and sacred principles, then we shall inevitably come to assume that on one side (our side, of course) lies absolute truth, and on the other total error. Out of this conviction there arises a fanatical spirit which will brook no compromise, which clamours for a war of righteousness, for the extermination of all those heretics who refuse to accept our principles and share our "way of life".

This intransigent interpretation of the Cold War has been fostered by two other tendencies of thought which are common to the whole of North America and which, to a certain extent, Canadians share with citizens of the United States. The first is a casual readiness to adopt quick, harsh, violent methods of getting our ends; and the second, which is really a corollary of the first, is a reliance upon the machine as the chosen—indeed, the ideal—instrument for all possible purposes. We are led to believe not only that we have a mission to rescue the rest of the world from error, but also that we must carry out our sacred duty uncompromisingly and probably by force. We are taught to expect, and almost to look forward to, "instant retaliation" by the terrible devices of "push-button" warfare. The most complimentary adjective which an American newspaper correspondent can apply to the foreign policy of his country is "tough". He is supremely happy when he begins a dispatch with the gratifying words "The United States today served blunt notice . . .". The ideal negotiator for the West, as he is conjured up in the columns of our newspapers, is a species of diplomatic gangster, with a truculent manner, a rasping voice, a short vocabulary consisting chiefly of negative expressions, and an up-to-date equipment of black-jacks and sawed-off shotguns which he is prepared to use at the slightest notice.

Conflict, we are taught to believe, is the real purpose of manly and straightforward diplomacy; peace is the dark goal of underhand and sinister intrigue. A while ago, in an English newspaper, there appeared a cartoon which depicted a board fence, with the word "peace" scrawled on it, and a little boy running importantly to inform his mother of the fact. "Mummy," he says, "Cyril's wrote a wicked word." Peace—or rather, perhaps, the acceptance of peace as a possible objective—has been revealed to us as morally reprehensible. Every concession, every compromise, even the mere acceptance of negotiation as a method in international relations, has been denounced as appeasement, betrayal, and capitulation. Diplomacy in its general sense, as any dictionary will tell you, means tactful and adroit dealing; but it has been indicated to us that this is an old and indecent European definition with which virtuous North Americans ought not to soil their minds.

III

This is the stuff on which we Canadians have been fed for a very long time, with three square meals and several snacks a day. These are the assumptions we must get rid of if we are to make a just appraisal of our recent part in world affairs. Diplomatic virtue, we must realize, does not necessarily consist in making faces at our opponents, delivering ultimatums, precipitating "showdowns", breaking off negotiations, forming military alliances, and, in general, throwing our weight pugnaciously around in all directions. The conflict between East and West is a conflict of interests as well as of principles; and interests, however highly we regard our own, are mundane and negotiable matters. Our real aim, as Prime Minister St. Laurent and Prime Minister Churchill have both declared, is to make an honourable settlement which will enable us and the Communist countries to live side by side in peace. The form of government and social organization which other countries adopt is their business and not ours. Dreams of great crusades for the extermination of Communists and the liberation of their dupes are nightmares from which we must pray for deliverance. Our legitimate task—and it is not only legitimate but also desperately necessary—is to erect defences for ourselves and our friends against external aggression; and this is a labour which in various ways has occupied us ever since the War.

What part has Canada taken in it? In 1945, at San Francisco, Canada accepted commitments for the maintenance of collective security which were quite as large as those she had accepted twenty-five years before at Versailles, and much more precisely defined. The Dominion Government had spent the years from 1919 to 1939 in regretting and explaining away its obligations under the enforcement clauses of the Covenant of the League of Nations. But in 1950, when the first test of the Charter of the United Nations came with the invasion of Korea, there were apparently no regrets and no apprehensions in Ottawa. I was in the capital in the early summer of 1950, and the tense spirit of enthusiasm and dedication which prevailed there must have been very similar to that of some medieval town in Europe after Peter the Hermit had passed through, drumming up recruits for the First Crusade. The League of Nations, everybody seemed to say, had failed to prevent the rape of Czechoslovakia; and now the United Nations, the new organization for collective security, must demonstrate its moral and physical superiority by rescuing this Czechoslovakia of the East, the Republic of Korea, from its peril. In the next four years it became obvious that Syngman Rhee was hardly of the same moral stature as Beneš and Masaryk, and that the shoddy, irresponsible régime at Seoul was not fit to be mentioned in the same breath with the great vanished republic of Czechoslovakia. A certain disillusionment set in. We suffered, moreover, like other crusaders in the past, from confusion and argument in our collective councils. Was the war being fought by the United Nations, or by the nations with troops in Korea, or by the United States, which, we were reminded on all possible occasions, had put the largest forces into the struggle, or by General MacArthur, who seemed irrepressibly eager to turn it into a general war of righteousness against Asian Communism? There was bickering over the conduct of the war, and over the negotiation of the cease-fire, and even yet no permanent settlement has been won. Korea is not, on all counts, a shining example of the efficacy of the new collective system. Nevertheless, the Korean War taught the world—and the Communist-controlled world in particular—a highly important lesson. It proved that the United Nations could be used, as its makers had intended, to resist, and to stop, external aggression.

Will the United Nations be able to take the same drastic action, in similar circumstances, in the future? The motives behind the Korean intervention were not above suspicion; and the record of the Security Council in the recent invasion of Guatemala must arouse grave doubts for the future.* The government headed by Arbenz may have been Communist-supported or even Communist-controlled, but this fact ought to have made no difference to the United Nations, which is, or should be, ideologically neutral. Yet plainly the suspicion of Communism made a lot of difference to the most important member of the United Nations, the United States. A vigorous propaganda campaign, in which the press enthusiastically co-operated, was organized in the republic against Guatemala; Guatemala was subjected to a thorough blockage of arms; and the amazing climax of the whole affair was reached when

*In 1953, Guzmán Jacobo Arbenz, the democratically elected President of Guatemala, expropriated the banana plantations of the American United Fruit Company and distributed the land among the Guatemalan peasants. The emigré opponents of the Arbenz reformist régime, led by Colonel Castillo Armas, threatened invasion from Honduras; and Arbenz ordered arms from Czechoslovakia. The United States regarded these steps as proof that Arbenz had become the tool of international Communism. It signed military agreements with Guatemala's neighbours, Honduras and Nicaragua, and provided Armas with guns and planes. Armas invaded Guatemala and Arbenz appealed to the United Nations. Under pressure from the United States, the Security Council refused to intervene and the Arbenz government fell.

the country which for well over a hundred years has stood forward as the avowed champion of the sacred principle of the freedom of the seas actually had the temerity to demand the right to search Atlantic shipping. In the meantime a fairly large-scale offensive was being mounted on the frontiers of Guatemala, with the apparent connivance of its nearest neighbours, and with arms whose origin will remain a subject of curious speculation for some time to come.

It was a growing realization of the possible failure of the United Nations together with a growing fear of the possible ambitions of the great Communist countries that has led, in recent years, to the growth of an alternative system of security, the regional defence pact. In 1949 the North Atlantic Treaty Organization was established with Canada as one of its members. An exclusive body, it does not pretend to offer general and equal protection: and it is, in effect, the old-fashioned military alliance writ large. But in the circumstances in which the West was placed after the second collapse of Czechoslovakia, NATO was desperately necessary. It is a viable organization. It has its own territories, its own rich resources in men and materials, its own defensible position. It is, above all, a union of mature powers which have come together spontaneously, and of their own free will, to defend their collective homeland. NATO was not something which the United States imposed on Europe, or which Europe was cajoled or threatened into accepting. Canada accepted the pledges in the same fashion, as a free agent. She is united with her closest relations and her nearest neighbours. She is defending her own.

The project of a South East Asian Treaty Organization is in a very different category. Until Mr. Dulles, on the eve of the Geneva Conference,* began to press for the immedi-

---

*The most important concern of the Geneva Conference (April-July 1954) was the settlement of the struggle in Indo-China. The French and their Vietnamese allies had been unable to overcome the resistance of Ho Chi Minh and the Communists, and early in 1954 their failure was confirmed by

ate creation of such a pact, we had not heard a great deal of talk about it. We had, as a matter of fact, heard relatively little talk for some time about Southeast Asia itself. It was therefore with something of a shock of surprise and consternation that the Western world began to realize that the position of the French was rapidly deteriorating and that there was a growing body of opinion in France which was prepared to end the costly struggle at almost any sacrifice. At this point, Mr. Dulles produced his suggestion of a defence pact, and Mr. Eden made an alternative proposal—a proposal the inspiration of which goes back to a period much more peaceful than this—of an eastern Locarno agreement.

The Canadian government has announced that it does not propose to join a Southeast Asian organization, presumably of either of these two kinds, or, indeed, of any kind. This is an eminently sensible decision. But the reasons which have been advanced in support of it are not quite so satisfactory. The Canadian government has explained its disinclination to accept this new obligation on the ground that it is already too heavily committed elsewhere. There is a good deal of sound sense in this argument; but in the particular case of Mr. Dulles's new defence scheme, it is the dubious nature of the enterprise itself, as well as Canada's inability to take part in it, to which the Canadian government should have frankly pointed in explanation of its

the loss of the stronghold of Dien Bien Phu. Great Britain believed that compromise was now essential and that the partition of Vietnam along the lines already adopted by Korea was the best solution. The United States, in the full flight of its messianic campaign for the containment of Communism in the Far East, was reluctant to accept any recognition of the authority of Ho Chi Minh, and urged joint American and British military intervention in aid of France. France, which at first considered these proposals, suddenly decided to seek an immediate ceasefire. The agreement that was finally reached at Geneva provided for the temporary partition of Vietnam along the 17th parallel and for a tripartite commission (Canada, Poland, and India) which would supervise the armistice and subsequent elections in Vietnam as a whole. The United States refused to sign the agreement.

refusal. What territories in Asia would we be defending? Where would a defensible line be drawn? Is this a genuine movement of a self-defence which has developed spontaneously in Asia, and, if so, what important Asian powers are sponsoring it? Would we be co-operating with Asians for their own protection, or would we be merely assisting Western imperialist powers to retain their holdings and their influence in southeast Asia? The new prime minister of France has triumphantly carried out his promise to negotiate an armistice in Indo-China. Great Britain, France, and the Netherlands have ended, or nearly ended, the colonial period in Asia. Should we put ourselves in the position of seeming to perpetuate colonialism, at the behest of the United States?

IV

For nearly ten years now the West has been creating defences, first against aggression in general, and secondly against the aggression which the uncertain ambitions of the Soviet Union appeared to threaten. On the whole, the task of building up the economic and military power of the West has now been done. And Canadians, who have accepted large commitments, general and particular, to the United Nations and NATO, should be satisfied with the part they have played in it. It was an imperatively necessary labour. But it was, nonetheless, a negative one. It made no positive contribution to the attainment of a general peace. It increased, rather than relaxed, the dreadful international tension of the last few years. The relaxation of that tension has now become the chief aim of foreign policy; and at Geneva the world made more progress in a shorter time towards its goal than people would have believed possible six months ago. Although the press of North America characteristically tried to belittle and misrepresent the Geneva Conference, its importance was nevertheless very great.

What can Canada contribute towards the achievement of a general settlement? Canada's first duty is to remember that she is a separate and autonomous nation in North America. Her most important contribution will be to speak her own mind politely but firmly on all occasions. In March Mr. Pearson made a very reasonable protest against the assumptions implied in Mr. Dulles's famous statement that in future the United States would "depend primarily upon a great capacity to retaliate instantly, by means and at places of our choosing". The phrase "our choosing", Mr. Pearson reminded his Washington listeners, could mean only an agreed collective decision; and an agreed collective decision could be reached only after consultation and discussion. Discussion, moreover—and it is an important point—may reveal differences of opinion; and these differences must not be hushed up, by a species of political blackmail, on the ground that their publication will cause gratification in Moscow or displeasure in Washington. The glory of Western civilization lies in the rich diversity of the nationalities and cultures which compose it; and what Mr. Pearson calls the "overriding claims of unity" must not be taken to justify an enforced and sullen uniformity. In a society of free nations, as in a community of free men, the right of private judgment and the right of free speech are basic.

Canada must use these rights and use them in the interests of realism, moderation, and good sense. No encouragement should be given to Far Eastern security pacts which include such discredited satellites as the Chinese Nationalist régime in Taiwan and in which independent Asian nations are unwilling to participate. No support should be granted to those who wish to impose some hasty solution upon a problem which has aroused such obvious and serious division in Europe and Great Britain as German rearmament. Our aim ought to be to enlarge the circle of nations which maintain ordinary diplomatic relations with each other, just as it is our natural human impulse to keep on speaking terms with those with whom we have to live and work. The Geneva Conference effectively dispelled the self-righteous fiction that the Chinese are diplomatic untouchables, and the acceptance of the government of the Chinese Republic as the effective government of China and its admission to the morally vacant seat in the Security Council of the United Nations are decisions which Canada and the rest of the world cannot afford to postpone much longer. Canadian opinion is something which the world now regards with a measure of interest and respect; and in the United Nations, in NATO, and in the Commonwealth, Canada occupies positions in which she can exercise considerable influence. NATO links us with Europe: the Commonwealth brings us in touch with the East. And it is vitally important for Canadians to use and rely upon associations which unite contrasted cultures and bridge continents. North America is not the world; and the world will not willingly accept North American domination.

Brian Mulroney's free trade
("opening up world markets")

The Myth of Biculturalism

For six years, ever since the lately deposed Premier Jean Lesage won power in the Province of Quebec, English Canadians have been subjected to what is undoubtedly the most extreme example of the political hard sell in their entire experience. For six long years, the advocates of French-Canadian "nationalism" have used every conceivable form of persuasion, compulsion, shock, and menace to compel English Canadians to buy a particular view of Confederation and of French Canada's place in it. This prolonged siege of promotion, like every other well-organized campaign of commercial pressure, has certainly had its conquests. A good many English Canadians, faced with this rapid, interminable flow of sales talk, have acted as simple, gullible, badly informed consumers often do: they have bought the product.

Like all successful promoters, the French-Canadian nationalists hit upon a completely novel approach, a gimmick, for their campaign. English Canadians had always known about French Canada and the problem of its relation with the nation as a whole. Our fathers and grandfathers had called this "the race question". But the phrase had an antiquated, nineteenth-century look. It plainly wouldn't do as a modern slogan. Something much more up-to-date, more impressive, more vaguely "sociological" was obviously required. And, in a happy moment of inspiration, the French-Canadian theorists found it. They began to insist that "ethnic and cultural values" were, and ought to be recognized as, the fundamental values in Cana-

First given as a lecture to the Alumnae Association of University College. University of Toronto, 12 March 1966 and published in *Saturday Night*, September 1966.

dian society. They appropriated two fine, big words, "bilingualism" and "biculturalism", to describe the ideal at which Canadian society ought to aim. Their campaign had not got very far when it was given magnificent official recognition and approval by Prime Minister Pearson, who obligingly established a Royal Commission on Bilingualism and Biculturalism. This was the contemporary equivalent of the coat-of-arms on labels and cartons which used to signify that certain products, "By Appointment", enjoyed the patronage of the royal family. Prime Minister Pearson, By Appointment, had decided to patronize bilingualism and biculturalism. And, after that, they were all the rage.

The acceptance of these values as basic implied a completely new way of looking at Canada and Canadian Confederation. It grotesquely exaggerated the importance of language and culture; it absurdly minimized the importance of everything else. Until then, Canadians had regarded the political, economic, and financial relations of the Dominion and the provinces as the most significant features of the Canadian federation—or, for that matter, of any other federation. They were now informed, in the most authoritative fashion, that these classic aspects of federalism were completely subordinate to what ought to be its real essence in Canada. Its real essence, they were told very firmly, must henceforth lie in the formal recognition of the Canadian cultural duality. It didn't matter very much whether Canadian Confederation provided good government and promoted economic growth. It didn't matter very much whether Canada was united at home and respected abroad. All that really mattered was whether Confederation satisfied French-Canadian cultural needs and fulfilled French-Canadian cultural aspirations.

This revolution in our way of thinking about Confederation—it is certainly not a "quiet" revolution, but extremely vociferous—has been brought about within the last half-dozen years by two sets of people: by the spokesmen for the Province of Quebec, and by the advocates of

French Canada as a whole. A fairly clear distinction should be made between the two groups, for in the main they have sought different objects. The advocates of French Canada have tried to improve the position of the French Canadian in the nation as a whole; the spokesmen for Quebec have exalted their province as the sole adequate expression of the French fact in North America. The first group believed—and believes—in a bilingual, bicultural, but still united Canada; the second group has pinned its faith to a virtually independent Quebec. There is, of course, a third group, whose members apparently hope to attain both goals at once, though there is an obvious and basic contradiction between them. It is hardly possible, at one and the same time, to co-operate in a bilingual but united Canada, and to shut oneself up in the cultural isolation of Quebec.

Though they differ in their ultimate aims, both groups regard cultural values as basic. And they insist that radical changes are necessary to give these values their place in Canadian Confederation. The advocates of French Canada argue that it ought to be possible for a French Canadian to participate in every aspect of Canadian life from coast to coast and yet to retain his language and to maintain his cultural identity. The spokesmen for Quebec insist that there are two nations in Canada, not one, and that an increasingly detached Quebec state is the only satisfactory expression of French-Canadian nationalism. At its fullest extent, the program of the first group might include the establishment of French as an official language in the provincial legislatures, courts, municipal bodies, and public administration of all or most of the English-speaking provinces, as well as provision for education in French from the nursery school to the graduate school, whenever and wherever it is desired. The demand of the second group, at its most extreme, is for the complete separation and independence of Quebec; but theorists of the "associate state" for Quebec go almost as far and even supporters of the

THE MYTH OF BICULTURALISM

"special position" for Quebec are not a very long way behind.

Obviously either or both of these programs—the bilingual but united Canada and the "separate" or "special" Quebec—would mean a revolution in the present structure of Confederation. That structure is, of course, an inheritance of the past; and anybody who desires political and social change, or is merely interested in its possibility, must concern himself with history. Revolutionaries realize this necessity; and over the centuries they have developed two different and, in fact, quite contradictory ways of coming to terms with history. The first method is to reject the past as irrelevant to the present; the second is to identify the past with the revolutionary aims of the present.

Both these tried and tested methods have been used by those who want to remake Canadian Confederation with cultural and ethnic values as their guide and inspiration. It has been said, by those who ought to know better, that the British North America Act of 1867 is hopelessly outdated and ought to be thrown out, and a handsome new constitution triumphantly installed in its place. This, on the whole, is the more popular method of dismissing Canadian history; but, as I have said, there is another method, more subtle, more sophisticated and, to some, more plausible. This is not to dismiss the Confederation settlement of 1867 as outworn and inappropriate to the present, but to argue that it has been misunderstood, that its true meaning has been lost or forgotten, and that the truth has finally been rediscovered by, of course, the revolutionaries themselves. Confederation, the historical revisionists now insist, *looks* as if it were merely a political union of a few British North American provinces; but these appearances are completely and woefully misleading. The real, inner truth is that Confederation is a compact between two ethnic groups, the two founding cultures, English and French, of Canada.

What is the truth of these theories when tested by the actual decisions of 1864-7? Have we lost the true meaning of Confederation or have the changed circumstances of a century of history made it invalid for the present?

II

The bases of Confederation were laid at three conferences: at Charlottetown, Prince Edward Island, at Quebec, and at London, England. The conference at Charlottetown was preliminary and the discussions of federal union there were purely unofficial. The real work was done at the Quebec Conference, which arranged a federal scheme in seventy-two resolutions, called the Quebec Resolutions. The third conference, which was held in 1866, two years later in London, revised the Quebec Resolutions; and they were then embodied in the British North America Act of 1867.

The theorists of Confederation as a bicultural compact insist, by implication, that we must look at these events in a very special way. We are invited to regard the Quebec Conference as a mid-Victorian Royal Commission on Bilingualism and Biculturalism in British North America, with John A. Macdonald anticipating the great role of A. Davidson Dunton, and George E. Cartier that of André Laurendeau. We are asked to picture the four French Canadians at Quebec—Cartier, Taché, Chapais, and Langevin—sitting on one side of the table and resolutely confronting twenty-nine assorted English-speaking Canadians, Nova Scotians, New Brunswickers, Newfoundlanders, and Prince Edward Islanders on the other. In fact, of course, nobody would have dreamed in 1864 of constituting such a meeting along ethnic or cultural lines. The Quebec Conference, as well as the other two, were meetings of provinces. Voting was by province, with Nova Scotia, New Brunswick, Newfoundland, and Prince Edward Island each being given one vote, and the Province of Canada two. Canada's two votes, however, were not given because the Province was divided into two ethnic groups, but because it was organized politically in two administrative divisions, Canada East and Canada West, which had previously been the two separate provinces of Lower and Upper Canada, and were soon to become the two separate provinces of Quebec and Ontario.

The conferences were not organized on ethnic or cultural lines, and their purpose was not a bilateral cultural agreement. On the contrary, their purpose was a political agreement between Canadians, both English-speaking and French-speaking on the one hand, and Maritimers on the other. It must always be remembered that the great aim of Confederation was a strong federal union of all the British provinces and possessions on the North American continent; and therefore the first object and the most difficult task of the Canadians at the conferences was to persuade the Maritimers to unite with them in founding the new nation. It was the Maritimers who had to be convinced; it was the Maritimers who offered criticisms and objections. There were twenty-one Maritime delegates at the Quebec Conference, nearly twice as many as the twelve Canadians. They talked more than all the Canadians and far more than the French Canadians, most of whom, according to the surviving records, had very little to say.

None of the delegates, moreover, either Canadians or Maritimers, showed much concern for ethnic or cultural values; they gave the French language and the French civil code comparatively little attention. What took up the greater part of their time at Quebec and London was the discussion of federal institutions, the two houses of parliament, and the division of powers between the Dominion and the provinces; and these are, of course, the classic problems of every federal country, whether it is culturally homogeneous or culturally heterogeneous. The special aim of these British Americans at Quebec was to create a strong, centralized federation which would avoid the decentralizing weaknesses of the American federal system, and would never break apart, as the American union then seemed to be doing, in a civil war. It is sometimes suggested or implied that this ideal of a strongly centralized federation was merely a private whim or notion of John A. Macdonald's, which was never completely accepted by the other delegates and dubiously regarded by many of them. This is another of the many myths of Canadian history. Two attempts were made at Quebec, by a tiny group of delegates, to challenge Macdonald's theory, and both were decisively beaten.

These were the major themes of the debates at the conferences. In comparison, the discussion of ethnic and cultural questions occupied a very minor part of the proceedings. The resolutions adopted on cultural matters were important and essential; but they were few, very precise in their wording, and limited in their scope. There was nothing that remotely approached a general declaration of principle that Canada was to be a bilingual or bicultural nation. All the intentions of the Fathers of Confederation concerning language are summed up in Section 133 of the British North America Act. This section provides that English and French shall have equal official status in Parliament and the courts of Canada, and in the legislature and courts of Quebec. A Canadian therefore has the constitutional right to plead in English or French in the courts of Canada or Quebec, or to speak in English or French in the Parliament of Canada or the legislature of Quebec; the laws of Canada and of Quebec and the records and journals of the Parliament of Canada and of the legislature of Quebec are to be printed in both French and English. Even on the face of it, these rights are obviously very precise and limited; and there are other, more serious limitations which are perhaps not apparent on the surface. The most important of these limitations is that there are only two courts of Canada: the Supreme Court and the Exchequer Court at Ottawa. All the other Canadian courts are provincial courts, constituted and maintained by the provinces; and this means, of course, that the French language has no official standing in the courts of any of the provinces, except in those of Quebec. The second limitation is that only the acts, records, and journals of the Canadian Parliament and the Quebec legislature must be printed in English and French. There is no constitutional requirement that the Canadian government should use both languages in any of its other publications, or in any of its administrative activities.

There is no evidence that the French-speaking delegates at the Conference, or the French-speaking members of the Canadian legislature, were dissatisfied with these provisions. There is no evidence that they tried to extend these language rights to the legislatures, courts, or schools of any or all of the other provinces. If any such proposals had been made, one can be reasonably certain that they would have been rejected. No special concessions to the French language had ever been considered, or even suggested, in Canada West (the future Ontario) or in Nova Scotia, Newfoundland, or Prince Edward Island. In New Brunswick, a few years earlier, it had been proposed, not that French should be permitted in the legislature, but simply that a French translation of the debates should be printed. S. L. Tilley, who led the New Brunswick delegation to the Quebec Conference, had rejected this proposal on the ground that the Gaelic, Welsh, and German minorities in the province had just as much right as the French to a translation in their own language.

The case for Confederation as a bicultural compact is so

completely imaginary that its advocates are prudently inclined to define it as an "extra-legal", "implicit", or "tacit" agreement. If they were honest with themselves, and with the Canadian people, who have had to put up with enough nonsense on this subject, they would admit candidly that there is no evidence for their theory at all. Instead they keep insisting that a bicultural compact did exist, not perhaps in the letter of the law but in an unspoken moral commitment. They go on to argue that this moral commitment to biculturalism, though perhaps not adequately expressed in the British North America Act, was carefully honoured by the Fathers of Confederation when they took over the northwest from the Hudson's Bay Company and established the first governments on the prairies. It is true, of course, that French was given official standing in the legislatures and courts of Manitoba and the Northwest Territories and that separate schools, in which French was frequently the language of instruction, were established at the beginning; but to argue that these facts prove the existence of a deliberate bicultural commitment and demonstrate its political wisdom is simply to perpetuate another wishful invention. There is evidence which suggests strongly that these decisions were taken, not deliberately, but reluctantly, or under duress. There is no doubt that the attempt to make Manitoba and the Northwest Territories western replicas of the Province of Quebec was made prematurely and unwisely before the prairies had time to develop their true and permanent character. As soon as its true character had been formed, the west turned with determination against the inappropriate constitution which had been imposed on it; and the resulting controversy, which was as prolonged and bitter as anything in Canadian history, ended in the virtually total rejection of biculturalism.

III

From all this evidence, there is only one possible conclusion. The idea of a bicultural compact, implicit in the B.N.A. Act, explicit in the original constitutions of Manitoba and the Northwest Territories, is a myth. The language rights which the French Canadians asked and which the Fathers of Confederation intended they should be given are as they stand in the B.N.A. Act—nothing less and nothing more. No moral commitment has been dishonoured and no contract broken; there is no reason for a sense of guilt and no case for making amends. The simple truth is that French Canada and the Province of Quebec have not got less than they were promised in 1867; they have, in fact, been given infinitely more. The B.N.A. Act merely stipulates that both English and French may be used in the debates, and shall be used in the records, journals, and acts of the Parliament. Obviously the federal government has not kept within these precise and narrow legal requirements. As the state has enlarged its sphere in the Canadian economy and multiplied its services to the Canadian people, the usage of the two languages on a basis of equality has been extended through all the multifarious publications of the modern welfare state, and in such national enterprises as the Film Board and the Canadian Broadcasting Corporation.

But this, of course, does not finish the argument. To contend, as I have done, that the idea of a bicultural compact at Confederation is a myth, does not provide a convincing answer to all those who demand drastic constitutional changes in the interest of French Canada as a whole or of an autonomous Quebec. There remains the second revolutionary argument, which, as I have said, is the direct antithesis of the first. The people who use this second argument announce with beautiful and disarming simplicity:

"We have not the slightest interest in what happened in 1867; we don't care in the least whether the meaning of Confederation has been misunderstood or whether its spirit has or has not been honoured. We regard the British North America Act of 1867 as an obsolete relic of the past which is completely irrelevant and valueless to the circumstances and needs of the present. We believe that constitutional changes which will give cultural values their true place in Canadian Confederation are necessary for one simple reason: The French fact in Canada has changed."

At this point, we are entitled to ask: changed in what way, and how far? Not very much statistically, it would seem at first sight. Canadians of French origin amounted to about 31.06 per cent of the population in 1871, the first census after Confederation, and to 30.37 per cent in 1961. Though the proportion of French by ethnic origin has declined very little, it has certainly not gained. It looks fairly stable; but when we turn from population by ethnic origin to population by mother tongue—which is, of course, the only accurate index of the number of people actually speaking French—it quickly becomes clear that this stability is far more apparent than real. The portion of the Canadian population which is French by mother tongue amounted in 1961 to 28.09 per cent; in other words, a considerable number of Canadians of French origin have ceased to speak the French language. About 7.5% of the total population of French Canada has changed languages in this way; but if Quebec is excluded from the calculation, the decline of French appears much more steep, particularly in Ontario and the western provinces. In Ontario, nearly one out of three persons of French origin now speaks English; in Manitoba, a little more than one out of four; in Saskatchewan, nearly two out of five; in Alberta, one out of two; and in British Columbia, two out of three.

The plain fact is that a large number of French Canadians have found it to their interest or advantage to speak

English rather than French. And there is every evidence that this tendency will increase rather than lessen in strength. In North America, north of Mexico, there are close to two hundred million people who either speak English now or will learn to speak it shortly, in all normal activities of life. English, so firmly established in international business and technology, is becoming the language of the world; and the centre of its dominance lies in North America. If we Canadians had decided—and the decision should have been made a long time ago—to turn our backs upon the Canadian-American border, if we had determined to live our own life and develop our own resources in comparative isolation, if we had declined American techniques, and rejected American standards, and refused American capital, then we might, conceivably, have fostered a fair measure of biculturalism. But, of course, we did none of those things. For two generations at least, English Canadians have increasingly insisted that they are North Americans of the first class; now—and this I take to be the real meaning of the so-called "quiet revolution" in Quebec—French Canadians are demanding the same status. We all want the good things North America has to offer. But if we insist on the North American way of life, we cannot avoid the dominant North American way of speech.

This is, if you like it, a change since Confederation; but it is not a change which holds out much hope for biculturalism in Canada. Moreover, there is a second change, in the Canadian constitution itself, which narrows the prospect still further. Canada has ceased to be the strongly centralized nation which the Fathers of Confederation intended. The balance of power, which the Fathers believed should incline decisively towards the Dominion, has now fallen sharply towards the provinces. This is partly because certain provincial resources and provincial functions of government have become vastly more important than was

Forsey's Co-fathers, or

ever expected. Mainly it is the calamitous result of a series of nineteenth- and early-twentieth-century decisions in the courts, particularly in the Judicial Committee of the Privy Council, decisions which have reduced the Dominion's legislative powers to a small fraction of what they were meant to be.

The Dominion's control of the Canadian economy has been perilously weakened; its place in the national life of Canada as a whole has been drastically reduced. And the consequence is that a great many important things that ought to be done nationally in Canada are done no longer by the Canadian Parliament; instead, they are done by the federal-provincial conference, a conference of the eleven sovereign governments of Canada, which has no place in the Canadian Constitution, but which meets more frequently and for much longer periods than it used to do, and decides our destinies in secret.

In these circumstances, what are the chances for constitutional changes that will promote bilingualism and biculturalism? Outside Quebec, the federal government is the one Canadian government which has any constitutional obligations to the French language; but the decline of the federal government's role in Canadian affairs sharply reduces the effect on the nation as a whole of any attempts it may make to promote biculturalism. The enlargement of the language provisions of Section 133 of the B.N.A. Act would require, under any amending formula likely to be adopted, the unanimous consent of all ten provinces and the Dominion; and for the moment the possibility of this can be dismissed. There remain the provinces. Could they and—what is equally important—should they attempt to improve the position of French by constitutional and administrative changes? It is, I think, highly unlikely that such attempts will ever be made in the western provinces or in British Columbia. The west has rejected biculturalism once; it will not voluntarily accept it a second time. Nor, it seems to me, will Ontario. Even if Ontario could be persuaded to make a considerable change in the status of the French language in the province, would the consequences be desirable? The plain truth is that the only positive result of such an attempt would be to increase the number of Ontarians who are not fluent in English and who are therefore handicapped in all the main activities of the province.

No, the movement to reconstitute Canada in the interest of bilingualism and biculturalism can have only one probable outcome—the creation of a separate, or virtually separate, Quebec. This could happen in one of two ways—either gradually and tacitly through the present decentralizing policies of the federal government, or suddenly and openly as a result of a positive decision to break up the federal union. The process of decentralization could conceivably go so far that Canada would lose the power to cope with a serious political or economic crisis and would simply disintegrate under its pressure. Or alternatively, the campaign for French-Canadian nationalism could be carried to the point at which English Canada would finally decide, in disgust and indignation, that it had had enough.

Either of these outcomes is now possible. If present tendencies continue, one or the other may become the probable destiny of Confederation. The division of Canada into two unequal parts, English and French, would mean an uncertain and hazardous future for both; but it would carry a far greater and more fundamental danger for the smaller than for the larger of the two divisions. It might result in the political disintegration of English Canada; but for French Canada its consequences would be cultural as well, in the broadest and deepest sense of the word. Separation would leave French Canada a small, exposed, culturally indefensible community in a monolithic English-speaking continent. Separation would probably mean the loss of political independence for both English Canada and French Canada. It would also mean the rapid decline and eventual extinction of the French language in North America.

The French language has survived in North America for one reason only: because Canada has survived. The Fathers of Confederation reached a settlement which gave the French language the best chance it will ever have on this continent. And if we try to improve on that settlement, we do so at our peril. ? Donald, Donald...

Nat. - Cdn. not as aware of Nat. identity at Confed. as were following WWII.
- Situation not same
ie Can - still closely tied to Brite & a continental mkt dominated by us not as developed at Confed and right up to WWII

Canadian Nationalism
and Its Opponents

IT IS ALWAYS difficult to set a date for the beginning of a political movement. Yet it seems to me that the conscious movement for the defence of Canadian nationalism had its origin in the famous debate over the trans-Canada pipeline in the parliamentary session of 1956. The first important fact to note about its career is that it began so late. Seventeen years had elapsed since the opening of the Second World War; and these seventeen years had utterly changed Canada's position in the world, seriously weakened her traditional defences, and left her isolated and vulnerable. But Canadians remained curiously unaware of the vast changes that had occurred in their circumstances. Our leaders made no attempts to devise national policies for a nation that was becoming increasingly solitary and unprotected. And then the trans-Canada oil pipeline—a project not vastly more significant than others that had passed unnoticed before—suddenly awakened us for the first time to an acute sense of the danger of our position.

Of course, there was nothing new at all in our freshly perceived state of perilous insecurity. It had come slowly but inexorably into existence over a great many years, and the Second World War had simply hastened the completion of its development. The war accelerated the decline and gradual dissolution of the British Empire–Commonwealth, and it brought the United States to a position of dominating authority and influence in the world of Western Europe and the Americas. It was the combination of these two enormous world changes that completely altered the Canadian situation. Until after the First World War, Canadians had assumed that membership in the British Empire–Commonwealth would help to ensure their survival as a separate nation in North America and at the same time extend their influence throughout the world. For the first half-century after Confederation Great Britain had remained Canada's chief market and the principal source of her immigrants and capital. Above all, the imperial connection—what I have called the Anglo-Canadian alliance—provided the only counterweight which could correct the huge imbalance of power on the North American continent.

After the First World War, this close association—political, economic, and social—between Canada and Great Britain began to lose its vitality, and the Second World War and its consequences hastened the decline. It became increasingly obvious that neither the United Kingdom nor Canada regarded the Commonwealth as the mainstay of its protection or prosperity. Under Churchill and his successors, England sought security in a special relationship with the United States and began seriously to consider the economic advantages of membership in the European Common Market. Canada was left alone in North America, in the immediate presence of the greatest military and industrial power on earth, a power which had successfully grasped the leadership of the Western world and whose authority in North America would henceforth be completely unchecked and uncontrollable.

This was the fate which nineteenth-century Canadian thinkers had always feared. For them, independence and separation from Great Britain simply meant isolation and weakness. How could four million Canadians, confronted by forty million Americans, achieve any real independence, George M. Grant, the principal of Queen's University, asked in 1872. Seventy-five years later, in the 1940s and 1950s, the same hopeless disparity of numbers existed; but nobody had yet grasped the fact that this huge American preponderance might seriously threaten Canada's identity and its control of its own destiny. A continental economy, dominated by the United States, was rapidly coming into existence, and a continental defence system had already supplanted the military and political alliance of the Commonwealth. The moral and cultural personality of Canada—the sum total of its values, standards, traditions, and beliefs—was assailed on all sides by the pervasive influence of the mass media—newspapers, periodicals, books, radio, television, and movies—of the American Republic.

In 1956, for the first time, Canadians seemed to awake from their supine inertia. For a moment they gained some dim, confused idea of what had been happening to them. The angry pipeline debate proved that the Canadian people could at last be roused to protest the takeover of their natural resources by American capital; but it also proved how difficult it was going to be to prevent or limit this growing and dangerous economic invasion. Despite the desperate resistance of the Opposition, the pipeline bill passed, only a few hours after the deadline C. D. Howe had set; and its passage was an ominous indication of the strength of the forces of American continentalism and of the relative ease with which it could overcome the obstacles that Canadians might try to put in its path.

From that moment, Canada did make occasional attempts to resist the gradual, persistent erosion of its independence; but no comprehensive and systematic strategy of defence was ever adopted. The Canadian efforts were isolated and piecemeal, tentatively advanced, and hurriedly abandoned at the first sign of risk or retaliation. In the fifteen years since the pipeline debate, there have been more retreats than advances on any of the three Canadian nationalist fronts, political, economic, and social. And while the political and economic leaders who negotiated the retreats have remained securely in power, the nationalists who tried to lead the advances have been dismissed, or defeated, or repudiated.

The heavy pressure of American influence is obvious in Canadian defence and foreign policy. The Ogdensburg Agreement of August 1940 established the Canada–United States Permanent Joint Board on Defence; and the military co-operation on a continental scale which it inaugurated was continued during the Cold War by the North American Air Defence Agreement (NORAD) of 1957. Like Great Britain and Australia, Canada gave general support to American power politics in the Cold War and even went so far as to contribute military assistance to that first inglorious endeavour of American imperialism in the Far East, the Korean War. It is true—and we must all be profoundly grateful for the fact—that Canada has never stooped to take any active part in that most criminal of all imperialistic ventures, the American intervention in Indo-China. But it is equally true—and must be admitted—that the Canadian sale of large quantities of war materials to the United States makes it impossible for us to escape the charge of complicity in this evil conflict. The only Canadian in power who dared seriously to question the wisdom of American leadership in defence and foreign policy was John G. Diefenbaker. He declined to make the automatic response to American initiative in the Cuban crisis in the autumn of 1962; he dared to postpone the adoption of nuclear weapons for the Canadian Armed Forces against the wishes of the Kennedy administration; and, as a result, he was attacked by the Kennedy administration, as well as by the official Liberal Opposition in Canada, and defeated by the Canadian people in the election of 1963.

The efforts to defend the Canadian economy from the

invasion of American capital have been equally short-lived and vain. It is ten years now since James Coyne, the governor of the Bank of Canada, tried to convince Canadians that they "must live within their own means"; and it is nearly eight years since Walter Gordon failed to persuade the Liberal Party to accept his takeover tax of thirty per cent on the sale of shares in Canadian corporations to foreign interests. Three years ago the Task Force headed by Melville Watkins completed its official government survey on the extent of American ownership and control in Canadian industry; and since that time a dozen books and scores of newspaper and magazine articles have kept Canadians fully informed about the steady onward march of American investment in almost every division of our economy. The popular protest has grown stronger with each successive takeover: the expansion of the Mercantile Bank, the transfer of the Denison Mine and the Home Oil Company, and the huge sale of natural gas to the United States have all provoked strong and prolonged critical comment. But in the main the government has remained unmoved by this nationalist clamour. If it has acted, it has acted indirectly, privately, and sometimes at the last moment; and, despite repeated promises, it has not yet produced a comprehensive plan of defence. The 3 Be Option - Plus 1988

In the face of all this, the moral and cultural identity of the Canadian people has had a hard struggle to survive. The Canada Council has done much for Canadian scholarship and the arts; and successive regulatory bodies have tried to save the airwaves for Canadian interests, issues, and talents. But the struggle to compete with American television programs and to combat the changing technology of American broadcasting has overtaxed the resources of the Canadian industry, just as the popularity of American periodicals has proved too much for Canadian magazines. Ten years ago a royal commission made recommendations for the promotion of a genuine Canadian periodical press. The bill, based on this report, which was passed a few years later, placed certain tax disabilities on foreign publications; but the two most popular American periodicals in Canada were specifically exempted from these provisions. American publishing houses have become increasingly active in Canada in recent years; one veteran Canadian house and a division of a second have been taken over by American interests. A third, the largest wholly Canadian-owned and controlled publishing business in the country, was put up for sale a few months ago and was rescued only by the intervention of a provincial government.

II

The story of the Canadian national movement during the fifteen years that followed the pipeline debate is a dismal story, full of retreats and defeats and frustrations. The nationalists have had some good leaders, a copious and effective supply of statistical ammunition, a good deal of interest and some support from the press, and apparently a large and vocal following among the Canadian people. Yet they seem to have achieved virtually nothing. What has gone wrong? Why are the results so tragically disproportionate to the effort expended? Was the Canadian nationalist movement doomed from the beginning? Or is its comparative failure up to now attributable to some vital defect in its strategy and tactics? Who are the principal opponents of Canadian nationalism? What are the reasons for their opposition and what forces can they bring to the attack?

In Canada, as in most other nations in the late twentieth century, nationalism has been opposed by two forces of great potency—by internationalism on the one hand, and by provincialism and localism on the other. These two forces are complementary in their destructive effects; they are the upper and nether millstones between which the nineteenth-century national state has been steadily ground down and weakened. Nationalism, the great creative force of nineteenth-century politics, has for the last two generations been increasingly subjected to criticism and disparagement; and perhaps the most important of the powerful solvents which have led to its disintegration is the group of ideas, interests, and aspirations implied in the word internationalism. Internationalism can, of course, have an economic, a cultural, or a political meaning; but fundamentally it rests upon a single ideal—the belief that the only hope of humanity rests on the possibility of a peaceful world order. Nationalism, these idealists assume, breeds division and conflict; internationalism will bring peace. Nationalism is therefore morally inferior to internationalism; and nationalists are ordered, as I was ordered recently by a censorious reviewer, to abandon what he called my "parochial proclivities" and to look on Canada in the "broader context of international society".

Stated in these impressive terms, internationalism appears as a noble and appealing idea; but, under a more critical scrutiny, its specious excellence begins to take on a curiously spurious appearance. Logically, I suppose, the ideal of complete world concord can be realized only through the establishment of a homogeneous and universal state; and whether this would be desirable, even if it were possible, is a question many of us might find difficult to answer. In the meantime, we know very well that the present division of the world into a large number of supposedly sovereign states is likely to continue indefinitely into the future. We are also well aware of the fact that the second attempt in the twentieth century to found an organization—the United Nations—for the maintenance of international peace and security has grievously disappointed the high hopes of its creators. The first attempt—the

League of Nations—collapsed in the Second World War, after only twenty years of existence. The United Nations has survived longer; but how tragically has it failed to attain the first of the declared objectives of its charter, "to save succeeding generations from the scourge of war".

The truth is that the international ideal has not yet succeeded in creating an effective world organization. On the other hand, it has helped to bring into being several regional associations of states, often on a continental scale, and usually dominated by a superpower. Ever since the beginning of the Cold War, the superpowers, each with its attendant string of satellite states, have become the dominant fact of modern politics. They are now the empires of the twentieth century; and it is their imperialistic rivalries, and not the contentions of the smaller states, which alone seriously endanger the peace of the world. If nuclear war, which will destroy the world, ever breaks out in Europe, or the Middle East, or the Far East, it will come, not as a result of the quarrels of the small powers of the region, but because of the intervention on a grand scale of the superpowers. It is imperialism, not nationalism, which poses the greatest threat to the peace of the world. And yet, in the absence of any effective system of international security, the imperialistic pull of the superpower is so great as to be almost irresistible. Canada has succumbed to it; and since that genuine international organization, the British Empire–Commonwealth, to which she once belonged, has now virtually dissolved, she has become a dependent member state of the American Empire.

When Canadians defend or extol internationalism, this is the strictly limited kind of internationalism that they have in mind. Dale Thomson, the Canadian critic who sanctimoniously invited me to see Canada "in the broader context of international society", is at present resident in Washington, the capital of the United States of America; and from that vantage point it is easy and natural for him to comprehend the whole of North America in a truly imperial vision. The Canadian advocates of internationalism are not really talking about internationalism at all; they are talking about North American continentalism. The international ideal is not the justification, but merely the excuse, for the continental empire dominated by the United States. Our first task is to expose this pious fraud and to free ourselves from its spurious moral compulsions. Our second and much more difficult need is to gain a clear view of the enormous and varied power of continentalism, and of the tight grasp it has already acquired on our actions and our thoughts. *Sounds like Free Trade*

Continentalism means the increasing organization of the activities of North America along continental lines under the leadership and direction of the United States. Political sovereignty may remain formally separate for a long time to come; but the chief governing decisions in defence, foreign policy, economic growth, and cultural development will increasingly be made, not by Canadians, but by Americans. This system, which has come gradually into existence over the past half century, has already conferred enormous material benefits on Canada and will no doubt continue to do so. It cannot give us security, for this is impossible in the nuclear age; but it can at least ensure us the protection of the greatest of the superpowers. The capital, the enterprise, the technology, and the technological skills of the most heavily industrialized and economically powerful nation in the world are all freely available to us on terms not very different from those required of its own citizens. We can enjoy the comforts, the luxuries, and the excitements of the most affluent and spendthrift continent in the world. We can continue to fill the ever-increasing hours of our leisure time with the endlessly varied products of the most elaborate entertainment industry on earth.

Canadians, of course, do not get all this largesse for nothing. They pay for it and the price is extremely high. In effect, they put themselves and all that they possess or may acquire under the control and direction of their neighbours. Their natural resources—their metals, oil, gas, water, and water power, the very birthright of the Canadian people—will be offered up to meet the voracious demands of the American military and industrial machine and unappeasable appetites of a lavish American society. The knowledge, the abilities, the professional and technical skills which the expensive Canadian educational system has created, will go to serve, not companies owned and controlled in Canada, but huge international or multinational corporations whose plans and policies are adopted in the United States. The rapid growth of industrialism and urbanism in Canada and the increasing dependence of the Canadian people on the proliferating marvels of technology will gradually weaken and break down the native Canadian moral standards and cultural values, and undermine the inherited Canadian belief in an ordered and peaceful society and a gentle and simple way of life.

These predictions are not baseless or extravagant. They may very well take place. And a good many Canadians are uneasily aware of this frightening possibility. Yet they shrink back, intimidated, if not appalled, by the risks and the costs which seem inextricably involved in any decisive change in the steady course Canada has followed so long. The truth is that Canadians, in accepting American capital, American management, and American technology, have unwittingly received the spirit that animates all three. Not only have they become subjects of the American continental empire, but they have also become converts to its characteristic philosophy of life, to what might legitimately be called its religion. The central doctrine of this religion is the belief that progress is the only good in life and that progress means the liberation of man through the progressive conquest of nature by technology. In the satis-

faction of man's wants lies the only meaning of his existence; and human wants can, of course, be altered, multiplied, and endlessly refined by modern advertising. There
must be no limitation on the indefinite expansion of man's
desires, no limitation on the capacity of modern industry
to satisfy them; and, as an inevitable consequence, the conquest of nature and the exploitation of its natural riches
must proceed swiftly and continually forward without stop
or hindrance. This new doctrine—the doctrine of contin-
ual economic growth—has captured the minds of Canadians, just as it has those of every other people in the
Western world. To achieve economic growth, they are prepared to sacrifice their independence, pillage their natural
resources, contaminate their environment, and endure all
the hideous evils of modern industrialization and urban-
ization. The American Empire is taking over the birthright of Canadians; and its imperial religion has taken
over their minds.

III

Continentalism, the only aspect of that question-begging
term "internationalism" that has any meaning for Canadians, is with little doubt the strongest opposing force
with which Canadian nationalism has to contend. But continentalism is merely the upper millstone; the lower millstone, parochialism or provincialism, is its complement;
and it is the attrition by these two powerful forces that has
ground down the solid fabric of Canadian nationalism.
The pressure from without may be the more powerful of
the two; but division within is a persistent enduring tendency in Canadian history going back to the disruption of
the British Empire in North America and the coming of
the Loyalists. The presence of the Loyalists led to the crea-

tion of a new province in the Atlantic region and to the division of the old Province of Quebec into Upper and Lower Canada. The mountain barrier of the Appalachians prevented any easy communication between the Canadas and the Maritime provinces. From the beginning, there was a strong strain of provincialism and localism in the history of British North America.

Confederation was the culmination of another and completely contradictory tendency in Canadian history—the urge towards unity and centralization for defence. Geographically, Canada is a western extension of the St. Lawrence River system, and the St. Lawrence has been a centralizing force in Canadian history. It is at once the symbol and the inspiration of the main style of Canadian endeavour, a transcontinental empire based on the east-west axis. From the days of the French régime, successive generations of Canadians have struggled to frustrate and defeat their rivals and to extend the dominion of the St. Lawrence to the western plains and the Pacific slope. These rivals, the Thirteen Colonies and the United States, were from the beginning more numerous and powerful than the northern provinces; and in order to compensate for their relative weakness and to adjust the balance of power on the continent, the British North American colonies which had survived the American Revolution began to follow two basic policies. They sought to retain the political, military, and economic support of Great Britain as a makeweight against the preponderance of the United States; and they drew slowly closer to union for better self-protection. The modern British Commonwealth, and the vital Anglo-Canadian alliance that underlay it, was the realization of the first aim; Confederation was the highest achievement of the second.

Both these strong supports of Canadian nationalism have declined. The slow dissolution of the British Empire–Commonwealth began half a century ago and the Anglo-Canadian alliance has ceased to act as a buttress of Canadian independence in North America. The descent from the high level of unity and centralization achieved in 1867 began early and has continued, with only brief interruptions, since. In part, this gradual diminution of national authority is an accident—the unexpected result of a series of legal decisions, particularly in the Judicial Committee of the Privy Council, which gave the provinces far more power than the Fathers of Confederation had ever intended them to have. But, if repeated strokes of meaningless bad luck have played a part in the process, the dismemberment of Canada must also be attributed to certain clearly discernible causes. At the centre of the decline lies the deterioration of the St. Lawrence itself as the chief factor in Canadian history. The east-west axis, transcontinental and transatlantic, has ceased to represent the main thrust of Canadian ambition and endeavour. In the nineteenth and early twentieth centuries, the settlement and exploitation of the west was the great national enterprise in which all Canadians joined; but now Canadian economic activity has largely shifted its direction from west to north. The national economy created by east-west transport and traffic has been broken up into a number of regional or provincial economies, each of which is controlled and used for its own purposes by the province to which it belongs. The main trade routes, which used to run east-west across the continent and the Atlantic Ocean, have now been sharply diverted south. The United States has become the chief market for Canadian exports and the chief source for Canadian imports of capital and technology.

Much of the provincial assertiveness and national disunity of the last two decades can be traced back to economic sources; but much of it also has equally deep cultural origins. The aggressive cultural forces of present-day politics are not national but local, provincial, regional, inspired by race, language, or religion; and the sudden out-burst of separatism in Quebec is one more example of this angry divisive trend. The so-called Quiet Revolution be-gan as an attempt to preserve French-Canadian culture and to give French-Canadian citizens a larger place in the life of their province and of the nation as a whole. From the start, two methods were advocated as a means of achiev-ing this object: the first was the creation of a united, bilin-gual Canada and the second was the recognition of Quebec as a distinctly different province with a right to a special, separate status in Confederation. As time went on, the leaders of all political parties in Quebec have increasingly emphasized the second of these methods, and have steadily enlarged the scope of the legislative autonomy which they claim for their province. The differences among the Liber-als, the Union Nationalists, and the various kinds of sepa-ratists are no longer differences of kind, but simply of de-gree; and the consequences of all of them for Canadian na-tionalism would be almost equally disastrous. At the con-stitutional conference last June, the new Victoria charter, designed very largely to guarantee the official position of the French language and to protect other French-Canadian interests, was deliberately rejected by Quebec because it failed to satisfy her insatiable demand for provincial inde-pendence. When Claude Castonguay remarked with brutal candour that he had no interest whatever in Canada be-yond the borders of Quebec, he seems to have voiced only too accurately the feelings of its government, if not of all of its people.

This, then, is our troubled state at the present moment. The forces opposed to Canadian nationalism—American continentalism and Canadian particularism—are extreme-ly powerful and pervasive. None of the political parties by which the public life of this country is carried on has yet adopted a comprehensive program for the defence and preservation of Canadian nationalism. The Liberals hesitate to restrict the American economic invasion; the Conservatives have not urged them to adopt vigorous measures of protection; and the NDP, the one party which has taken a positive stand against all aspects of American domination, is split between those of its members who are willing to grant separate status to Quebec and those who are determined to refuse it. But Canadian nationalism can be preserved only by a comprehensive program in which resistance to excessive particularism and defence against aggressive continentalism is each an integral part.

We can save two cultures in a single nation; but not two separate nations and not ten quarrelling provinces. Our politicians have refused to acknowledge this truth because, like politicians the world over, they fear that, if they really tackle an important national issue, they will antagonize a powerful interest or an influential minority. Canadian nationalism is one of those causes, deep in people's hearts, that ordinary politicians never dare to touch. The nationalist movement in Canada must remain an apolitical movement, in the hope that if it cannot capture one party, it can influence them all.

Thank you Creighton — a term appropo to the Canadian provinces and yet never used — until now
:)

Continentalism and the Birthright of Canada

URING THE PAST twelve months, Canadians have become increasingly engaged in an earnest and ani-
mated public debate. Its subject is that most fundamental of all possible Canadian questions, the prospects
for Canada's survival as an independent nation. The debate has been centred mainly on various vital aspects of
our relations with the United States: the disputed Canadian claim to territorial sovereignty in the Arctic, the
steadily continuing takeover of Canadian industry and natural resources by American capital, and the gradual weakening of the Canadian cultural identity under the constant
hammering of the American mass media. The debate has
moved rapidly over the whole broad range of our political,
economic, and cultural relations with the United States,
gathering in intensity as it proceeded; but in the last few
months, it has become increasingly concentrated on a particular subject, the future of our key Canadian sources of
energy for modern industry and modern industrial society.
Mr. J. J. Greene, the Minister of Energy, Mines, and Resources, with his leonine head, deep-set, mournful eyes,
and poetic expression, has become the central protagonist
in the controversy, and the sale of natural gas to the
United States has emerged as the outstanding issue. It was
brought to a head at the end of September by the an-
nouncement that four companies had been given licences

First given as a convocation address at Laurentian University in November 1970, and published in the *Laurentian University Review*,
vol. 3 (3). February 1971, under the title "Reflections on the Amer-
icanization of Canada".

to export 6.3 trillion cubic feet of natural gas to the United States over the next fifteen to twenty years, and this in addition to the export licences for 12 trillion cubic feet which had already been granted. The very magnitude of the deal—it will commit, by Mr. Greene's own admission, 34 per cent of Canada's established gas reserves to the United States—partly explains its prominence in the eyes of many Canadians. But their disquietude goes deeper than this. And it is, it seems, important to understand the reasons for this anxiety.

In the first place, Canadians instinctively regard their natural resources in a very special light. They have grown accustomed and hardened, by constant repetition, to the American takeover of an endless variety of Canadian industries; but there are, nevertheless, certain key sectors of the national economy—its financial institutions, and its transport and communications systems, for example—over which they have tried with considerable success to retain control. The instinct to guard our natural resources—electric power, oil, gas, water, and forests—is perhaps even more powerful and profound. These natural resources are not looked upon as ordinary assets—things the Canadians have built or acquired themselves. They are regarded as part of the original endowment of nature, as the birthright of Canada. Many of them are not owned absolutely, as they would be in the United States, by private enterprises. They are properties in which the Crown retains a right, which it has sometimes converted into public ownership, for the beneficial interest of the people of Canada.

A very large part—a third, in fact—of one of these precious national assets has now been pledged to the exclusive use of the citizens of the United States. The size of the sale is huge, even if it stood alone as a solitary transaction; but a good many Canadians nurse the suspicion that it is very far from being a solitary transaction and that it will speedily be followed by others on a similar large scale. A great and powerful nation which becomes dependent on the energy it buys from its neighbour has a strong moral claim, which it will be quick to enforce, for the continuance of the original supply. The tap, once opened wide, cannot be abruptly turned off. On the contrary, it will probably be opened still wider. The Americans can be expected to insist, not only on the renewal and the substantial enlargement of the export licences for natural gas, but also on secure and uninterrupted access to most or all other Canadian sources of energy. The aim of the American economic and military establishment is to induce the Canadian government and people to acknowledge that Canada's natural resources—oil, gas, electric power, nuclear energy, and water—are in fact continental resources, freely available to Americans in exactly the same way as their own domestic supplies.

It is partly for this reason that the American government has been restricting the import of Canadian crude oil into the United States. It hopes in this way to compel the Canadian government to pay for an enlarged American market in oil by guaranteeing copious supplies of other sources of energy more urgently needed at the moment in the Republic. These prolonged negotiations, the first round of which has obviously been won by the United States, have been cynically but not inaccurately described as the "energy poker game". Canada, in all its relations with the United States, is very much like a poor man in a big poker game. He must match the big stakes in order to stay in the game, but his capital resources are very limited. His blue chips have now been nearly all lost and he is down to his original inheritance, his birthright. And a man who plays poker with his birthright is a fool. He is only too likely to be cleaned out.

It is this fate—the pillage of our basic resources and the destruction of our natural environment—that haunts the minds of Canadians. It alarms them all the more because, as they can see quite clearly, this is exactly what has happened in the United States. American natural resources have been wasted, contaminated, and depleted. The voracious requirements of the American industrial and military machine and the insatiable demands of an affluent and wasteful American society have now outstripped what the most richly endowed half-continent in the world can provide. The recent power failures and the discovery of a shortage of natural gas are only two indications that there is an end to the riches of even the most opulent country on earth. Canadians, like Americans, have been brought up to believe, as a cardinal article of national faith, that their natural resources were unbounded and inexhaustible. But now that complacent North American doctrine has been proved false—false at least so far as the United States is concerned. Why should we continue to believe it to be true for Canada? If Canada had decided to reserve its inheritance for its own people, this belief might have remained valid for generations to come. But we have now denied ourselves this choice; it will never be open to us again. We have come close to admitting that Canada is expendable in the service of the American technological empire.

The United States has become the most advanced technological society of modern times. The American people subscribe, with fewer reservations and qualifications than any other people on earth, to the belief that progress is the only good and that progress means the liberation of man through the progressive conquest of nature by technology. The possibilities of the future, it has always been confidently assumed, are infinite; there must be no limitation on the satisfaction of whatever human wants industry decides to create by modern advertising. But the resources of this small planet are not infinite: they are finite. They can either be used, wasted, and in the end completely exhausted, or, if they are renewable, they or the environment in which they grow can be so damaged and polluted by modern technology that they will disappear. These hard truths are being slowly, grudgingly admitted, even in the United States; and the Canadian government and the Canadian petroleum industry have been busily trying to soften their impact in Canada. They have sought to convince us, basing their case on the present trend of discovery and on the volume of Canadian sedimentary rocks, that our reserves of oil and gas will last indefinitely into the future. But these, of course, are estimates. The simple truth is that nobody knows, with any degree of exactness, what our resources are, and how far and how fast the domestic and foreign consumption of them is likely to grow.

The risk of depletion and the threat to the environment of vast areas of our Canadian north are, at the present moment, incalculable; but, in the meantime, we can be perfectly certain that this intensified exploitation of our sources of energy will soon have its effect on our export trade and on the Canadian economy as a whole. American and Canadian capital, effort, experience, and expertise will be flung into the production of this new staple; and its rapid and inevitable growth will deepen our already profound dependence on the export of natural products. Canada has always been a tributary and dependent country, producing huge supplies of raw materials for more specialized industrial nations; but latterly there has been a gradual shift towards greater diversity and refinement in Canadian industry. In the last twenty years crude materials have declined as a proportion of the total Canadian exports, and end products, or fully finished manufactures, have increased. All this slow movement towards greater economic strength through diversification and maturity will now be slowed; it might even be arrested if, as seems only too possible, the sale of natural gas is to be followed by a comprehensive deal in our other sources of energy, electric power, oil, gas, nuclear energy, and water. At this point, Canada, the recognized hinterland of the American metropolis, will have become fully integrated in a continental economy dominated by the United States.

Is this the future that the Canadian people want? And if they wish to escape from it, what are their chances of success? The forces of continentalism, actively encouraged by Canadian governments for nearly two generations, have become almost irresistible. They have virtually converted Canada into an economic, political, and cultural colony of the United States; and in the process of this recolonization they have profoundly altered the character of the Canadian people. Canadians now believe as fervently as Americans that progress consists in the conquest of nature by technology for the satisfaction of human wants. Our belief in economic growth has become a manic obsession; our faith in the wonders of technology is unlimited. Why not make a quick buck out of selling our natural resources now, when in twenty years' time we shall be getting our energy from nuclear power or solar heat? And why should we jealously reserve our riches for ourselves, in a selfish nationalistic spirit, when a far less well-endowed world is crying out for them? These arguments may carry conviction with Canadians, for their Canadian nationalism is as weak as their belief in material progress is strong; but they are spurious arguments nevertheless, which should not be permitted to delude us. All that technology has done so far is to ransack the treasures of a finite world; and all that the sale of our resources to the United States could do would be to strengthen the American military and industrial machine. We would not be promoting a genuine internationalism or helping to raise the world's standard of living. We would simply be feeding the gaping maw of the giant American corporations. They are often called multi-national or international corporations, which suggests that they serve the interests of all countries in which they operate with beautiful impartiality. Of course, they do nothing of the sort.

They serve their own interests, and they obey the laws and promote the aims of the government and people of the United States. They are, in fact, imperialist organizations. Internationalism is powerless to resist them; world peace and the world state are as far away as ever. The only power strong enough to prevent the destructive onward march of economic and military imperialism is the national state.

History and the Constitution

I APPEAR BEFORE this Committee reluctantly, and only because my friend Senator Forsey has overpersuaded me. I expect you will find what I have to say irrelevant and gloomy, and that you will think I have wasted your time. I have no changes of my own to propose in the constitution of Canada. I simply want to examine, very briefly, some of its origins and part of its development. It seems to me that reformers who are preparing to chart the future should know something of the past. But, if history can be used with profit, it can also be abused. This afternoon I should like to discuss some of the wrong conclusions that have been drawn from it, and some of the valuable lessons which I think it has to teach.

All those who advocate drastic constitutional change must adopt some attitude to history. A constitution which has developed with a country for even as little as a hundred years and has gradually adapted itself to every function of the national life inevitably acquires recognition and acceptance, and sometimes wins respect and affection. The first task of revolutionaries in all ages is to undermine and break down this established position, this prescriptive right, as Burke called it; and they usually set about it by taking one of two distinct approaches to history. Either the past can be dismissed as "the bad old times"—the times of ignorance, immaturity, tutelage, and oppression; or it can be extolled as "the good old times", the times of generous promises that have been forgotten and high ideals that

Originally delivered as a Brief to the Special Joint Committee of the Senate and the House of Commons on the Constitution of Canada on 6 April 1971 and published here in a slightly revised version.

have been killed by the letter of the law. In other words, history can be denigrated, or it can be idealized. Either it can be got rid of, or it can be re-interpreted to serve a revolutionary purpose or justify a revolutionary program.

The first of these two attacks has been much the more popular in Canada, and for two reasons. It is extremely simple and it looks thoroughly modern. The idea that everything old is worse and everything new is better has an irresistible appeal to the credulous; and the belief that rapid obsolescence is the basis of the good life has become the principal dogma of the popular religion of the age of affluence. In reality, of course, there is nothing new about these ideas at all: they are simply debased variants of the nineteenth-century belief in progress; and they are invariably expressed, by Canadians eager to alter the constitution, in appropriately hackneyed language and broken-down old metaphors. Thus, the Canadian constitution is denounced as "the dead hand of the past" which prevents Canada from keeping its "rendezvous with destiny". The British North America Act is derided as "a battered old hulk", "a relic of the horse and buggy days" or "a piece of antiquated mid-Victorian plumbing". And, in North America, everybody knows what must be done with antiquated plumbing. To mend it or repair it is unthinkable. It must be yanked out and replaced by what is invariably called in the advertisements "a new unit". And a truth which is incontestable for toilets and bathtubs must be equally valid for constitutions.

The phrases "mid-Victorian times" and "horse and buggy days" are used, of course, to insinuate that the past is irrelevant and valueless for the present. They are useful for purposes of disparagement; but the word "colonial", which also has a political meaning, is even more effective. "Horse and buggy days" calls up the picture of a simple, primitive, rustic age which Canada has outgrown; "colonial" suggests the idea of an inferior status of tutelage and subordination from which Canada has freed herself. The nation, say the constitutional revisionists, has now gained its maturity and won its independence from British imperial control; but, of course, this could not have been true in 1867. The Fathers of Confederation were colonials. They were the mental prisoners of the British imperial system. Their retention of the monarchy, parliamentary government, and membership in the British Empire was not—could not have been—their free choice; it was forced upon them by the dictation or the moral pressure of the imperial authorities. The burlesque climax of this travesty of our history is reached in the assumption that the British North America Act was not only passed by the Imperial Parliament but also drafted by imperial ministers and civil servants.

That these crude myths should have a certain currency in educated circles today is an indication of the depth of our historical ignorance. The Fathers of Confederation clung to constitutional monarchy because they believed that it was the best government ever devised for free men; they were determined to retain the imperial connection because they were convinced that it was essential to Canada's survival as an independent nation in North America and because they regarded the British Empire as the greatest secular force for good in the world at that time. If they had wished to separate from Great Britain in 1867, nothing would have been easier. Anti-colonial sentiment was running very strongly in England in the 1860s. Macdonald, Galt, and Brown were all sadly aware of the fact that a great many British Tories, Whigs, and Liberals would have preferred them to declare for separation and independence. Constitutional monarchy and the British connection were retained in Canada at Confederation, not because of British influence, but in spite of it. The British North America Act was the work, not of British ministers, governors, or civil servants, but of the thirty-four British

American delegates to the conferences at Charlottetown, Quebec, and London. When the London Conference ended, all the amendments to the Quebec Resolutions had been settled, except the provisions designed to overcome the resistance of the Senate in the case of a deadlock with the House of Commons, and even this had been agreed upon in principle. The British North America Act is exactly as the Fathers planned it, with one significant exception. They wanted to call their new nation a Kingdom; they had to be content with Dominion instead.

The historical fictions I have been discussing so far are assumed to prove that the Confederation settlement of 1867 has little or no meaning for modern Canada. To dismiss, to get rid of the past is the first impulse of most constitutional reformers; but some, in all ages, have adopted a more subtle approach. They believe that the past can be used for their purposes. History can be re-interpreted, if not rewritten, to provide a justification for the revolutionary cause. History thus becomes not "the dead past" or "the bad old times", but "the good old times", when a fine liberal spirit prevailed, when promises, since forgotten, were made, and pledges, never implemented, were given. There is at least one good illustration of this approach in the constitutional debate that has been going on in Canada for the past decade. Those who believe that Canada is, or ought to be, a bilingual and bicultural country have sometimes tried to find a warrant for their conviction in history. They have sought to prove that Confederation was not a political union of several provinces, but a cultural compact between two "nations", English and French. There is no evidence for this belief in the original Confederation settlement, and very little in the subsequent admission of the other provinces; but the absence of documentary proof does not always silence the advocates of the bicultural compact. They take refuge behind the defensive argument that the idea of the equal partnership of the two nations was an

unrecorded moral commitment which was the basis of the
agreement.

There are several expressions of this belief: one rather
simple example will have to suffice. It was said a while ago
in Parliament that in 1867 French-speaking Canadians accepted the language provisions of the British North America Act on "a temporary basis" only. "It is evident," the
speaker argued, "when we read the views then stated, that
the French Canadians expected eventually to secure the
constitutional equality of the two languages." *"When we
read the views then stated"*. What views, we may ask, and
when and where stated? In the winter of 1865, when the
Quebec Resolutions were submitted to the Canadian legislature for its approval, there were four French-speaking
ministers in the cabinet. Three of them, Cartier, Taché,
and Langevin, took an active part in the debate that followed, explaining, interpreting, and defending the Quebec scheme. If any one of them had been dissatisfied with
the language provisions, or had promised or predicted
their enlargement, this would have been the time and
place—and the only legitimate time and place—to make
himself clear; but not one of them uttered a word that implied such anticipations. Clause 46 of the Quebec Resolutions, which dealt with language, did come in for some criticism during the debate; but this was because of its phras-
ing, not its scope.

II

It is wrong to denigrate or idealize the past; but history
has its legitimate uses which should not be forgotten. A
nation which neglects or repudiates its past is very unlikely
to have a secure or prolonged future. In general, English-
speaking peoples have realized that the depreciation of

their heritage is dangerous, and this principle is often expressed in a special, formal declaration by the head of state. Our Queen took a coronation oath; the President of the United States promises to protect and defend the constitution. This does not mean, of course, even for the United States, and *a fortiori* for Canada, that the constitution is, and must be, what it was when it was first proclaimed. It is not a petrified relic of a bygone age, but a living creation, which should accommodate itself to changing conditions and respond sensitively to new demands. But at the same time it must not be false to its origins. Circumstances may modify a constitution; but they must not alter its essential character. If in the long run environment triumphs and ruins the original endowment of heredity, the constitution loses its integrity, and the nation whose political life it governs faces a very ambiguous future. This, it seems to me, is exactly the calamity that has overtaken Canada.

It is important to note that the constitution of 1867 was essentially a Canadian creation, a native product. Parliamentary government was indeed British in origin; but the northern provinces had adapted it, over a long period of time, to suit their special needs, and in the process had made it Canadian. In 1867 the provincial legislature of Nova Scotia was 109 years old, that of New Brunswick 82, and those of Ontario and Quebec both 75. It was these provincial legislatures, in which British Americans had gained control of their own affairs through the practice of responsible government, that provided the model for the institutions established in 1867; and it was the special British American experience and the distinctive British American needs that governed the division of powers. The federal constitution of 1867 was a characteristic Canadian creation, shaped by Canadian history, designed for Canadian purposes, and deliberately different from the constitution of the United States.

This constitution we have virtually lost. It has been altered radically and almost beyond recognition. And it is only when we go back to the declared intentions of the Fathers of Confederation that we can measure the extent of its mutilation. In Macdonald's eyes, the two principal features of the constitution of 1867 were parliamentary institutions and a strong central government. "The primary error at the formation of their [the American] constitution," he declared in his opening speech at the Quebec Conference, "was that each state reserved to itself all sovereign power save the small portion delegated. We must reverse this process by strengthening the general government and conferring on the provincial bodies only such powers as may be required for local purposes." The federal residuary power was the instrument with which Macdonald hoped to achieve this aim, and to it he attached enormous importance. "It is a wise and necessary provision," he told the Canadian Assembly in February 1865. "We thereby strengthen the central parliament and make the confederation one people and one government instead of five peoples and five governments with merely a point of authority connecting us to a limited and insufficient extent." The residuary clause would give the national legislature power and scope; it would provide room for future developments and thus ensure the flexibility which Macdonald thought so essential. "Our constitution," he said, "should be a mere skeleton and framework that would not bind us down. We have now all the elasticity which has kept England together."

There can be no doubt about Macdonald's convictions; but it is sometimes argued or assumed that his belief in the importance of the federal residuary clause was his own personal view, or perhaps that of himself and Tupper, and not the opinion of the Quebec Conference as a whole. This, like so many more of the strange fictions about Confederation, can be easily refuted by the evidence. The residuary clause was not passively accepted or unwillingly endorsed by the Conference; it was directly challenged by Chandler of New Brunswick and Coles of Prince Edward Island, who submitted a resolution exactly reversing Macdonald's proposal and giving residuary power to the provinces. In the end, after a long debate, Coles's resolution was rejected, with not a single provincial delegation voting for it.

It is impossible, and unnecessary, to describe in any detail the complete miscarriage of this great design in the courts. Gradually the general power of Parliament to legislate for the peace, order, and good government of Canada has been swallowed up by the examples which were intended to illustrate but not to restrict its scope; and the provincial power to legislate in respect of property and civil rights in the province has virtually replaced it as the real residuary clause of the Canadian constitution. The ominous words of Sir Montague Smith in the case of *Russell* v. *the Queen* have proved only too accurately prophetic. "Few, if any, laws," he said, "could be made by Parliament for the peace, order and good government of Canada which did not in some incidental way affect property and civil rights; and it could not have been intended to exclude Parliament from the exercise of this general power whenever such incidental interference would result from it." Of course, it was never intended that Parliament should be so excluded; but excluded it was, nevertheless. In 1896 Lord Watson did admit that questions which in origin were private and local might attain such national dimensions as to justify federal legislation, but Lord Haldane succeeded in restricting these possibilities to national emergencies such as war, pestilence, famine, and massive national intemperance. It is true that the attempt in 1946 to confirm this restrictive interpretation and to expunge the decision in *Russell* v. *the Queen*—that pale ghost of Macdonald's residuary clause—failed. Yet Lord Simon's judgment did no more than barely open the door which had been tightly closed against a more liberal interpretation.

In effect, the residuary clause, one of the two dominating principles of Macdonald's federal system, has been destroyed. The federal government has lost much of its power to deal with national issues on a national scale; and it has been deprived of most of the flexibility which the residuary clause was intended to ensure. The constitution which Macdonald hoped and believed would be simply "a skeleton and framework that would not bind us down" has in fact become intensely rigid and restrictive. It has failed to adapt itself, as it might so easily have done, to the myriad new functions of government which have developed with the rise of public ownership and state regulation. Without doubt, the Fathers intended that the control of the economy should be in the main a federal responsibility. In the debate on the Quebec scheme in the Canadian legislature, Cartier took care to reassure the businessmen of the future Province of Quebec that the protection and promotion of their interests would fall, not to the provincial, but to the general, government. The virtual nullification of this intention has left Canada without a known and recognized method of dealing with the successive crises which punctuate the onward march of technology and industrialism. Parliament, for example, is constitutionally incapable of dealing with the twin problems of inflation and unemployment by the methods recently proposed in Great Britain and now adopted in the United States; since the crucial constitutional decisions of the early 1920s, Canada has lacked the authority to control wages, prices, and rents in times of peace. In such circumstances, national action is possible only in the highly unlikely event that Ottawa and ten provincial governments could agree upon a common plan; and thus the federal-provincial conference takes over duties which the Parliament of Canada was intended to perform, and in effect becomes a fourth, dominating, but irresponsible level of government.

III

It is not only Macdonald's chief federal principle—the federal residuary power—which has been undermined and eaten away until nothing more than a shell remains. His second great principle—constitutional monarchy—on which the new political institutions of Canada were based, has suffered also, though in this case the decline is not outward and obvious, but hidden and unacknowledged. In part, this moral degeneration can be explained, as has been seen, by the popular assumption that the monarchy and parliamentary institutions were imposed on Canada by the imperial government, or accepted submissively by docile colonials without wills or minds of their own. Modern Canadians are ignorant of the fact that constitutional monarchy was maintained and continued by the Fathers, not simply because it was an inheritance which they enjoyed and valued for 100 years, but also because its superiority could be proved by reason and experience. During the 1850s and 1860s the new democratic and republican régimes in both Western Europe and North America had all collapsed tragically in defeat, authoritarian reaction, and civil war. British constitutional monarchy, which had outlasted them all and was tranquilly and successfully broadening its own popular base, stood at the apex of its prestige.

"In our constitution," said George Cartier, "the monarchical element would form the leading feature." Macdonald believed that the monarchy was a unifying institution to which all classes, creeds, and parties in the state would look up. The defect inherent in the constitution of the United States, he thought, was that the president was incapable of playing this role. "He is never considered as being the father of his people," Macdonald said. "He is at best but the successful leader of a party." This suspicion and dislike of a head of state who was the creature and servant of a temporary partisan majority was very strong in both Macdonald and Cartier; it is part of their fear of what Cartier called "mob rule", the tyranny of majorities; and it found expression in Macdonald's desire for "a strong and lasting government in which we can work out constitutional liberty as opposed to democracy". Constitutional monarchy, parliamentary institutions, and responsible government were the inseparable elements in such a system; and Macdonald frequently pointed out how superior this constitution was to the uneasy association of congress and president, each with its separate electoral base. In his opinion, the American president could be, and sometimes was, "a despot for four years".

There can be no doubt that these views were shared by the vast majority of Canadians at Confederation; but it is almost equally certain that in the last ten or twelve years the traditional Canadian belief in constitutional monarchy has been gradually weakened, not only by the opponents who hope to abolish it completely, but also by its alleged friends, who insist that they wish only to modify it with a few constitutional improvements, borrowed, of course, from the United States. At a time when an American president, whose policies have been rejected by his own legislature and whose government would have fallen in Canada or England, can look forward complacently to another eighteen months in office and the possibility of re-election, there doesn't seem to be a great deal of point in imitating the American system. Yet many prominent Canadian citizens, including some who have appeared before your committee, have urged the adoption of a variety of American constitutional or political devices, including the congressional committee system, the presidential executive, the bill of rights, or the Senate with special powers. As these American institutions and methods grow more attractive, our own are steadily losing their prestige. A while ago, Dr. Corry, appearing before your committee, described the terms "Queen", "Queen's", "Crown", and "royal" as mere "tags and labels" which were expendable. One cannot help wondering what would happen if a professor of political science from Harvard or Princeton were to appear before an American Congressional Committee and gravely propose that the words "president", "presidential", "constitution", and "republican" were unimportant terms which the United States could very well do without.

A constitution is a living creation which develops slowly according to the changing circumstances of its history. But the experience which the Canadian constitution has undergone can no longer be regarded as development and growth, for it has ended in almost total change and increasing disintegration. The Canadians have permitted, and encouraged, their courts and government to divorce them from their past and to disown their constitutional origins; and they have now suddenly awakened to the awful truth that their great nineteenth-century creations have been lost or damaged or destroyed. They have almost literally nothing of their own to put in the place of what has irrevocably vanished. The great creative period in Canadian constitutional history came in the middle of the nineteenth century. It is unlikely to be repeated and there are certainly no signs of its return now. In 1867 a basic agreement about first principles existed; now there is only a confusion of discordant proposals. In 1864 the Quebec Conference took only a few weeks to draft its scheme of federal union; but the modern constitutional conference, begun in 1968, is now well into the fourth year of its prolonged deliberations, with virtually nothing to show for the time and effort expended. The constitutional proposals of June 1971, pompously announced as the "Victoria Charter", dealt only with political rights, language rights, the Supreme Court, and the amendment of the constitution; they had nothing whatever to say about the division of legislative powers between the federal government and the provinces, the division which is the heart of any federal system and which urgently requires revision in Canada today. Yet, even though the "Victoria Charter" so studiously avoided the real crux of Canadian federalism, it was rejected by Quebec; and the long struggle to devise acceptable solutions for a few selected problems proved vain. Canada has lost its sense of unity and purpose, and with these it has lost its creative powers. What was in the middle nineteenth century a recognizably Canadian body of political thought has now vanished. Canada is bankrupt, and like all bankrupts who have not been discharged, it tries to go on borrowing from the nearest available creditor, in this case the United States.

These, it seems to me, are the real lessons that Canadian history has to offer. I expect that you may find them imprecise as well as very gloomy; but I think nevertheless that they should be kept in mind. I believe that Canadians in general, and the members of this committee in particular, should be under no complacent delusions about what has happened to Canada, about its present divided condition, or about its doubtful prospects for the future. At this moment in our history, a spirit of critical realism is what we need most.

Index